THE HUGUENOT SETTLEMENTS
IN IRELAND

M = *Military Settlement*
T = *Trading Community*
W = *Settlement of Weavers*
✠ = *Huguenot Church*
Λ = *Huguenot Minster,*
    but no Church.

ULSTER W

Lambeg
Belfast M
Lisburn ΛW
Lurgan W
Dromore
Armagh

Sligo

Killala

Castleblayney

Killeshandra

Dundalk WΛ

CONNAUGHT

Collon

Chapelizod W

Dublin MTW
✠✠✠✠

Portarlington
M✠

LEINSTER

Wicklow

Galway

Carlow ✠

Killaloe

Kilkenny
ΛW

Limerick

Enniscorthy

Clonmel W
Carrick-on-Suir

MUNSTER W
Waterford
TM✠

Wexford Λ

Mallow

Tallow

✠✠T Cork
Youghal M

Innishannon
WΛ

Bandon

Kinsale

The
HUGUENOT
SETTLEMENTS
in
IRELAND
English Miles

0 10 20 30 40 50 60

The Huguenot Settlements in Ireland

Grace Lawless Lee

HERITAGE BOOKS
2008

HERITAGE BOOKS

AN IMPRINT OF HERITAGE BOOKS, INC.

Books, CDs, and more—Worldwide

For our listing of thousands of titles see our website
at
www.HeritageBooks.com

A Facsimile Reprint
Published 2008 by
HERITAGE BOOKS, INC.
Publishing Division
100 Railroad Ave. #104
Westminster, Maryland 21157

Originally published
London
1936

International Standard Book Numbers
Paperbound: 978-0-7884-2005-4
Clothbound: 978-0-7884-7185-8

DEDICATED

TO MY FATHER

PHILIP GEORGE LEE, M.D.

IN LOVE AND GRATITUDE

PREFACE

THE following work is based on a thesis which was awarded the Blake National History Scholarship of Trinity College, Dublin. It does not pretend to give a comprehensive account of all the Huguenot families in Ireland—such a task would prove a Herculean if not impossible one to-day—but an attempt has been made to trace the history of each settlement with that of the more important families therein. In doing so it will be proved how large a share was contributed by them to the history of Ireland, and how great was the influence they exerted over the trade, the professions and the social life of the country, and thus it is hoped that a gap may be filled not only in the history of the French refugees but in that of the country which became their home.

The origin of the term Huguenot is open to controversy, and the problem which it raises has been discussed by many writers. It forms no part of the author's intention to enter upon it here but, since the name has been often applied so loosely to Flemish and even to German as well as to French refugees, it must be stated that here it is used solely as a synonym for French Protestant. That writers such as Gimlette can find an early precedent for their elastic use of the term will be seen in Fitzmaurice's demand of 1569 referred to in the chapter on Cork (page 28), but such a use seems both incorrect and confusing and has therefore been avoided in a work which concerns itself solely with the French settlements in Ireland.

No writer treats of this subject in its entirety. Smiles in

vii

his "Huguenots in England and Ireland" dismisses the latter country in one chapter. Weiss introduces the Irish settlements only incidentally in the section of his "Histoire des Réfugiés Protestants de France" devoted to the Huguenots in England. Agnew's "Protestant Exiles from France" contains much valuable information concerning individual families in England and Ireland, as does Haag's "La France Protestante," but there is no attempt to trace each settlement. Lane Poole, in the Lothian Essay "The History of the Huguenots of the Dispersion," devotes only half a chapter to their activities in Ireland, and Burn's "History of the Foreign Refugees" dismisses the Irish contingent in a matter of four short pages. Dr. Gimlette of Waterford intended to compile a "History of the Huguenot Settlers in Ireland," but his death occurred before he had completed more than a short and somewhat untrustworthy portion of the work, which was published for private circulation, without editing or correction, at a later date.

There remain the useful series of articles on Lisburn, Belfast, Portarlington, Youghal and Waterford in the old "Ulster Journal of Archæology"; a short mention of Cork in the "Cork Historical and Archæological Journal"; and a mine of information scattered throughout the proceedings of the Huguenot Society of London, such as the paper on the "Projet de Colonisation en Irlande" by the Baronne de Chambrier, and that dealing with the "Huguenot Churches of Dublin and their Ministers" by Mr. T. P. Le Fanu. Of inestimable value also are those volumes among the transactions of the Society which have preserved the Registers of the French Churches of Dublin and Portarlington, and the Letters of Denization granted to the Huguenots in England and Ireland. The sections of the "Journal of the Association for the Preservation of Memorials of the Dead," which have noted the inscriptions on Huguenot graves throughout the country, are also of importance.

Apart from these scattered, and at times conflicting, notices of the settlements, the history of the Huguenots in Ireland has yet to be compiled. Cork especially has been left in obscurity probably because, the Church Registers having disappeared, few data remain easily accessible for a satisfactory history. Nevertheless in corporate records and private papers much knowledge may be gained, and in the following pages special attention has been paid to this southern colony.

Much of the information dealing with individual families has come to the author from private sources, and she would here take the opportunity of thanking all those who so kindly allowed her access to family papers and manuscripts, or who brought to her notice facts which she could not otherwise have obtained. Her gratitude is also due to the Librarian of the French Hospital, London; to the Deputy Keeper of Manuscripts in the British Museum; to the Librarians of University College, Cork, and of Dublin University; and in particular to the Board of Trinity College, Dublin, for their generous aid towards the expenses of publication, and to Professor Edmund Curtis and Mr. Thomas Le Fanu, whose invaluable criticism of and guidance in her work has made possible this small contribution to the history of the Huguenots.

G.L.L.

CONTENTS

MAP

CHAPTER I

THE FLIGHT FROM FRANCE AND THE ORIGIN OF THE HUGUENOT SETTLEMENTS IN IRELAND

THE Wars of Religion in France and the Campaign of William III in Ireland; the Siege of La Rochelle and that of Derry; the machinations of Madame de Maintenon and Louvois in the *salons* of Versailles, and the deliberations of the Linen Board of Ireland are widely separated in time and environment, so widely that their juxtaposition would seem a paradox but for the fact that they are blended in the history of French Protestantism and that each forms a stage, as the following pages will show, in that tragic story of persecution which, from the middle of the sixteenth century, lost to France one of the finest elements in her population, and for over two hundred years correspondingly enriched those countries in which the refugees found a home.

" Some persons," wrote Calvin of the Vaudois in 1545, " who previously slept in false security, buried in profound slumbers, have begun to consider what they ought to do. But because it is very hard to the flesh to neglect its own interests so far as to endanger life—to become the object of public hatred, or abandoning prospects at home, to enter upon a life of voluntary exile—these prevent a constant and firm resolution."[1] The words were momentous, not only did they point to the early stirring of that need for spiritual independ-

[1] Calvin to Luther. Letter dated Jan. 21st, 1545.

ence which set the Huguenots apart from their fellow-country-men, but to the growing persecution which forced them to throw themselves on the protection of foreign nations rather than to lose their freedom of thought in their own. It was indeed " hard to the flesh to neglect its own interests," but already many had chosen this course, and from the martyr-dom of Le Clerc, the wool-carder, at the stake at Metz in 1525,[1] to the execution of François Rochette, the last Protest-ant minister to suffer for his faith, in 1762,[2] successive waves of Huguenot settlers sought refuge in Switzerland; in Prussia; in Denmark, Sweden, Poland and Russia; in Staten Island, Virginia or South Carolina;[3] in the Berg Valley at the Cape of Good Hope; in Holland, that " great ark of the fugitives ";[4] in England, and, both from there and directly from the Continent, in Ireland.

It is with the French refugees in the last country that this work proposes to deal, and the accompanying map will prove how numerous were their settlements therein and how varied in character from the aristocratic congregation of Portarling-ton to the trading communities of the ports, and from the weavers of Clonmel and the linen manufacturers of Lisburn to the military colonists in Youghal.

The flight of the Huguenots to England and Ireland occurred in four waves. The first during the second half of the sixteenth century when French and Flemish fled together from the persecutions under Catharine de Medici in France and the Duke of Alva in the Netherlands; the second during the early years of the seventeenth century when Richelieu's

---

[1] " If not actually the first martyr of the French Reformation, as has commonly been supposed, Jean Leclerc deserves to rank amongst the most constant and unswerving of its early apostles." Baird, " History of the Rise of the Huguenots," Vol. I, p. 89.

[2] Baird, " The Huguenots and the Revocation," Vol. II, p. 496.

[3] As early as 1564 René de Laudonnière had attempted to found a Huguenot colony in Florida, though this was wrecked by the Spaniards. Baird, " Rise of the Huguenots," Vol. II, p. 200.

[4] Bayle, quoted by Smiles, " Huguenots in England," p. 187.

centralizing policy brought about the siege of La Rochelle; the third when the Edict of Nantes was revoked in 1685 and a code of Penal Laws was instituted which "maintained a perpetual St. Bartholomew in the country for about sixty years";[1] and the fourth when the Peace of Aix-la-Chapelle ended the war of the Austrian Succession in 1748 and set free the soldiery to help the Jesuits in hunting down the remaining communities who met in the "Church in the Desert," though by then all who could do so had fled and these refugees were principally from the peasantry, small farmer and small manufacturing classes who had lacked the wealth or opportunity to escape as their richer co-religionists had done.

I

In each age the supreme misfortune of the Huguenots lay in the fact that, willingly or unwillingly, they were forced to become the tools of party policy. Thus they were regarded in the sixteenth century not only as an heretical sect, an offshoot of the Albigenses or Waldenses and therefore a part of the new spirit which the forces of the Counter-Reformation were sworn to destroy, but as a dangerous political force, adherents of the House of Navarre, by whom they were protected, and the enemies therefore of the Guise faction and of the Crown. The Wars of Religion which devastated the country during the latter half of the century were undertaken less from motives of conscience than of policy, and the Massacre of St. Bartholomew's Eve in 1572 was but a move in the game played by the wily queen of Henry II. As he had supported the Protestants in Germany while persecuting them in France, so she, in the Peace of Saint Germain of 1570, sided with Navarre and granted a measure of toleration to the sect which two brief years later she sought to exterminate.

[1] Coquerel, "Histoire des Eglises du Desert."

A*

But even before the Religious Wars and the organized attempt at the destruction of the Huguenots throughout France in the massacres of 1572, attacks had been made on them by the Provincial Parliaments, such as that of Aix, in the reign of Francis I, when Lefevre, whose translation of the New Testament became the basis of the Huguenot Bible, was forced to leave the University of Paris. It was in answer to the persecutions set on foot by the Aix Parliament that the bold " Confession de foi faite d'un commun accord par les Eglises Réformés du Royaume de France " was adopted by the first National Synod of French Protestants, held in Paris in 1559, as the charter of the Huguenots.

The first refugees to come to Ireland appeared during the reigns of Henry VIII and Edward VI, though these, like Bernadin de Valoys,[1] an official in Dublin Castle, and Martin Pierre and Oliver d'Aubigné,[2] respectively Under-Treasurer and Controller of the Mint, were chiefly officials sent from London. The jealousy evinced towards the foreigners in both countries is best illustrated by the attacks made upon the Flemish refugees employed in the silver and lead mines sunk in County Wexford in 1551,[3] and when, in the reign of Mary, proclamations in the seaports ordered their departure, envy sided with Romanism to drive them out. Edward VI had proved more hospitable than his subjects to these strangers from France and the Netherlands. He gave them the Church of the Austin Friars[4] for their services in London and encouraged their industry, not only for their own sakes, but because it was thought that the English wool trade, which had suffered during the unrest in the Netherlands, would

[1] C.S.P., Ire. (1509-1573), p. 45.
[2] Ibid., p. 127.
[3] One petition of the many against them stated that " English and Irish-men can better skill of that work than the Almains can." C.S.P., Ire. (1509-1573), p. 123.
[4] To this, writes Weiss, " La plupart des Eglises françaises d'Angleterre, d'Ecosse, d'Irlande, et même d'Amérique doivent leur origine et leur première organisation."—" Histoire des Réfugiés Protestants de France."

benefit by the presence of skilled weavers from Flanders. In the same spirit of mingled charity and self-seeking, Sir Henry Sidney during his Viceroyalty in Ireland was empowered by Elizabeth to establish at Swords a colony of these Flemish immigrants. Others, too, might have found refuge there, for the Queen restored all the privileges granted to them by Edward VI and protected them against native jealousy, but Ireland of the later sixteenth century was too disturbed to attract settlers, and save for some petitions by John Van Trere to establish salt works,[1] by Pierre Briet, Jean Carré and Antoine Becku to engage in the manufacture of glass,[2] and by Peter Back of Brabant to set up a tanning industry,[3] no great desire is evinced by the refugees to come to Ireland. Dublin, safe within the Pale, harboured merchants from Rochelle and Bordeaux with a few Huguenots who, like John de Beaulieu, had left the over-large Southampton colony.[4] Cork, too, must have possessed some refugee inhabitants,[5] but no attempt at a definite settlement was made, and Sir Henry Sidney's little colony laboured alone at the " Diaper and tickes for beddes and other good stuffes for man's use," and the "excellent leather of deer skynnes, goat and sheep fells " of which he was so proud.[6] As these settlers were not French their history lies beyond the scope of this work, but many of the Huguenots who at the same period were taking up their abode in England came later to Ireland, and this early settlement must have pointed the way to later refugees and shown such rulers as Strafford or Ormond that a plantation of the kind would be feasible.

Towards the end of the century immigration ceased for

[1] C.S.P. Dom., Eliz., Aug. 1569.
[2] C.S.P. Dom., Eliz., Aug. 1562, Sept. 1568.
[3] C.S.P., Ire. (1509-1573), p. 338.
[4] *Vide* p. 216.
[5] *Vide* p. 28.
[6] Sir Henry Sidney's " Summary Relation of all his services in Ireland," 1582. Cal. Carew MSS , II, 350.

a time. The Religious Wars in France had culminated in the establishment of Henry IV on the throne, and the Southern States of Holland had yielded to Spain. In England, after the attempted invasion of 1588, all foreigners were suspect as spies, riots broke out against them, and in 1593 a Bill to restrict their privileges was introduced. But, above all, in 1598, Henry IV promulgated the Edict of Nantes, granting "perpetual" and irrevocable security to the Protestants in his dominions. "Complete freedom of conscience; complete civil equality; closely limited freedom of worship; excellent guarantees for the administration of justice; and a large state subsidy for the maintenance of Huguenot troops and ministers "[1] were obtained for the Protestants, and one of the Articles invited those Huguenots who had fled to other countries to return, and declared that children born to French parents abroad should be considered French citizens. Many refugees, such as John de Beaulieu, availed themselves of the opportunity of returning to the Continent, though of these some fled again during the next century and were followed by the descendants of the remainder when the Edict was revoked.

II

The very Edict, however, which protected the interests of the Huguenots in the one reign was to bring about their political ruin in the next, for the great measure of independence which they had obtained under it was certain to prove an obstacle to the centralized government of Richelieu's desire, and was as certain to be swept away by him as a dangerous *imperium in imperio*. Their intrigues with the Queen Mother and with foreign powers proved that they had not as yet learnt the danger of associating their religious principles with politics, and when their General Assembly,

---

[1] Grant, "The Huguenots," p. 66.

meeting at La Rochelle without the royal sanction in 1621, proceeded to publish a declaration of independence and to justify its conduct by an appeal to the Courts of Europe, it laid them open to the charge of rebellion and prepared the way for their downfall when the Cardinal-Minister should come to power.

The Huguenots were declared guilty of high treason; their church at Charenton was demolished; massacres occurred throughout the country; and in 1628 La Rochelle fell. Again many fled from the country, where the towns which had been granted to them by the Edict gradually became royal garrisons; though Richelieu, content with having broken their political power, allowed them the free exercise of their religion and full equality with the Roman Catholics in law.[1] Some of the Huguenot nobles went over to the conquering side and thus, deprived of those leaders who had embroiled them in politics, the Protestants who remained in France returned to the peaceful pursuits of the professions, trade and agriculture. In the next reign Mazarin could say of them, " I have no cause to complain of the little flock; if they browse on bad herbage at least they do not stray."[2]

Those who fled to England found in James I and his son, if not ardent champions, at least friendly hosts. " Si aucun était si osé que vous molester, vous adressant à moi, je vous ferai—justice," was James's assurance to the French Church in London in 1603.[3] Collections were made for the refugees in England in 1621;[4] in Scotland in 1622; and generally throughout the kingdom in 1628;[5] and Charles, on his

[1] Peace of Alais, 1629.
[2] Rulhière, " Eclaircissements Historiques," quoted Baird, " The Huguenots and the Revocation," Vol. I, Ch. 7.
[3] Weiss, Bk. III, Ch. 1, p. 262. Letter dated May 21st, 1603. Original in French.
[4] This was intended especially to aid refugees from Normandy. Baird, " The Huguenots and the Revocation," Vol. I, Ch. 4, p. 220.
[5] Ibid., Ch. 6, p. 324.

accession, commanded all officers of the Crown "to permit all strangers, members of the foreign Churches and their children peaceably to enjoy all the privileges and immunities which had been formerly granted to them."[1]

As in the previous reigns a certain amount of jealousy was evinced towards these strangers, and the Irish merchants were not the more reconciled to them by the disorganization in trade with France caused by the Rochelle privateers who preyed on French shipping.[2] Nevertheless Frenchmen found their way to the country, as Charles Anthonie and Jean Baptiste who worked in the Irish mint;[3] Adam de Croquigni and Cornelius Melin who were in royal service and obtained Letters of Denization in Ireland;[4] and Anthonie Ballatier from Languedoc who was made "a free denizen" in 1618 and licensed "to plant and sell mulberry trees and other trees and herbs in both England and Ireland."[5]

Sir Pierce Crosby who fought at La Rochelle, the Earl of Cork and Sir William Beecher, the friend of their leader Soubize,[6] aided the exiles, many of whom, as will be seen throughout the course of this work, became landed proprietors; and Strafford employed them to further the establishment of his linen industry. "I have sent," he wrote to the Master of the Rolls in 1636, "for workmen out of the Low Countries and South of France and set up already six or seven loomes which, if it please God to bless us this year, I trust so to invite them (i.e. the native Irish) to follow it when they see the great profit arising thereby that they shall generally take to it and employ themselves that way."[7]

---

[1] Gimlette, "Huguenot Settlers in Ireland," p. 155.
[2] *Ibid.*, p. 152.
[3] C.S.P., Ire., Vol. IX. 1604.
[4] Gimlette, p. 151.
[5] *Ibid.* The Denizations in Ireland from 1603 to 1800 have been printed in Vols. XVIII and XXVII of the Huguenot Society's Publications.
[6] *Ibid.*, p. 161.
[7] Letter to Sir Christopher Wandesford dated July 25th, 1636.

Láud's attempt to suppress the foreign Churches in England in 1632 and to force the refugees to "Conforme themselves to the laws of the Kingdom as well ecclesiastical as temporal,"[1] drove some of them to Ireland, where they found protection from his enemies in the Privy Council; and when Cromwell swept away Charles and his ministers and reduced the country to obedience after the 1641 Rebellion, he employed in his army some of the French settlers from the eastern counties of England and rewarded them with grants of the land which had been taken from the Irish.[2] That his sympathy for the Huguenots was keen is evinced by his championship of the Vaudois whom, Gimlette states, he wished to transplant to Ireland. He employed Huguenot clerics as John Durant and Paul Amiraut;[3] and in his instructions to the Lord-Deputy and Council in 1656 commanded "that for encouragement of foreign nations to come into Ireland to purchase or take to farm houses and lands there, letters patents of denization be granted under the Great Seal of Ireland to all persons of what nation soever professing the Protestant religion."[4]

III

If Richelieu were justified in his attack on the Huguenots as a political force, Louis XIV had no such excuse in his destruction of them. If by 1600 La Rochelle had become such a byword that the Earl of Thomond could write to Cecil of the townsmen of Limerick that "If in time they be not looked unto they will become as ill as Rochelle for disobedience,"[5] no such charge could be laid at the door of those

[1] Manifesto Laud to Council, quoted Gimlette, p. 171.
[2] Gimlette, p. 180.
[3] *Vide* pp. 118, 121.
[4] Dunlop, "Ireland under the Commonwealth," Vol. II, p. 583.
[5] Thomond to Sir R. Cecil. C.S.P., Ire., Jan. 1600, p. 402.

who had remained loyal to Louis during the Wars of the Fronde; who served him as did Duquesne in the Navy, Turenne or Schomberg in the Army, and the Marquis de Ruvigny at Court; who brought honour to France as did a divine such as Claude; and wealth as did the linen manufacturers of Normandy, the tanners of Touraine, the hat and paper makers of Caudebec and the Angoumois, the iron workers and stocking weavers of the Sedanais and Languedoc, the serge manufacturers of Gévaudan, or the silk and ribbon weavers of Lyons and Tours.

The Revocation of the Edict of Nantes is taken, like the Massacre of St. Bartholomew, to mark an epoch of flight; but as in the first case some left France who could foresee the doom of the Huguenot party under Catharine de Medici, so many fled long before the Revocation took place. They had been spasmodically persecuted before the Massacre, they were systematically persecuted before the Revocation. As long before it as 1660 the termination of the Synod of Loudun marked the close of the last legal meeting of Huguenot deputies; in 1665 the Chambers of the Edict in Paris and Rouen were suppressed; a comprehensive act of fifty-nine articles was passed against the Protestants in 1666, and by 1669 so much emigration had occurred that it was prohibited by edict. "They are forbidden to quit their country," stated Dean Drelincourt in 1682, "and yet, by their hard usage and persecution, in effect not suffered to stay."[1]

The persecution had slackened while Louis was engaged in the war with Holland, but increased after the Peace of Nimeguen and the failure of the attempt to unite the Catholic and Protestant interests in an "Eglise de France." In 1681 Louvois, his Minister of War, instituted the "Dragonnades" by sending those soldiers who had been mustered for a threatened war with Spain to terrorize the Huguenots into

---

[1] "A Speech to the Duke of Ormond." Pamphlet, Dublin, 1682.

conversion, and at last, on October 22nd, 1685, the Edict of Nantes was revoked.[1]

No writers agree as to the numbers who fled from France or were converted therein. The Intendants falsified their returns from the provinces in order to prove their own zeal in the conversion of the Protestants, and Weiss states that the Consistories of Huguenot Churches in foreign countries did not submit complete lists of their congregations to the authorities, "de peur d'inspirer de l'ombrage à un peuple hospitalier, il est vrai, mais jaloux a l'excès de la possession intégrale de son territoire."[2] He places the total number of *émigrés* at over 600,000, of whom 70,000 fled to the British Isles.[3] Lane Poole[4] asserts that the tale of the refugees was above 300,000, and of these England, Ireland and Scotland obtained 80,000. Baird[5] states that of every score of fugitives seventeen fled to England and Ireland, and Dubourdieu,[6] writing in 1718, speaks of nearly 100,000 in the two countries. Smiles computes the total number of emigrants at a million, and states that 400,000 left France in the twenty years previous to the Revocation, and 600,000 in the twenty years after that event.[7] Of these estimates that of Weiss appears nearest to the truth.

Amongst the Protestant powers who universally condemned the religious policy of Louis, England took a foremost place. " I conjure you in the name of the great Henry, whose precious blood circulates in both our veins, to respect the Protestants whom he looked upon as his children. If, as is reported, you wish to compel them to renounce their

[1] *Vide* Smiles, "Huguenots in France," Introduction, p. 9, and Grant, p. 172.
[2] Weiss, p. 272.
[3] Weiss, Bk. III, p. 323.
[4] "Huguenots of the Dispersion," p. 169.
[5] "The Huguenots and the Revocation," Vol. II, p. 93.
[6] "Appeal to the English Nation."
[7] "Huguenots in France," pp. 17, 18.

religion under pain of banishment from your Kingdom I offer them an Asylum in that of England," wrote Charles II,[1] and despite his francophile and often hypocritical policy the refugees found protection and encouragement under him.

As early as 1662 the Duke of Ormond introduced into the Irish Parliament " An Act for Encouraging Protestant Strangers and Others to Inhabit Ireland." This laid down that " all persons of the Protestant Religion born out of the King's Dominions—which at any time within the space of seven years from the end of this Parliament shall transport their stocks and families into any part of this Kingdom with intention that themselves and children shall inhabit here— after taking the Oaths of Allegiance and Supremacy—shall be reputed the King's Natural Born Liege Subjects," and that " all persons as well Strangers and Aliens as the King's Subjects of the Protestant Religion who enter any city, borough, privileged and incorporated town—with intent to dwell there, shall, upon reasonable request and payment of 20 shillings, be admitted a freeman of any such place, Guild, Brotherhood, Society, or Fellowship of any trade, craft or other mystery, and enjoy all privileges of trading, buying, working and selling in as ample manner as any freeman," although they might not employ more than six apprentices. This was re-enacted by William and Mary, Anne and George I,[2] and, owing to its abuse by foreign merchants, who pretended to be settlers in order to avoid Customs dues, a proclamation to explain the true meaning of the Act was later made.

Despite this generous measure the Huguenot settlers

---

[1] Quoted Gimlette, p. 84.
[2] 4 Will and Mary, c. 2. 2 Anne, c. 14. 4 Geo. I, c. 9. No general Act of Naturalization was passed in England owing to the jealousy felt towards the refugees. Charles II unsuccessfully tried to introduce it in 1681, and naturalizations continued to be doled out by Letters Patent and Private Acts. In Ireland, naturalization followed automatically on taking the Oaths.

found that they, with other aliens, were expected to subscribe twice as much as the native citizen to the fund raised in the same year as compensation to the Duke of Ormond.[1] The Tonnage and Poundage Act, too, discouraged Huguenot merchants, as did the restrictions on the use of foreign coin.[2] The Bill which passed the English Parliament in 1666, forbidding the import of Irish cattle and fish into England, also, it was thought by the Irish Privy Council, would " defeat the intent and benefit of a late Act for encouraging Protestant strangers to settle in Ireland."[3] Nevertheless the refugees continued to arrive and "under the Act" to become citizens and freemen of the corporate towns. Grants of land were made to them; and Ormond, in an endeavour to industrialize the country so as to defeat such measures as that prohibiting the export of cattle, established Huguenot linen weavers in Chapelizod, and woollen manufacturers in Clonmel and Carrick-on-Suir. Ore smelting was undertaken by the foreigners in Enniscorthy, and settlers from the colony at Norwich were attracted to Ireland by Sir Peter Pett's Memorial to the Viceroy for " the setting up of a manufacture of fine worsted stockings and Norwich stuff in all parts of the Nation."[4]

The cloth manufacture soon became such an important feature in export that an Alnager was appointed; the first to hold office being Joseph Scardeville, a naturalized Frenchman.[5]

In 1672 " New Rules " were provided for the Irish Corporations, and Gimlette[6] states that an idea of the distribution of Huguenot settlers by this date may be gained by the fact that, in the rules drawn up for certain cities, those

---

[1] Gimlette, p. 192.
[2] Ibid.
[3] Carte, "Life of Ormond," Bk. VI., p. 331.
[4] Vide p. 117.
[5] Gimlette, p. 198.
[6] Ibid.

of Dublin, Cork, Waterford, Limerick, Kinsale, Youghal, Cashel, Clonmel, Athlone, Derry, Galway, Carrickfergus, Coleraine, Strabane, Charlemont, Tuam, Drogheda, Dundalk, Kilkenny, Wexford and Ross, a special clause was inserted with reference to Protestant Strangers which was omitted in the others. It would seem, however, either that " Protestant Stranger " was an elastic term not necessarily implying "Refugee,"[1] or that the clause was included rather as a preparation for future eventualities than as the regulation of a *fait accompli,* for it has not been possible to trace settlements, or even individual refugees, in many of these towns at the period.

James II recalled the City Charters and expelled, and in some cases attainted, the Protestant freemen. The pastor of the Huguenot congregation which had been permitted under Ormond to meet in St. Patrick's Cathedral was imprisoned, and the Act which had granted naturalization and free admission into all corporations to the refugees was annulled. Nevertheless " An Account of the Persecutions and Oppressions of the Protestants in France " was printed in Dublin in 1686,[2] and in England public opinion was too strong for the King.[3] Although he ordered the burning of Claude's "Les Plaintes des Protestants," he was forced to renew the privileges given to the Huguenots in 1681 by Charles II, which provided free passports, Letters of Denization, and free import for the goods of the refugees; offered them assistance in moving from place to place; allowed them freedom to exercise their callings and placed them under the special protection of the Archbishop of Canterbury and the Bishop

---

[1] Thus in the Cork Freemen's Register in 1781, Edward Davies, manufacturer of lamp-black, is made free as a " Protestant Stranger," though at that date, and with a Welsh name, he can scarcely have been a Huguenot.

[2] Pamphlet, Dublin. Reprinted for Joseph Howes, bookseller, 1686.

[3] *Vide* the many references to the French refugees throughout Evelyn's " Diary."

of London.[1] The collections which had been ordered in the churches in the previous reign were also continued.[2] Indeed " the people of England were more especially liberal on this occasion because they began to think it might be their own case and must be everywhere the effect of popery and arbitrary power."[3]

The victory of William of Orange meant a renewed asylum for the Huguenots in Ireland. The refugees who sought to enter his service before the descent on England were so numerous that the States General of Holland wished to prohibit their employment. William, however, offered himself to support the expense of their maintenance, and so they were enrolled in great numbers and later formed into three regiments of foot under La Melonière,[4] Du Cambon[5] and La Caillemotte Ruvigny,[6] and one of horse under Marshal Schomberg.[7] Another regiment of Dragoons was subsequently formed, thus completing the " Five Irish Regiments." The last, commanded by Miremont, was not originally French, but refugee officers and men were gradually incor-

[1] These privileges were published in the *Gazette* and caused a large influx of immigrants. (Hug. Soc. Pub., XVIII, pp. 124-5.)

[2] *Vide* Evelyn's " Diary," March 14th and April 25th, 1686. The whole sum collected in England, Ireland and Scotland, and called the Royal Bounty, amounted, according to Weiss, to £200,000, or, as stated by Lane Poole, to £124,553 by 1695. For its "obscure and partly discreditable" history see Lane Poole, p. 193. Sums were administered by the "Comité Laie " and the " Comité Ecclesiastique " to distressed laymen and ministers, and Weiss states that in 1688 as many as 27,000 claimed assistance.

[3] Bishop Kennett, " History of England," quoted Lane Poole.

[4] He served later in Flanders, was pensioned on the Irish Establishment, and died in 1715. (Agnew, II, 183.)

[5] Chief Military Engineer. Died 1693 and was succeeded in command of the regiment by the Comte de Marton, later created Earl of Lifford. (*Ibid.*)

[6] Killed at the Boyne and succeeded in the regiment by Pierre Belcastel, who opened the siege of Limerick in 1690. (*Ibid.*)

[7] Raised in England in 1689. Arrived in Ireland after the surrender of Carrickfergus, and served at the Boyne where Schomberg was killed. The Marquis de Ruvigny took over its command in 1691. (*Ibid.*)

porated into it, and at the time of its disbandment it was wholly Huguenot.[1] The numbers in each regiment were maintained by recruits from Geneva and Lausanne dispatched to Ireland by the agency of the Baron d'Avejan and the Marquis d'Arzilliers.[2] At the conclusion of the campaign they were sent to serve in Flanders and were disbanded after the Peace of Ryswick, although many of the officers and men were re-employed under different colonels for the wars of Anne.

The history of the Irish Campaign has been told by Huguenot as well as native writers. In the " Mémoires " of Dumont de Bostaquet, who was one of William's officers to settle in Portarlington, and those of Samuel de Péchels who later resided in Dublin; in the " History of England " of Rapin de Thoyras who fought throughout the war and eventually became tutor in the household of the Earl of Portland;[3] and in the " Journey " of Gideon Bonnivert who served in the North in 1690,[4] a contemporary picture of the army life of the period may be gained with some insight into the motives which induced the refugees to engage in such numbers on the side of William. " Les Français réfugiés ne contribuèrent pas peu a la conquête d'Irlande," wrote d'Avejan. " Ils regardaient la conquête de cette île comme la cause de Dieu et la preálable de leur retour en France."[5]

It was this spirit which contributed materially to the victory of the Boyne. " Duke Schomberg's Regiment of Horse," says Rapin Thoyras, " behaved with undaunted resolution, like men who fought for a nation amongst whom themselves and their friends had found shelter against the

[1] *Ibid.*
[2] Weiss, Bk. III, Ch. 2, p. 305.
[3] Smiles, " Huguenots in France," p. 316.
[4] From Sloane MSS., Brit. Mus. Lib., quoted U.J.A., Vol. IV, p. 78.
[5] Court MSS., quoted "Mémoires Inédits de Dumont de Bostaquet," Introduction, p. 26.

persecution of France."[1] In James and his army they saw the epitome of all from which they had suffered. "Allons, mes amis," Schomberg himself is reported to have cried, "rappelez votre courage et vos ressentiments. Voilà vos persécuteurs."[2]

The gratitude of William to his Huguenot allies was evinced in a practical manner. He declared "that all French Protestants that shall seek their refuge in our Kingdom shall not only have our Royal protection for themselves, families and estates—but we will also do our endeavour in all reasonable ways and means so to support, aid and assist them in their several trades and ways of livelihood as that their living—in this realm may be comfortable and easy to them,"[3] and titles, offices and grants of the forfeited lands in Ireland rewarded many of those who fought in the campaign. Thus the young Marquis de Ruvigny, who was created Earl of Galway, obtained the Portarlington estate,[4] René De La Fausille was appointed Governor of Sligo,[5] and the third Duke of Schomberg was created Duke of Leinster in 1692,[6] when Ruvigny obtained the Lieutenant-General-ship of all the forces in Ireland.[7]

William's partiality for the Huguenots provoked much jealousy in England. It was possibly because of this that he encouraged the Irish settlements and planned the establishment of the disbanded regiments therein. His grant to Galway, who sublet his estate on easy terms, wisely provided a place of residence for the military pensioners, and Luttrell[8] writes, on November 2nd, 1697, that the French

[1] "History of England." Quoted Smiles, "Huguenots in France," p. 347.
[2] "History of England."
[3] Proclamation, quoted Gimlette, p. 256.
[4] *Vide* p. 138.
[5] *Vide* p. 211.
[6] Irish Patent Rolls.
[7] Agnew, "Henri de Ruvigny."
[8] Narcissus Luttrell, "A Brief Historical Relation of State Affairs."

B

refugees living on charity in England were ordered to go to Ireland, where they would be encouraged to follow their several trades.

One hundred and twenty-one officers, whose names are recorded by Dumont de Bostaquet, were placed on the Pension List in 1692, and when the disbandment took place after the Peace of Ryswick[1] the number was raised to 590, including a few civilians and 57 non-commissioned officers and private soldiers. These settled chiefly in Portarlington, Dublin, Youghal, Waterford and Belfast. An interesting volume in the Public Record Office of Dublin[2] contained the names of these pensioners, with statements submitted by them to the Auditor General in 1702 specifying the amount of their private property with details regarding their families. In 1714 sworn declarations were again obtained from pensioners on the Civil List, and 281 of these were made by Huguenots. The volumes were lost when the Dublin Four Courts were destroyed in the Irish Civil War of 1922, but an abstract of the 1702 returns had been submitted in tabular form to the Lords Justices and transmitted to the English Treasury,[3] where it is fortunately preserved; in addition a list of military and civilian Huguenots pensioned on the Establishment appears in the appendix to the House of Commons Journal for 1719.

But William's energies were not only directed towards the settlement of the military Huguenots in his dominions. For many years the establishment of a manufacture which should take the place of the Irish wool trade had been agitating the minds of statesmen. This had become increasingly necessary as the jealousy of the English manufacturers caused duties to be levied on the export of woollen goods from Ireland, and when this taxation culminated in the Act of

[1] The names of the officers pensioned at this period were published in a Dublin Tract entitled "Hiberniæ Notitia" in 1723, but they are very incorrectly spelt.
[2] 18th Rep. Dep. Keeper Records, Iré., Appendix V.
[3] This has been printed in Vol. VI Proceedings Hug. Soc., Lon., p. 295.

1699, which effectually ruined the industry, it was imperative to encourage another. "There is no country has a better land or water for flax and hemp, and I do verily believe the navy may be provided here with payling and cordage cheaper by far than in England," wrote Molyneux in 1696,[1] and in the same hope Strafford and Ormond had both attempted to set up the manufacture of linen. Now William, with the help of the Crommelins, was to bring this undertaking to fruition.

Holland had never been a satisfactory place of residence for the Huguenot linen manufacturers. The Dutch spinners were incapable of producing yarns as fine as those to which they had been accustomed in France, and weavers were hard to find.[2] Thus, when in 1697 a Bill was passed "For the encouraging the Linen Manufacture of Ireland, and bringing flax and hemp into and the making of sailcloth in the Kingdom,"[3] and William invited Louis Crommelin from the Low Countries to set up the manufacture, the offer was at once accepted, and with seventy-five French families, 1,000 looms and £10,000 capital supplied by Crommelin in machinery and raw material,[4] the venture was started in the ruined town of Lisnagarvey, rebuilt for the purpose by the refugees.[5]

Crommelin was made overseer of the "Royal Linen Manufactory of Ireland," and received a salary from the State of £200 per annum, with interest on the manufacture at 8 per cent. for twelve years. This contract was renewed by Anne on her accession, and interest at 8 per cent. for ten years was extended to all those who brought looms into Ireland.[6] Spinning schools were instituted in response to a

---

[1] "Letters between Locke and his friends," p. 167.
[2] Gill, "The Rise of the Irish Linen Industry," pp. 16, 17.
[3] 8 Will. III, c. 39.
[4] U.J.A., Vol. I. Art. "Lisburn."
[5] *Vide* p. 177.
[6] Gill, p. 18.

statute of 1707, in order to assist the Huguenot manufacturers who were used to working with a finer yarn than the Irish knew how to prepare. Funds for distribution were entrusted to a committee of twenty, and this was replaced in 1711 by a Board of Trustees which continued until 1828. In 1728 a Linen Hall was opened in Dublin.[1] Encouraged by the Irish Parliament, which in 1705 took off export duties on linen and freely admitted machinery for its manufacture, and unhampered by the jealousy of English manufacturers, which had ruined the wool trade, the linen industry grew rapidly. By 1710 1,688,574 yards of linen were exported, while by 1779 the number had increased to 18,836,042.[2]

Besides the linen manufacture which spread from Lisburn to Waterford and Kilkenny, the Huguenots engaged in silk and poplin weaving in Dublin,[3] in sailcloth manufacture at Cork,[4] and in the making of cambric at Lurgan and Dundalk.[5] They introduced Dutch bleachers and organized the brown linen markets. Indeed they seem to have possessed a constructive and organizing ability to a marked degree, and Professor Gill states that "It was probably as organizers of trade and manufacture rather than actual makers of linen cloth that they affected the industry in Ulster."

In addition to the Huguenot soldiers and manufacturers William wished to find room in Ireland for several thousands of the refugees whom the Swiss cantons were unable to house; though in this he was less successful. The Bill failed to pass through Parliament[6] and the project was abandoned in 1693.

The whole story of this attempted colonization has been told by the Baronne de Chambrier in an interesting though

---

[1] Warburton, Whitelaw and Walsh, "History of Dublin," Vol. I, p. 227.
[2] Young's "Tour in Ireland," Ed. C. Maxwell. Note, p. 221.
[3] Under the La Touches.
[4] Under the Besnards.
[5] Under Goyer and de Joncourt.
[6] Lane Poole, p. 105.

not always accurate article entitled "Projet de Colonisation en Irlande par les Réfugiés français 1692-1699," printed amongst the Proceedings of the Huguenot Society of London,[1] and it is too long to enter into here, but it is of interest to note what localities were suggested as places of settlement, and who among the landed gentry of Ireland were willing to assist the foreigners. Henri de Mirmand abroad, Lord Galway and his agents, de Virazel and de Sailly in Ireland, laboured to bring the scheme to fruition, but the money promised by the Treasurer Godolphin in the English Parliament towards the settlement was diverted for purposes of war, and though, in 1698, Galway wrote to de Mirmand that " Si quelques réfugiés ont des fonds a placer ils ne pourraient le faire mieux et plus avantageusement qu'en achetant des terres en Irlande," he finally discourages any hope of help for the indigent exiles therein—"Les émigrés qui n'ont ni fonds ni métier, ne peuvent pas réussir dans ce pays, pauvre et épuisé et qui, malgré cela, donne annuellement huit mille livres sterling pour des pensions aux réfugiés."

When the scheme was at its height Charles de Sailly was sent to examine the country from Dublin to Cork. He made his journey in March of 1693, and sent his notes to de Mirmand in the following month. Kilkenny, Waterford, Cork, Bandon, Carlow and Wicklow, " le Montpellier irlandais," he considers suitable places of settlement. At Waterford Mr. Walkin would let 1,860 acres with sixteen houses and wood for their construction. At Cork it would be possible to establish manufactures in silk, wool, hats and gloves. Sir Richard Cox would receive Colonists on his estates. The "Count of Tipperary " offers a house, twenty cabins and 1,000 acres of land at Cloyne. In Cashel, which is in ruin, there are many houses needing inhabitants, and the barony of Blarney can take fifty gentlemen with their dependants. Many other landowners who would welcome the immigrants are mentioned, and as well

[1] Vol. VI, p. 370.

"il y a une série d'offres trop longues à detailler." Despite the failure of the scheme some refugees from Switzerland did find their way to Ireland,[1] as did six hundred French families from Holland in 1690.[2]

That many thinkers in Ireland looked to the Huguenots to bring prosperity to the country is proved in a pamphlet published in Dublin in 1697.[3] "The present desolation of France," states the writer, "may be a means of raising the power and wealth of those neighbouring Protestant countries which have wisdom and goodness enough to take hold of the opportunity." The Dutch and Palatines he considers worth bribing to come to Ireland, but "the French Protestants are the people that we have the greatest expectation from at present." He stresses their skill in various trades and in husbandry and concludes that "if we could draw in great numbers of French Protestants, this would be an Act of great Charity to them; a great blow to the French King, and the greatest kindness that we can do ourselves"—and it was in this spirit of encouragement that in an address to the Crown in October of the same year the House of Commons proposed " to endow a foreign clergyman in every parish where Protestant foreigners exceeded fifty in order that religious worship might be performed in their own language."[4] This is of importance since it serves as a guide to the number of colonists in each settlement. The clergy were encouraged to conform to the Church of Ireland, and frequently were ordained for benefices which they held in addition to their French ministry. They used the French version of the Scriptures

---

[1] "Projet de Colonisation."

[2] Lane Poole, p. 109 note. When the Palatinate was attacked by Louis XIV in 1698 a dispersion of the Palatines occurred; some settled later in Limerick and Tipperary, but as these were mostly Germans they, like the Walloon settlers, are outside the purpose of this book.

[3] "The True Way to Render Ireland Happy and Secure." Dublin, 1697. Pamphlet in form of letter to the Rt. Hon. Robert Molesworth.

[4] U.J.A., Vol II. Article on Youghal.

translated by Martin of Languedoc[1] and the Book of Common Prayer which had been translated into French as early as the reign of Edward VI, for use in the Savoy Church in London and the Islands of Jersey and Guernsey, and had been revised by Jean Durel in 1662.[2]

In their organization the French Churches approached nearer to Presbyterianism than to the Anglican ritual. Under the pastor *anciens* were appointed to deal with church matters, and each congregation was disciplined by a Consistory which, says Agnew, " corresponded with a Scottish Kirk Session " and was a " local court for superintendence over the members of one congregation."[3]

Not all the clergy, however, subscribed to the Church of Ireland. Fontaine of Cork and Daillon of Portarlington proved refractory,[4] and there were two Calvinistic as well as two "Conformed" churches in Dublin.[5] In all ten Huguenot churches were established in Ireland: four in Dublin; two in Cork; and one in Lisburn, Portarlington, Carlow, and Waterford respectively. The colonies in Dundalk, Wexford, Innishannon, Clonmel and Kilkenny had each a minister, though they do not seem to have possessed a special place of worship; and those of Belfast, Lambeg, Killeshandra, Castleblayney, Youghal and Bandon lacked both church and pastor. The Baronne de Chambrier[6] adds Tallow and Wicklow to the list of settlements but omits Wexford, which, as will be seen, had a definite French congregation. So had

[1] Gimlette, p. 230 note.

[2] *Ibid.*, p. 233 note. An earlier revision had been made by Pierre de Laune of Norwich in 1616, but Durel's was adopted by the churches of London and Dublin.

[3] " Protestant Exiles from France," Vol. I.

[4] *Vide* pp. 36, 148.

[5] In 1712 the refugees published in Dublin " An apology for the French Refugees established in Ireland " as an answer to the accusation brought against them by Convocation that they had " broken into non-conforming congregations."

[6] " Projet de Colonisation."

Collon in the County Louth, while Huguenot names are also found in Galway, Limerick and Kinsale. None of these communities, however, was large enough to warrant a minister or church, and they can scarcely be termed colonies.

IV

The last wave of emigration from France occurred about 1752, and was the result of a general tightening up of the Penal Laws against the Huguenots despite, or perhaps because of, a memorial which had been addressed by them to the King in 1750.[1]

By now they had become chiefly localized in Languedoc, where the Camisard Insurrection under Seguier and Cavalier had raged between 1702 and 1705, and where, under Antoine Court and Paul Rabaut, the "Church in the Desert" had been reorganized after the Rising.[2] While France was engaged in war the Huguenots largely increased, but in the intervals of peace persecution raged owing to the numbers of military who could be employed against them.[3] By 1748 the War of the Austrian Succession had ended and the Dragoons were sent into Languedoc, where the new Intendant, the Comte de Saint-Priest, carried out the law with such ferocity that the Protestants fled in their hundreds to Switzerland,[4] whence some, passing down the Rhine through Holland, came to Ireland and settled as silk and poplin weavers in Dublin. Other refugees left Normandy and Poitou for England, but the most extensive emigration was from the South.

Public opinion, however, was stirring against persecution. In 1712 the Marquis de Rochegaude published a list of the

[1] Smiles, "The Huguenots in France," p. 246.
[2] Ibid., Chs. 5-12.
[3] Thus the Irish Brigade was employed in suppressing the Camisards. Ibid., p. 142.
[4] Weiss, Bk. III, p. 281.

Huguenot captives in the Galleys and succeeded in interesting the Queen of England in their cause. Agnew states that the list contained 321 names and that, through her intercession, the French Government set all these at liberty.[1] Smiles[2] maintains that 136 were freed out of the 742 Huguenots who were then enslaved, and that amongst the number was Marteilhe, whose "Mémoires d'un Protestant condamné aux Galères de France pour cause de Religion," published in Rotterdam in 1757, formed a corollary to Jean Bion's "Relation des Tourments que l'on fait souffrir aux Protestants qui sont sur les Galères de France,"[3] and drew much attention to the cause of the French Protestants.

The last two "Galley slaves for the faith" were liberated in 1775. In 1764 the Jesuits were suppressed and the Huguenots lost their most inveterate enemies. The new age of scepticism worked in their favour since its anti-religious spirit made for the toleration of all creeds, and by 1766 Voltaire, the sceptic, had fought and won the cause of the Huguenot Calas. From 1780 de Rulhière had been employed by Louis XVI to draw up evidence from the State Papers of the necessity for the Revocation. His work[4] threw such light on the persecutions that, in 1787, the year following its publication, an Edict of Toleration was signed. Rabaut Saint Etienne, speaking before the National Assembly, voiced the feelings of the majority when he claimed the rights of Frenchmen for two millions of useful citizens who were Protestants,[5] and by the Declaration of Rights of 1789 Huguenots were admitted to public office.

But this freedom came too late to induce the French Protestants who had made their homes in other countries to return, nor was the National Assembly, although it professed

---

[1] "Henri de Ruvigny." Many came to England.
[2] "The Huguenots in France," p. 204.
[3] Published in 1708, and dedicated to Queen Anne.
[4] "Eclaircissements Historiques."
[5] Smiles, "Huguenots in France," p. 276.

itself willing to restore forfeited estates to their Protestant owners, over anxious to welcome any who came. In June 1792 the son of Louis Geneste of Lisburn wrote to his father from France, where he had returned to prefer his claim: "All matters relative to the fugitive Protestants are enveloped in darkness and the clerks and persons attending at the different offices seem disinclined to draw aside the veil—It is their wish to suppress such information as would tend to throw light on the subject."[1]

Most of the Huguenots in Ireland by this date had become so identified with the life of their adopted country that their French origin had been almost forgotten. During the wars with France they had remained loyal to England, and the Act of Naturalization passed in that country in 1708 recognized this fact.[2] In some cases they changed their names into English, possibly owing to the anti-Gallican feeling these wars aroused, or misspelt them in order to facilitate their correct pronunciation. Thus Le Fevre became Smith, or Jacques, Jack or Jaikes, and the de Foy or de Foix family called itself Defoe.[3] Many names were maltreated by the communities amongst which the refugees settled,[4] while those who had possessed landed property usually called themselves by their title, thus the Chevalier de Robillard, Seigneur Champagné was known in Portarlington simply as de Champagné.

But apart from their names, they were, by the early nineteenth century, indistinguishable from the Irish society around them, and it has therefore been thought unnecessary to trace them beyond this point. It is true that a French minister was employed in Portarlington as late as 1841, that

---

[1] Quoted U.J.A., Vol I. Article on Lisburn.

[2] It was repealed in 1712, but from this on the Huguenots were recognized practically as British subjects. Agnew, "Protestant Exiles."

[3] Smiles, "Huguenots in England," Appendix, p. 382.

[4] Smiles cites as an example "Coach and Six Lane" in Cork, so called because a Huguenot, Couchancex, had once resided there, but it has not been possible to trace this name amongst the Huguenots in Ireland.

one of the Huguenot burial-grounds in Dublin was continued in use until the present century, and that the refugee families were held together by intermarriage and, in the trading communities, by the apprenticeship system; but they took their places naturally in Municipal Corporations, in the Church, at the Bar, as Members of Parliament, in the Army and in the Administration. The Chagneaus, who represented Gowran in the Irish Parliament; the Fleurys and Maturins, who were eminent in the Church; Chief Justice Lefroy and Judge Perrin of the Irish Bench; the Right Honourable William Saurin, Attorney-General; Colonel Barré, Vice-Treasurer of Ireland; Mayors, like Sir Vesian Pick of Cork; Bankers, like the La Touches; Manufacturers, like the Besnards; and Merchants, like the Boileaus—all were of Huguenot descent, though they have become so identified with the interests of the country that the fact is easily forgotten.

Names such as these, so eminent in such a variety of professions, attest the impossibility of divorcing the French element from Irish social life. No history of the country can be complete which fails to recognize this fact, to give due credit to the refugee families for the intelligence and resource which carried many of them to such high positions in so short a time, and to acknowledge, as the following chapters will endeavour to prove, the very large part played in the history of Ireland by the Huguenot settlements.

CHAPTER II

THE City of Cork, owing largely to its geographical position and facilities for trade, has always had a foreign element amongst its citizens, and a list of their names taken at any time during the eighteenth century will have a strangely cosmopolitan sound. Thus Coppinger, said to be of Danish origin, will appear with the Pomeranian Crone;[1] the Suabian Cramer[2] will be listed with the Dutch Voster, and the English Quaker Pike will hold a place near the French Huguenot Perrier.

The earliest reference to the settlement of Huguenots in Cork is to be found in a demand made by James Fitzmaurice of Desmond on July 12th, 1569, to the Mayor and Corporation, that they " should aboolessh oute of that cittie that old heresy, newely raised and invented, and namely Barnaby Daaly, and all them that be Hugenettes boothe men and woomen."[3]

How many " Hugenettes " were then resident in the city it is impossible to state, and any that at that date sought refuge there were probably from Flanders. Pierre Briet, Jean Carré and Antoine Becku, who at various times from 1567 petitioned

---

[1] Daniel Crone from Troylson (recte Stralsund), Pomerania, took the Oaths and was naturalized 1663. A descendant was Mayor 1748.

[2] Col. Tobias Von Kramer made denizen 1639. A descendant married into the Coghill family.

[3] C.S.P., Eliz., Ire.

Elizabeth that they might be allowed to set up in Ireland " a
Glass Manufactory on the model of the Venetian Glassworks,"
have already been mentioned.[1] Carré fled, according to
Burn,[2] from the Low Countries or from Poitou, where Smiles[3]
locates this family, and, Gimlette[4] believes, settled in County
Cork, where the name Carré or Quarré is found during the
next reign. This has been contradicted by Mr. Westropp,
who states that " nothing more appears to be known concerning this project and probably neither Briet nor Carré set up
any glass house in Ireland."[5] But it is possible that some
other member of the Carré family found refuge in the
country, for a George Carré represented Naas in the Parliament called in 1661,[6] and in 1686 an Ezéchiel Carré was
priested at Cork.[7] In 1698 Augustus Carré is made free of
that City, and this must be the Augustus Carré who is Sheriff
in 1721.[8] In February 1735 his eldest son, Collombine Lee
Carré, is admitted a freeman, and in June 1740 another
Augustus Carré, probably a second son, " having served Jacob
Laullie " obtains this honour. A Mr. Gabriel Carré also
figures on the Freemen's List in 1713.[9] It may be added that
a Michael Quarry was a cotton manufacturer in Cork in 1792,
and in 1799 John Quarry was priested in Cloyne. He became
Rector of St. Mary's, Shandon, Cork, and died in 1837, leaving a son who became Archdeacon.[10] The Quarrys married
into the Robinette family, given by Burn as of Huguenot
stock, which will be dealt with amongst the goldsmiths of
the City.

[1] *Vide* p. 5.
[2] " History of the Protestant Refugees," p. 253.
[3] " Huguenots in England," Appendix.
[4] " Huguenot Settlers," p. 129.
[5] " Irish Glass," p. 20.
[6] Gimlette, p. 189.
[7] Brady, " Records of Cork, Cloyne and Ross."
[8] Council Book, Cork. Ed. Caulfield.
[9] Register of the Freemen of the City of Cork, transcribed from the
original MSS. by Richard Caulfield.
[10] Brady.

Gimlette implies that the Réné Mezandière who was appointed Customer of Cork under the Duke of Ormond in 1664 was of Huguenot origin,[1] and the Goble family, which, like that of Robinette, figures amongst the Cork goldsmiths, was already residing in the City by 1656; but it was not until the close of the seventeenth century that the real wave of foreign refugees reached Cork, and that the French Huguenot settlement therein was definitely founded. Since all Church Records of this settlement have disappeared,[2] information as to its history is necessarily limited, and it is unfortunate that the records for the years 1643-1690 are missing from the Corporation Book, as edited by Caulfield, as this period is of particular interest in the study of Huguenot history in the City. It is, however, possible partly to fill the gap by reference to the Register of Freemen, and at a later date the Apprentice Indenture Enrolment Book, with the Court of D'Oyer Hundred Book, all three transcribed by Caulfield, is invaluable as a guide to the trades and parentage of the Huguenot apprentices. For the rest, Vestry Books, as those of Christ Church, the municipal church of the City; old Directories, as those of Edward and West, and family records enable the student to piece together something of this lost chapter in the history of the Huguenot settlements.

From 1685 the Register of Freemen is full of references to the refugees. Thus on February 18th in this year appear "Peter Rogue; John James Ribet (or Riblet) Vigié; Peter Billon; and Samuel Ablin," sworn free gratis, "for yt they were poor distressed French Protestants forced to flee their own country by reason of ye persecution." Later in the same year Mathew Savory, Zacharia Trebuseth and Peter Segen are also admitted freemen gratis, "for that they were poor Pro-

---

[1] "Huguenot Settlers," p. 192.

[2] The late Dr. La Touche, the Deputy Keeper of the Records, endeavoured to trace them, but came to the conclusion that they had been destroyed.

testants and forced to fly their country on account of their Religion, ye persecution being then hott in France."[1] Despite the pitying tone adopted towards these newcomers in the civic records, the Corporation in 1693 stated that a committee should be ordered " from time to time to correspond with our Representatives in the next Parliament to have it passed into an Act the excluding of foreigners and such as will not take the Oaths mentioned in a late Act from trading in Corporation and taking away the livelyhood of His Majesty's faithful and loving subjects,"[2] and in August 1685, Anthony Semerat seems to have found greater difficulty than his fellow countrymen in becoming a Cork citizen. This " French refugee was admitted and sworn a member and freeman of ye society of Goldsmyths of Corke by Wm. Hovell, Esq., Mayor of sd. Cittie, for ye sum of 20s. according to ye Act. ye master of sd. Society first refusing ye same."[3]

On the whole, however, the Corporation and citizens of Cork were eager to welcome these fugitives, and put few obstacles in their way. Despite his inauspicious beginning, for instance, Semerat (or Simroe, as he is spelt in the Court of D'Oyer Hundred Book; or Semirot as he himself writes his name) rose to be Warden of his Company in 1710, and Master in 1712. He died in 1743,[4] but he left a son to carry on his name and profession, who was apprenticed to Thomas Dean, a Dublin goldsmith, in 1716.[5]

Peter Rogue, mentioned above, and Thomas Rogue, who was serjeant to the Sheriff of Cork in 1694, may have been connected with Jean La Roque, *maréchal des logis* in de Tuigny's Company under Schomberg in 1689,[6] who was pensioned after Ryswick, especially since a John Laroque,

---

[1] Freemen's Register.
[2] Council Book.
[3] Freemen's Register.
[4] C.H. & A.J., Vol. XII, No. 69. Westropp, " Goldsmiths of Cork."
[5] *Ibid.*, Vol. VIII, No. 53. Berry, " Goldsmiths of Dublin."
[6] De Bostaquet, " Mémoires Inédits."

merchant, was made a freeman in 1709. The famous map-maker of that name was probably a descendant.

Vigié removed from Cork to Galway, and held the office of Mayor there in 1703, where his future history is recorded.[1]

Samuel Ablin may have been a relative of the Jacob Ablin who was a merchant in Dublin in 1642,[2] or of the Isaack Ablin "late of Cane in Normandy" who received his Letters of Denization in Ireland in 1656.[3] He was appointed Sheriff of Cork in 1710,[4] and there seems to have been more than one refugee of the name in the City at that period, for a John Ablin was one of the churchwardens of Christ Church in 1708.[5] The name also occurs in the memoirs of James Fontaine, who writes of a "Mr. Abelin, an Elder of our Church," who kept a shop in Cork and to whom the minister entrusted a sum of money for the relief of certain French weavers whose manufactures were sold by him.[6]

Peter Segen may have come from the Southampton colony, where the name Seguin is found,[7] and it is possible that Savory may have been connected with the family of Tanzia de Savary of Perigord which fled to Holland after the Massacre of St. Bartholomew, and at a later date and in a new genera-tion, removed to England and settled at Greenwich under William III.[8] The will of Daniel Savery of Mallow appears amongst the Cloyne Diocesan Wills in 1704, and a Joshua Savery was one of the copyholders in Mallow in 1711,[9] so that it would appear that the family had become localized outside the City of Cork.

[1] *Vide* p. 212.
[2] Gimlette, p. 216.
[3] Hug. Soc. Pub., Vol. XVIII, p. 337.
[4] Council Book.
[5] Vestry Books, Christ Church.
[6] "Memoirs of a Huguenot Family" (compiled from the autobiography of the Rev. James Fontaine, written in 1722), p. 166.
[7] Gimlette, p. 136.
[8] "Huguenots in England," Appendix.
[9] C.H. & A.J., Vol. XXXIII, 1928.

In July 1699 another group of refugees was admitted to the Freedom of the City, when it was ordered that " And. Dupond; Jo[n]. Dela Croix; Matt. Ardouin, Jun; Peter Guillot; Peter Guillot, Jun.; Adam Billon; Jo[n]. Billon, in consideration that the above persons are all such as have fled their country on account of the Protestant Religion, be admitted free of this Corporation gratis, only paying the Town Clerk's fees."[1]

Dupond was entered in the Freemen's Register as a "Doctor of Physick." Other refugees of this name in Cork and Clonmel will be treated of in the account of the latter settlement.[2] The De La Croix, John, mentioned above, and his father, Isaac, who had been admitted a freeman in June 1696 on payment of five guineas,[3] will be dealt with amongst the settlers of Kinsale[4] where the name later occurs. The name Guillot was localized both in Lisburn and Youghal, and mention has been made of this family in both settlements.[5]

Adam and John Billon must have been relatives of Peter Billon already mentioned. The former took the Oaths at the Cork Assizes, held at the King's Old Castle, in August 1700 in company with a John Caillon.[6] It would thus seem that, unlike most refugees, he obtained the Freedom of the City before naturalization.

The Mathurin Ardouin, junior, who obtained his Freedom in 1699, must have been a son of the Ardouin who in March 1696 was granted the same honour;[7] in 1730 Peter, his son, was also made free.[8] This was possibly the Peter Ardouin who was apprenticed in 1719 to Daniel Pineau, a Dublin Huguenot

---

[1] Council Book.
[2] *Vide* p. 120.
[3] Council Book.
[4] *Vide* p. 87.
[5] *Vide* pp. 71, 183.
[6] Hug. Soc. Pub., Vol. XVIII, p. 347.
[7] Council Book.
[8] Freemen's Register.

C

goldsmith,[1] though he does not appear to have carried on this trade in Cork. He himself was a large enough business man to take apprentices in that city by 1753,[2] and in 1755 he was a member of the Market Jury.

These refugees had been recommended to the Council by the Bishop of Cork,[3] and that a keen sympathy was evinced towards them by both the clergy and laity of the City may be gathered from the Vestry Books of St. Mary's, Shandon,[4] where, under date June 25th, 1699, it is stated that the sum of £71 12s. 3d. was collected "upon receipt of a brief bearing date April 17th, 1699, for the relief of the Vaudoy [sic] and other Protestant refugees." This collection was authorized by Letters Patent, and it is worth noting that another for the same purpose and in the same year is recorded in the Vestry Book of the church at Lisburn as resulting in £24 10s. od.[5]

In the country, too, they were remembered. "Thousands of poor French Protestants fled into England and Ireland," records the Rev. Devereux Spratt of Mitchelstown in his diary on October 17th, 1685, "where they had great sums of money raised for them. I collected in the Union of Tipperary of persons, with myself, who gave no less that £7. I set apart a day of humiliation to seek the Lord for them for spiritual support under suffering."[6]

With the knowledge of this sympathy to cheer them the exiles soon settled down in their adopted city. "They were all," states Burn, "engaged in trade, as merchants, distillers, sugar refiners, etc,"[7] but, as will be seen, there were some

[1] C.H. & A.J., Vol. VIII, No. 53. "Goldsmiths of Dublin."
[2] Enrolment Book of Apprentices.
[3] Bishop Dive Downes.
[4] C.H. & A.J., Vol. X, No. 64. Caulfield, "Records of St. Mary's, Shandon."
[5] U.J.A., Vol. I. Art. "Lisburn."
[6] C.H. & A.J., Vol. XII, No. 70. "Notes on the Autobiography of the Rev. Devereux Spratt, Rector of Brigown, Mitchelstown, 1661-63" (died in 1688).
[7] "History of the Protestant Refugees," Ch. 11, p. 249.

exceptions to this somewhat sweeping rule. Most of them lived in the parish of St. Paul, near Godsell's[1] Lane, and here, when the settlement became sufficiently large and wealthy, they built a church.

In the early stages of the colony the Huguenots met for worship first in Christ Church, then in the County Court room, and later in " a spacious apartment—regularly fitted up for the purpose with pulpit, benches and everything necessary," in the house of their first minister, the Rev. James Fontaine.[2]

This remarkable man was the son of Jacques Fontaine, pastor of Vaux and Royan in Saintonge. He was born in 1658, graduated in the College of Guienne and fled, after imprisonment for his faith, from France. He reached Ireland in December 1694 by way of Taunton, where in 1688 he had been admitted to Holy Orders by the Protestant Synod assembled there,[3] and he entered on his duties as pastor at Cork in January 1695.[4]

Here he found a general welcome. On September 10th, 1694, the Council[5] recommended that " James Fountaine, the French Minister, be admitted free gratis," and he writes, " I have already said that the French had received me with much kindness, I may say the same of the people generally."[6] He established a manufactory of broadcloth in order to support his family, since the congregation was not yet rich enough to offer him a stipend, and as he had not conformed he could not obtain a grant from the Crown.

In 1698 a feud arose in the congregation on the question of his ministerial status. Fontaine offended Mr. Isaac De La Croix by certain references in one of his sermons, and the

---

[1] This name is believed to be Huguenot, and also occurs in Lisburn. In 1799 a James Godsell was a freeman of Cork (Nixon), and as early as 1700 the name appears in the Court of D'Oyer Hundred Book.

[2] " Memoirs," p. 168.

[3] *Ibid.*, p. 143.

[4] *Ibid.*, p. 168.

[5] Council Book.

[6] " Memoirs," p. 171.

latter incited members of the congregation to question his authority as minister, and even, as the pastor states, went about alleging "that I was not a Minister at all."[1] The Bishop[2] therefore recommended that he should be episcopally ordained, and Fontaine having heatedly objected, the matter was brought before the Lords Justices.[3] "Lord Galway," writes the pastor, "was disposed to sacrifice me to please the Bishop of Cork. . . . I wrote to Lord Galway and told him that if any change should be made in the mode of worship I had adopted, by the appointment of an English Clergyman, I should feel myself bound in spite of my resignation to officiate for that portion of the flock who preferred the French usage. I believe this threat was not without its effect in causing Lord Galway to recommend Mr. Marcomb for my successor, which was most satisfactory to me."[4]

On his resignation, the ruin of his manufacture owing to the Act prohibiting the export of woollen goods, and the death of his son, Aaron, in 1699, Fontaine removed to Bearhaven.[5] A writer[6] has stated that at one time the minister occupied and gave his name to Fountainstown, near Ringabella Bay, County Cork, but there seems to be no authority for this belief, and the name Baile Fionntain is said to indicate Fenton's Homestead.[7]

At Bearhaven Fontaine's energy and initiative were turned into the new channel of the establishment of a fishing industry. He induced some French merchants in London to join him in a company on a three years' agreement, and established "thirteen destitute Frenchmen who had served in the Army under King William and been dis-

[1] Ibid.
[2] Edward Wetenhall.
[3] Agnew, "Henri de Ruvigny."
[4] "Memoirs."
[5] Ibid.
[6] C.H. & A.J., Vol. XXIV, No. 117.
[7] C.H. & A.J., Vol. XXV, No. 121. "Place names of the Barony of Kerrycurrihy, Co. Cork."

charged, the War being over,"[1] in Bearhaven and Dursey Island. His aim had been to interest the people of the neighbourhood in the industry, but they were less ready to profit from his enterprise than those of Cork had been, and he writes of the ex-soldiers, " whether it was owing to their ignorance of agriculture or their habits of indolence engendered by a military life, or the perpetual injuries they received at the hands of the Irish, I know not, but certain it is they became discouraged, and most of them left me before the end of the three years."[2]

In 1700 Bishop Dive Downes visited the district,[3] and notes in his invaluable diary under June 10th, " I went from Bantry to Bearhaven in a hooker and returned to Bantry on Wed. 12th of the same month. In the whole Parish of Killaghneenah are about fifteen Protestant families, five of them French "; he gives " Mr. Fountaine " as one of those holding land in this parish.

Fontaine, like his settlers, was plundered by the Irish, and given no protection by the local Courts; his unpopularity in the district was due chiefly to the fact that he had been appointed a Justice of the Peace, and in this capacity he served as a check on the intercourse between the natives and the French privateers who infested the coast. He fortified his dwelling, half farm, half sod fort, which was attacked in 1704 and again in 1708 by the French. In the latter engagement he was taken prisoner, but released on ransom. He was now rendered practically destitute, but the Commander of the Forces in Ireland, and the County of Cork, granted him £100 and £800 respectively, in damages, and he retired to Dublin where he resided until his death in 1728. Here he once more proved his resource by establishing a school

---

[1] " Memoirs," p. 189.
[2] *Ibid.*
[3] Visitation Records. 1699-1702. Edited in C.H. & A.J., Vols. XIV and XV.

in Stephen's Green,[1] in which he proposed to board " Gentlemen's sons," and to " teach them the French, Latin and Greek tongues, also History, Geography, and Mathematics, and especially Piety, for £20 a year, and two guineas entrance."[2]

In his escape from France Fontaine had travelled with the two Mademoiselles Boursiquot, one of whom he subsequently married in 1686. This lady, who shared the bravery and versatility of her husband to the full, defended the sod fort at Bearhaven in his absence and gave valuable assistance in the engagements of 1704 and 1708. She died in Dublin in January 1721.[3]

They had six sons and two daughters; Peter and Francis both graduated in Trinity College, Dublin, took Holy Orders, and left Ireland for America, where they settled in Virginia with James who farmed there. Moses established himself as an engraver in London, and John, after fighting under Peterborough in Catalonia, eventually emigrated, like his brothers, to America, taking with him the famous " Mémoires " written by his father. One of their daughters married Mathew Maury, a refugee from Castel Mauron in Gascony, who settled in Dublin in 1714. In 1719 they also emigrated to Virginia, where Maury died in 1752. His grandson, James, returned to England and set up as a merchant in Liverpool. Mathew Fontaine Maury of the Confederated States Navy was another descendant, and a third was Anna Maury, who published her ancestor's memoirs in New York in 1852.[4]

Another James Fontaine (or Fountaine) was resident in

---

[1] " Memoirs."

[2] Prospectus of the school, quoted in " Dublin Fragments, Social and Historic," Peter, p. 112.

[3] Agnew, " Protestant Exiles," Vol. II, p. 23.

[4] " Huguenots in England," Appendix, and Agnew, " Protestant Exiles from France." Fontaine's mother, two aunts and three brothers settled in London. Details of the English part of his career are given by Smiles, pp. 303-4.

Cork during the early eighteenth century, though he seems to have had no connection with the minister. He was a Warden of the Cordwainers' Company in 1710 and Master in 1720,[1] and in 1711 he married Lucretia Leserve in St. Mary's, Shandon.[2] He may have descended from the James Fountaine, chirurgeon, who received his Freedom in 1656;[3] but a John Fontaine fought in Galway's Regiment of Horse,[4] and Gimlette states that a family of this name settled in Innishannon,[5] so that it seems to have been a common one in Ireland at that date. The surgeon of 1656 must have been the James Fountaine, first Chirurgeon-General in Ireland, who received his patent in Dublin in 1661. A Daniel de Maziers des Fountaines was made Physician General to the Army in 1668, who may have been of the same stock.[6]

Some of the Cork Huguenots of his day are referred to by Fontaine in this autobiography. A Paul Roussier and Claude Bonnet helped him to defend his fort in Bearhaven, and in Cork, besides Abelin, De La Croix, and Marcomb, he speaks of Caillon, P. Renue, P. Cesteau, M. Ardouin, and John Hanneton, to whom, as elders of the French Church and members of its Consistory, he tendered his resignation in June 1698.

Most of these have already been mentioned. Peter Renue (or Renew) was Sheriff in 1691 and Mayor in 1694,[7] and he may have been connected with the Hilary Renue who was naturalized in 1690. A Frenchman named Marcombes was tutor in the household of the Earl of Cork in the early

---

[1] Court of D'Oyer Hundred Book.
[2] C.H. & A.J., Vol. X, No. 64. " Records of St. Mary's, Shandon."
[3] Freemen's Register.
[4] " Hiberniæ Notitia."
[5] " Huguenot Settlers," p. 213.
[6] Cameron, " History of the College of Surgeons, Dublin," and *vide infra* p. 221.
[7] Council Book.

seventeenth century, but he returned to France,[1] and no connection can be traced between him and the pastor who succeeded Fontaine. The name also occurs in Portarlington, where a certain Moyse Marcombe was a surgeon in the early days of the settlement.[2] Of the minister nothing can be discovered in Cork records, and not until 1712 does the history of the Huguenot congregation again emerge.

In that year it was decided to build a church, and on April 29th a deed was executed by which " Joseph Lavit and Elias Lasarre demised to the congregation of French Protestants residing in the city, suburbs and liberties of Cork a plot of ground, containing fifty feet from north to south, situate on the north-east Marshe of Cork, which they had that day taken for the use of the Congregation, from Henry Lumley, to build a convenient house to meet in for the Service of Almighty God for a term of 999 years at £6 5s. od. per annum." The deed was witnessed by H. Mainardue and Jean Jagaultz,[3] the latter of whom was made a freeman in 1700. He was a merchant, as was Elias Lasarre, spelt Lasserris in the Freemen's Register, where he is recorded in 1701.

The situation of the plot of ground thus demised was exactly stated in the lease drawn up on the same day granted by Lumley to Lavit and Lasarre, described therein as " French Protestants." It was " bounded on the North with the Garden of William Kirkpatrick, on the South with the waste ground of the said Henry Lumley, on the East with Lumley Street and on the West with Ballard's Lane."[4] The

---

[1] Gimlette, p. 169.

[2] Hug. Soc. Proc., Vol. XIII, p. 560.

[3] Quoted by Burn (Ch. 11, p. 249), who transcribed the deed then in the possession of the Rector of St. Paul's. No trace of it now exists amongst the records of that church, which, with those of Christ Church, the author has been permitted to examine by the kindness of the present Rector, and no mention of any French Church occurs in these records, although it formed part of the parish.

[4] Copy of leases preserved amongst the Hardy MSS.

fact that there were three Ballard's Lanes in Cork has made for some confusion in identifying this site, but the Ballard's Lane here mentioned had become Carey's Lane, the title by which it is now known, by 1742. In January of 1733 an adjoining almshouse, comprising a frontage of thirty-eight feet and a depth of sixty feet, was also taken by lease from Hugh Lumley by Elias Lasarre and James Massiot at £4 a year and £100 fine;[1] the lease extended over the same term as the earlier one, and the ground was utilized as a graveyard.

That the church was in existence by 1737 is proved in the attack made by " Alexander the Coppersmith " in his " Remarks on the Religion; trade; Government etc., of the City of Cork," on the religious denominations of the City. These are divided according to the public edifices into " episcopacy, presbytery, quakerism, anabaptism, huguenotism, hypocrisy and popery," and they are all denounced but the Huguenots, who are passed over since he "will not reproach a set of exiles in their misery."[2]

In Caulfield's " Annals of Cork," prefixed to his edition of the Council Book, a king's letter is quoted from the " Irish Book " (IX, 463) in which it appears that by 1745 there must have been two French Churches in the City; but no trace of the second now remains. " We are acquainted by your letter that there are two French Churches in Cork which have conformed to the Liturgy of the Church of Ireland, and that several industrious French Protestant families have lately come over and settled in Cork, induced by the opportunity they have of worshipping God according to their conscience, and desiring a salary of £50 per an. for support of each of said Churches. We give you orders for placing same on Civil establishment." The communication is dated

---

[1] Copy of leases preserved amongst the Hardy MSS.
[2] Printed in Cork by George Harrison, 1737. Quoted Tuckey, " Cork Remembrancer."

at " St. James," November 25th, 1745. Further proof is given in an appeal made by John Pick (Pique), the minister of the church, on August 19th, 1774,[1] which is summarized in the " Irish Book." He had been " invited from Geneva by the French Protestants of Cork, received a salary of £75 by subscription. He has been Minister of said Church since 1732. The subscription has failed by the death of many heads of French Protestant families. In 1745 he had but £50 p.a. from both Churches in Cork, the duty of which he performed alone since the death of his colleague, the Rev. John Madras; he has no other means of support for his family and is now 67 years of age.—Prays that the whole sum of £100 on Civil List be granted to him. His case is supported by the present and late Bishops of Cork, Churchwardens and Elders of the French Church." He was ordered to receive £100 per annum, from November of the same year.

The Baronne de Chambrier[2] states that in 1745 new refugee manufacturers arrived in Cork, and that these founded the second French Church, and since it has been stated by a descendant of the Besnard family[3] that the linen manufacturer Julius Besnard was instrumental in establishing the French Church in Cork, and since no reference to him is made in the deed quoted above, it is probable that this new church owed its origin to him. Smith, however, writing of Cork in 1750, speaks of only one congregation, which, he says, uses the Liturgy of the Church of England,[4] and in the map appended to his history the locality of the former church alone is marked.

The church in Lumley Street continued until about 1813,

[1] " Irish Book," XII, p. 294. Quoted Caulfield's " Annals."
[2] Hug. Soc. Proc., Vol. VI, p. 423. " Projet de Colonisation."
[3] " Notes on the Besnard Family." Compiled by Canon Evans.
[4] " Ancient and Present State of the Co. and City of Cork," Bk. II, Ch. 9.

when "the congregation which had previously dwindled away to one or two individuals, entirely ceased to exist."[1] In 1797 Thomas Stopford, the then Bishop of Cork, granted the use of the French Church to the Methodist community, who occupied it until 1805, when their own chapel, situated in Patrick's Street, was opened, and in 1841 it was leased to the Primitive Methodists, who had held their services there from 1819.[2] In 1897 it was eventually sold to the Wesleyan Methodists, and has since become a sugar store, the property of the Messrs. Newsom.

By their great kindness the writer has been enabled to study their copy of the lease of 1841, which is of the greatest interest since a map is appended clearly showing the confines of the church and the extent of the graveyard which ran behind it, and which is now built over.[3] It also proves that recognized Huguenot families were still residing in Cork at that date, since the Rev. Robert Longfield, in whose possession the buildings and ground lay,[4] stipulates to the lessees that they shall hold the property " saving and reserving at all times unto the families of the French Huguenots in the City of Cork all such right of burial in the graveyard or ground to the rere of the said French Church fronting Carey's Lane . . . as they at any time heretofore possessed and enjoyed with full and free liberty for them at all times hereafter . . . to enter the same for the purpose of burial as aforesaid." The lessees were permitted " to rebuild and enlarge the said church," but only " so that such building or enlarging should not in any manner interfere with or prevent the families of

[1] Burn, p. 250.
[2] From information kindly supplied by Mr. Robert Walker of Cork.
[3] The French Church ran from north to south, that constructed by the Wesleyans from east to west, thus the graveyard which was on the northwest side of the original church was destroyed in the erection of the new building.
[4] The property had passed into the possession of the Longfield family in 1773. (Note supplied by Mr. Robert Walker.)

the said French Huguenots from the right of burial . . . in the said graveyard."[1]

In 1897, however, Mountifort Longfield, Esq., agreed to sell to the trustees for the Methodist Church." The preaching House, commonly called the French Church with the Graveyard, etc. . . . discharged from all the limitations, powers and provisions under the Settlement,"[2] and the cemetery behind the church has disappeared, a small part at the side of the present store being all that remains. This contains three slabs[3] and a piece of broken white marble said to be from the Hardy Monument which once adorned the western wall of the church and recorded the family motto, "Tout Hardi."

It seems, however, that long before 1897 the Wesleyan congregation had interpreted their permission to build and enlarge the church very liberally and without consulting the remaining clauses of the lease, for the Perrier Monument was removed from the French Church by Sir Anthony Perrier who died in 1845, owing to the fact that the church was then being pulled down to make room for the new Wesleyan Chapel, and that many of the old tombstones were being destroyed in the process.[4]

As far as may be ascertained the ministers of the Cork French Churches were as follows:

1694.   James Fontaine.
1698.   Marcombe.
1732–1783. John Pique, Senior.

---

[1] Copy lease, Rev. R. Longfield to Fras. Jackson and Ors, June 23rd, 1841. (Entered Registry Office, Dublin, July 5th, 1841.)
[2] Conveyance, Aug. 3rd, 1897. M. J. C. Longfield to Rev. Jas. Robertson and Ors.
[3] Two (those to the Malet and Hardy families) are of the nineteenth century. The third is indecipherable.
[4] J.A.P.M.D., 1901. Excerpts from Dr. Caulfield's MS. re the destruction of the graves.

1739–1773. John Madras.

1783–1810. John Pick, Junior.

1786. Justin de Mont Cenis. (Appointed to Dublin.)

1794–1813. Thomas Goetval.

Thomas Windandus Goetval was a native of Switzerland.[1] In October 1794 he was licensed to be Curate Assistant of the French Church on the nomination of the Rev. John Pick.[2] He resided in Anne Street,[3] and died about 1813, when the congregation broke up.

Mont Cenis was priested at Cloyne on letters dimissory from Cork in 1786. He was appointed to Cork[4] but removed to Dublin in the same year, and served in the French Church in St. Patrick's Cathedral until his death in 1795.[5]

John Madras, son of a Madras of Amsterdam, who came to Cork in 1735,[6] was ordained as French minister in 1739, and held that post until his death in 1773. In 1740 he was appointed chaplain to the Earl of Kingston, and in 1745 was created Precentor of Ross. He was twice married, and the Rev. John Henry Madras was the child of his second wife, Alice, daughter of Henry Baldwin of Curravody, County Cork. He was buried in the French Church.[7]

His son, John Henry, entered Trinity College, Dublin, in 1791, was priested in Cork in 1797, and was successively curate of Kilmichael, Durrus and Kinneagh and priest of Nohoval. In 1833 he was Vicar of Aglish and he died in 1852. He married in 1801, Martha, daughter of Richard Evanson, and their son, John, made freeman of Cork in 1826, was Prebendary of Donoughmore in 1851.[8]

[1] Burn, p. 250.
[2] Brady, " Records of Cork, Cloyne and Ross."
[3] West's Directory, 1810.
[4] Brady.
[5] Hug. Soc. Proc., Vol. VIII, p. 87. "Hug. Chs. of Dublin."
[6] Burn, p. 249
[7] Brady.
[8] *Ibid.*

John Pique was ordained deacon in 1742 and priest in 1744, presumably owing to the fact that the French Churches had then decided to conform to the Church of Ireland. He married in the same year a Miss Mary Pick, possibly a cousin, at St. Mary's, Shandon, Cork. He was succeeded in the ministry by another John Pick, probably his son, who was "Licensed on 3rd April, 1783, to the care of the French Reformed Church and Congregation in Cork City, vacant by the death of Rev. John Pick, late Minister, on nomination of the Duke of Portland, late Lord Lieutenant of Ireland."[1] In the Freemen's Register the Rev. John Pick, junior, appears under date June 1779, so that he may have assisted in the French or some other City church before his appointment in 1783. He seems to have been in more comfortable financial circumstances than his predecessor, and to have owned some property, for in the Council Book appears an order under date August 8th, 1786, that "£150 (be paid) to the Rev. John Pick for the purchase of his interest in his dwelling house in Princes Street, and the ground belonging thereto, on his making a sufficient title."

He had a son Thomas, Lieutenant in the Kilkenny Regiment of Foot, who fought in the battle of Waterloo, and for his gallant conduct was admitted a freeman at large of the City on October 28th, 1815, "The Board being desirous that a public testimony of their approbation should be recorded."[2]

Another John Pick, a wine merchant, was living in Cork in 1729. He seems to have been well-to-do, for in the Council Book an order is given in September of that year that "a bond under the City Seal be passed to Mr. John Pick, Wine Merchant, so much lent by him for that purpose (finishing the Church of St. Mary's, Shandon) at 5%."[3] He may have been the father of Mary Pick, wife of the French minister.

[1] *Ibid.* Quoted from Diocesan Registry.
[2] Freemen's Register.
[3] Council Book.

But the most interesting member of the Pick family in Cork was the famous Sir Vesian, Mayor of the City in 1796. He was the son of the first minister of that name, and in 1761 was bound apprentice by him to William Ricketts, a Cork merchant.[1] In 1779 he was appointed Sheriff, in 1796 Mayor, and he died in 1822, being buried in the family vault beneath the floor of the French Church. During his mayoralty the French attempted a landing in Bantry Bay, and for his activity in the defence of Cork he was knighted and voted the sum of £29 14s. 1d. by the Court of D'Oyer Hundred.

Many stories have been told of this Huguenot Mayor who found the intricacies of the English language and English Law equally difficult to master, but the most memorable is that of the letter sent by him to the Lord-Lieutenant in the height of Cork's panic on the arrival of the French, in which he assures His Excellency that he " wrote with a sword in one hand and a pistol in the other."[2]

His eldest son, Andrew, bound apprentice to his father in 1790,[3] was admitted a freeman in 1798, and Captain Vesian Pick of the '89 Regiment of Foot was also made free of the City in 1813.[4]

To turn from the clerical families of Huguenot extraction to the Huguenot business men is to find how very important was the part that they played in the commercial life of Cork. Sir Vesian was only one of the many Huguenot aldermen, and to deal with all the names appearing in the Municipal and Parish Records would be an impossibility. A few facts in the lives of the most important can alone be indicated.

The Goldsmiths' Guild of Cork in particular seems to have attracted the refugees, and in its records appear many of

[1] Enrolment Book of Apprentices.
[2] C.H. & A.J., Vol. I. " Old Cork Celebrities."
[3] Enrolment Book of Apprentices.
[4] Freemen's Register.

their names, such as Foucault, Pantaine, Semirot, Billon, Codier, Toulon, Tolekin, and Robinette. That of Goble is also said to be of Huguenot origin,[1] although this family appeared in Cork a considerable time before any of the others. "The influence of these immigrants upon the design and execution of the Goldsmiths' work which was wrought in the City," writes Sir Charles Jackson,[2] "may be seen in the numerous examples of the art still preserved, which resemble the contemporary styles prevailing on the Continent much more closely than the English work of the same period."

In 1656 when the Goldsmiths were incorporated, Robert and Edward Goble, Braziers, possibly sons of the John Goble who was a brazier in 1639, were appointed trustees of the Company. The former became Master in 1695, and Robert Goble, junior, probably his son, who died in 1737, was made Warden in 1719.[3] The Gobles were goldsmiths of note. Much of the Church plate of the period, such as that of Innishannon or St. Fachtna's, Ross, was their manufacture,[4] and in 1696 the Mace of the associated Guilds of Cork[5] was made by the junior Robert. The Silver Oar of the Corporation is also said to be their work,[6] and this is the more likely as their services were requisitioned by the Council whenever a box in which to present the Freedom of the City was needed.[7] From an entry in the Vestry Book of Christ Church, dated 1676, it would seem that they acted as bankers as well as goldsmiths, for the churchwardens ordered that a sum which had been bequeathed to the parish, the interest on

[1] C.H. & A.J., Vol. XXIV, No. 117.
[2] "English Goldsmiths and Their Trade Marks," p. 681.
[3] C.H. & A.J., Vol. XII, No. 69. "The Goldsmiths of Cork."
[4] Webster, "Church Plate of the Dioceses of Cork, Cloyne and Ross," p. 135.
[5] Now in the South Kensington Museum.
[6] C.H. & A.J., Vol. XXIV, No. 117.
[7] Council Book.

which was to go to the poor weekly "in bread," should be "lett out to Mr. Robert Goble, the Jeweller."[1]

James Foucault was another leading goldsmith, often employed by the Corporation. He must have been that Jacques, son of Peter Foucault, surgeon, of Dublin, who was apprenticed in 1700 to the Dublin goldsmith, John Harris.[2] The earliest notice of him in Cork occurs in 1714, and by 1729 he was dead, for, in July of that year, the Council ordered "that £8 6s. od. be paid the Widow Foucault, for seven silver boxes given with freedoms."[3]

Simon Peter Codier, who was one of Foucault's apprentices, was made free in 1725.[4] The latest notice of him occurs in 1759. Samuel Pantaine appears from 1678. He was Master of the Guild in 1679 and 1686, and he died three years later.[5] Semirot and Billon have already been mentioned. Tolekin was naturalized in 1768 as a foreign merchant, now of the City of Cork,[6] and worked as a silversmith from 1795-1836.[7] Robinette did not come to Cork until 1791, when he was apprenticed to Carden Terry. He is described as coming from Tullagh, County Waterford,[8] and may be the son of Roger Robinette of that county who was dead by 1781.[9] The family seems to have intermarried with that of Quarry.

William Teulon is given in the list of Goldsmiths in 1791, and S. Teulon in 1845.[10] The first settler of the name in Cork was Pierre, perhaps a brother of Antoine Teulon who settled in Greenwich, and was naturalized in 1708. If so, he was

[1] Vestry Book, Christ Church. The writer has been informed that the last representative of this family in the City took his mother's name of Barry.
[2] C.H. & A.J., Vol. VIII, No. 53. "Goldsmiths of Dublin."
[3] Council Book.
[4] Council Book.
[5] C.H. & A.J., Vol. XII. "Goldsmiths of Cork."
[6] Hug. Soc. Pub., Vol. XXVII, p. 236.
[7] C.H. & A.J., Vol. XII. "Goldsmiths of Cork."
[8] Enrolment Book of Apprentices.
[9] W. & S.E.I.A.J., 1915.
[10] C.H. & A.J., Vol. XII.

descended from Jean Teulon, who fled from Nismes at the Revocation, but "no evidence is forthcoming to confirm or disprove the tradition that the patriarch of the Irish family and Antoine were brothers, the books of the French Church at Greenwich and Cork being lost."[1]

A John Teulon, who had been educated at the Blue Coat School, was apprenticed to the Cork merchant, Westcombe Wood, in 1761.[2] That the 'prentice boy became himself a successful merchant is evinced by an entry in the Corporation Book in July 1789, ordering that a Bond for £500 at 6 per cent. should be passed to him. His son, Charles, was bound apprentice to him in 1800, but later seems to have abandoned business for the Army, if he was the Captain Charles Teulon of the 28th Regiment of Foot who was admitted freeman at large for his gallantry at Waterloo, in company with Lieutenant Thomas Pick.[3] Two John Teulons are mentioned as distillers by West in 1810.[4]

Amongst the civic families of Cork, those of Hardy, Besnard and Perrier, which have already been mentioned in connection with the French Church, were eminent.

Of all the Huguenot families connected with the City, that of Hardy is the most interesting, since a complete record of each step in its history may be pieced together from the treasure of original documents and manuscripts still extant in the possession of one of its members. Not only does the original passport of the first Hardy to come to England still survive, but certificates from the Walloon and Irish Huguenot Churches. Naturalization Papers, Marriage Licences, Apprentice Indentures, some in the original, some in contemporary copies, have all been preserved, so that a student, privileged as was the present writer to peruse these papers, has spread

---

[1] "Miscellanea Genealogica et Heraldica," 4th Series, Vol. II (1906-1907).
[2] Enrolment Book of Apprentices.
[3] Freemen's Register.
[4] Directory—County and City of Cork.

out before him a picture rich in contemporary detail, and valuable not only as a record of this particular family but as an illustration of many of the experiences met with by the Huguenots in general.

For this reason, and since these records have not before been published, it has been thought well to trace the history of the Hardy family in full.

This task has been considerably lightened by the inclusion among the papers of " A Simple Family Narrative by way of Preface to the Contents of these Manuscripts," written by Simeon Henry Hardy, the grandson of the original settler, in 1799.

In this he states: "I believe that my great-grandmother succeeded to, and continued in, the trade in which my great-grandfather was engaged on his death, which I believe to have been largely mercantile." This was in La Rochelle, and here the great-grandmother, Madame Hardy, née Gayott, who must have been a lady of some initiative, commenced the written records of the family by keeping a register, probably in her Bible, of the more important family events. It was transcribed by a niece or nephew and exists in this form amongst the papers; in it, it is stated that on Easter Sunday, March 30th, 1698, Henry Hardy was born.

Also amongst the papers is the original of the passport granted to the latter in February 1717, which allowed him to proceed to Holland " by the first vessel that will leave and to remain there for three years for the purpose of learning the language and commerce, at the end of which time he will be bound to return to France, in conformity with the bail and under the penalties attached thereto."[1] His age is given as sixteen, an obvious understatement, perhaps deliberately made by the boy himself.

---

[1] Original in French. Given at La Rochelle, February 17th, 1717, and signed by the Comte de Chamilly, "Lieutenant Général des Armées du Roy—Commandant en chef pour Sa Majesté dans les Provinces de Poitou, Saintonge, Pais d'Aunix et Isles y adjacentes."

In Holland he resided with a family at Edenberg, but two years later, despite the stipulations of the passport and perhaps thinking the opportunity of leaving France too good to be missed, he crossed to England, where he was received by his uncle, Monsieur Beteilhe (or Betheile or Bertheile or Bethaille—all four forms are found in the manuscripts), whose family had been naturalized in 1702. In May of the following year, according to the record written by himself in French and contained amongst the papers, he married Miss Martha Beteilhe, daughter of the above, when " Monsieur La Rivierre, Minister of the Greek Church, blessed our nuptials."

The Beteilhe family, according to the narrative of Simeon Hardy, " were in the height of affluence " before the failure of the South Sea Bubble, in which they speculated heavily, cost them their property. Henry Hardy obtained a handsome *dot* with his wife, and seems to have had plans for setting up as a merchant in London on a large scale. He took all the necessary Oaths, became a member of some of the City Guilds, and leased premises in Token House Yard. With the failure of his father-in-law, however, these plans were ruined. He became a mercer on Ludgate Hill, and by 1729, when his fourth son, Richard, was born, he had removed to Dublin. Here he engaged in the provision trade and, as stated by his grandson, " through his brother-in-law Rickard a merchant of Rochelle had the supplying of the French Government with Irish Provisions until the breaking out of the War with that Nation put a stop to that trade."

Amongst the manuscripts is a certificate given in January 1728 by the Town Clerk of Dublin, which states that " Henry Hardy Mercht. was admitted into ye Libtys. and Franchises of ye City of Dublin in Christmas Assembly, 1728, and was then accordingly Sworn and Inroll[d]." It is added that " the within Henry Hardy did not come in free of the City by the Act of Parliament and was not obliged to take all the Oaths, but took ye Oath of Allegiance to his Ma[e]tie, subscribed the

Deed and took ye Freeman's Oath." The "Certificate of his taking the Oaths" is also extant.

As far as may be ascertained from the papers, Henry Hardy had five daughters and four sons. Of these Henrietta married William Barbe of Dublin,[1] and secondly Thomas Lamphière, who died at Mallow in 1770; and Henry Barthélemy, who was born in London on November 26th, 1722, was apprenticed to his father in the business[2] and married in Dublin on March 14th, 1744, Mary, daughter of Charles Boileau, whose family will be dealt with amongst the Huguenots of that city. Their marriage settlement exists amongst the papers, as does an agreement made between the bridegroom and members of the Boileau family dealing with property which had come to him with his wife. The marriage was solemnized by the Rev. Jean Pierre Droz, brother-in-law of the bride, and his characteristic signature appears on both documents.

It would seem that in 1746 Henry Hardy, senior, had thoughts of settling again in London, for he procured a certificate from the French Church in Dublin, signed by the Nonconformist minister, Paul de St. Ferreol, and was recommended by the Consistory of London to M. François Noguier, "Ancien du Quatier de Temple," "l'Église ne se croyant obligée de reconnoitre pour membres que ceux quy sont sur le Catalogue de l'Ancien de leur Quatier." This certificate and recommendation covered the entire family, including "La veuve Me. Susanne Beteilhe, avec Monsr. Henry, père, et Me. Susanne Hardy, sa femme; Mr. Henry Hardy, leur fils ainé et Me. Marie Hardy, sa femme; et Mr. Richard Hardy, leur second fils,"[3] and in June and August of that year the younger members of the family crossed to England, Richard "by the direction of Mr. Edward Mason, Secretary to H.R.H.

---

[1] *Vide* p. 246.

[2] A copy of his Apprentice Indenture, enrolled in the Trinity Guild of Merchants, July 19th, 1740, is extant.

[3] Actually the fourth son, but by then two older children had died.

the Duke of Cumberland." The old man did not leave until October, and his residence in London only lasted for two years, for he returned to Ireland in August 1748, five months before his death.

Henry Hardy, junior, had also returned to Dublin, and on the death of his father he became a grocer in Pill Lane, and later a clerk to Digges La Touche. "My recollection," states his son Simeon, "just leads me to remember our residence in lodgings near the Linen Hall, Dublin, from whence we removed to Cork; My father coming in the situation of Book-keeper to Richard Bradshaw of that City, Merchant, at a salary of £60 per annum." Here he died on July 12th, 1783, having been predeceased by his wife by twenty-three years.

They had ten children, the record of whose short lives makes tragic reading, since one was stillborn, six died in infancy, and two at the early ages of fifteen and twenty-three years respectively. "My son John Hardy," records the father, "I sent to sea for a tryal on board the *Elizabeth*, Captain William Brown. He sailed from Corke 3rd January, 1769, for Gibraltar, Portmahon and Baltimore in Maryland and was drowned May 1769, 50 leagues from Maryland, aged 15 years. By all accounts he bore an excellent character even from Capt. Brown, nephew of my present wife." Of Peter Harmer Hardy, born in George's Street, Cork, in November 1759, he records in the family Bible " died in 1782 in East Indies when with his relative Governor Droz."

The "present wife" mentioned above had been a Miss Susanna Perdrian, a lady stated by her stepson Simeon to be fifteen years older than the widower, who had married her, it is somewhat unkindly added, "purely for the sake of his children living by his first wife." That this marriage occurred very soon after Hardy became a widower is proved by "Articles of Agreement" made in November 1760 between him and Miss Perdrian, and witnessed by Harmer Delahoide and Peter Ardouin, who were also appointed trustees for his children in his will. The latter has already been mentioned amongst the Huguenot families of Cork, and the bride must have been a descendant of the Osea Perdriau who was admitted a freeman of the City in 1683.

Simeon Henry Hardy, who was born on January 20th, 1748-9, and was baptized as stated in his father's Bible record " at home in Pill Lane by the Rev. Mr. Droz " and " received into the French Church of Cork after having passed his examinations under the Rev. Mr. John Madras, 4th August, 1765," was apprenticed to this Mr. Harmer Delahoide when twelve years of age. " God Allmighty," is the pious wish recorded by his father, " mark him with grace to be an honest man," and that this was fulfilled is attested on the back of the Apprentice Indenture preserved among the papers, where it is certified by Delahoide that " the within named Simeon Henry Hardy served me as apprentice for the full term of seven years and upwards and behaved very dilligent, faithfull and honnest."

In February 1771 he married Miss Jane Johnson, and in the summer of that year opened a " ware room for the sale of Linens." He died at his residence in George's Street in 1810, and was buried in the Huguenot graveyard, where a stone now indecipherable marked the grave of " the much lamented Simeon Henry Hardy, with his venerated parents Henry and Mary."[1]

He left a very numerous family, all listed in his " small Bible ": among them Henry, sworn Attorney at the King's Bench in 1794, who married Eliza, daughter of Charles Evanson, Mayor of Cork, and was the first Secretary of the Harbour Board; Andrew, who served in the Royal Navy, and died in the City in 1816; Robert, who died in 1847 and was interred in the French graveyard; Simeon, who left Ireland for Dominica, possibly owing to the fact that the family were shipowners and had by now become interested in the West

[1] J.A.P.M.D., 1901.

Indian sugar trade, but returned to Cork in the year of his father's death, and whose grave may still be seen in the Huguenot burial-ground; and John Peter, whose name was recorded on the monument erected in what was once the French Church, and whose burial may be taken as closing the long chapter of Huguenot history in the City.

This monument which has now been destroyed stated that:

The Burial Place of the
HARDY FAMILY,
French Huguenots,
Was outside this wall.   One of the first interments in it
Was that of MARIE, daughter of
CHARLES BOILEAU,
Lord of Castelnau, and wife of
HENRY HARDY,
Who died on the 17th June, 1760.
And the last was that of
JOHN PETER HARDY,
Who died on the 14th May, 1868.
" Tout Hardi."

The ancestor of the Besnard family, which established itself in Cork in the early eighteenth century, was an advocate of Paris who fled to Holland at the Revocation, and there found refuge with a sail-maker who taught him how to support himself by this art.[1]   He married Marie Du Bois, also a fugitive from Paris, and had twenty-two children, the eldest of whom, Pierre, emigrated to Ireland and settled as a merchant in Cork.   Besnard of Cork married a Miss Worthington and had three daughters and two sons, Julius and Jean.   The latter traded as captain of a merchant vessel to Portugal and

---

[1] These notes have been taken from a MS. history of the family, compiled by the late Canon T. E. Evans, now in the possession of the Very Rev. W. Wilson, late Dean of Cloyne.

the West Indies, and died without male issue. Julius[1] resided at Douglas near Cork, where he established a linen factory with a hamlet for the workmen,[2] and, as well as helping to establish a French Church in the City, he was instrumental in the erection of Douglas Church in 1785, where many of the family are buried. He died in 1815, leaving his factory in the hands of his eldest son, who was appointed Inspector General of the Southern Provinces for the Linen Board, and in this capacity toured the South in 1816.[3] The Besnards were successively Mayors of Cork: John in 1831, his brother Peter in 1835, and the latter's eldest son Julius in 1839, who was thus the last Protestant Mayor before the Municipal Corporation Act threw that office open to Roman Catholics, and the last occupier of the old Mansion House, now the Mercy Hospital.

The sailcloth factory established by the Besnards was, according to Smith,[4] "the largest in the Kingdom." "We had almost been led to believe that this Manufactory had become extinct," says West in 1810, "but . . . we found it had increased one half since the period at which Mr. Smith wrote. Upwards of 1,000 hands are now employed in these extensive concerns belonging to Messrs. Julius Besnard & Sons, who have also, at a short distance, an extensive Rope walk."[5] Sailcloth was in great demand during the Napoleonic War, but the trade collapsed in 1815 when the Government contracts ceased.[6] The junior Besnards emigrated for the

---

[1] Gimlette states ("Huguenot Settlers," p. 166) that the Besnards were connected with Sir Julius Cæsar, Chancellor of the Exchequer under Charles I. If this is correct it may account for the name Julius Cæsar, given to the second son of Julius Besnard, but no mention of this is made by Canon Evans.

[2] Edward, "Cork Remembrancer," 1792.

[3] Gill, "Rise of the Irish Linen Industry."

[4] "Ancient and Present State of the Co. and City of Cork." He describes the factory in full with statistics of the manufacture.

[5] "Directory."

[6] Gill, p. 126.

most part to Australia, Canada and the U.S.A., and the name is now extinct in Cork.[1]

The Perrier family derived from Brittany, whence Mark du Perrier emigrated to Ireland after 1685. His son, Antoine, a cavalry officer who fell at Malplaquet, had a son, John Perrier of Dublin, who married Louisa De La Mazière and died in 1737. Their son, Anthony, born 1712, became a leading merchant, and High Sheriff of Dublin, before his death in 1772.[2] He married twice, his second wife being Susanna, daughter of Ferdinand Spiller of Ross, County Cork, and their son, David, born 1765, established the family in Cork, where he had been apprenticed in 1779 to the merchant Thomas Burnett.[3] Tuckey records that on February 9th, 1795, "David Perrier, one of the City Sheriffs, and Strettell Jackson, Common Speaker, presented the Freedom of this City to the Lord Lieutenant. . . . His Excellency conferred the honour of Knighthood on the former."[4] In 1813 Sir David was made Mayor, a position, according to the *Southern Reporter* of October 1814, which he " maintained with dignity and splendour, with which was united an appropriate hospitality."[5] Tradition states that he lived at Lota, a large house on the River Lee at some distance from the City, and maintained a twenty-oared state barge in which it was his custom to visit the residences fronting the river. His brother, Anthony, born in 1770, appears as Sheriff in 1808, as Mayor in 1820, and was knighted by the Lord-Lieutenant on the latter's visit to Cork in 1829. In 1821 he was entrusted with the address sent by the Corporation to George IV on his Accession, and he died in 1845. His eldest son was Sheriff in 1832, and his daughter married a grandson of Julius Besnard.

---

[1] Canon Evans, MS.
[2] J.A.P.M.D., 1912.
[3] Enrolment Book of Apprentices.
[4] " Cork Remembrancer."
[5] C.H. & A.J., Vol. I, p. 46.

It has been suggested that the Perriers were not forced to fly from France, but were wine and general merchants from Bordeaux, who preferred, for business reasons, to reside in Ireland,[1] but this is disproved by Agnew, by the family records from which the writer has been permitted to quote, and by the fact that an Antoine Perrier, who must have been a relative, was sent to the Galleys at Bordeaux for his faith in 1698. Further details of the family, members of which are still resident in Cork, are given in the "Cork Historical and Archæological Journal" (Vol. XXII, No. 109, p. 80).

Lavitte, Dumas, Allenet, Laulie, Cossart, Perdriau, Mathis, Jappie, Plaincé, Bonbonous, Verdille, d'Altera and Malet are only a few amongst the other Huguenot names in the civic records which it is possible to notice, even shortly, here. Some, as Arnaud, Belesaigne, Mazière, Jacques, Le Grand and Le Febre, occur also in other settlements, where they will later be recorded, and De La Cour, De La Main and Lamellière are families which must be mentioned since they form exceptions to the general rule that the Huguenots of Cork were solely interested in commerce.

For the rest, Boileau, Demijour and Pothet are names mentioned by Crofton Croker;[2] Journeaux by Windele;[3] Bussy, Boneval and Pelion by Burn;[4] and Cazalette by Weiss.[5] John Lorie, described as " a French Protestant Stranger, now a Merchant of the City of Cork," was naturalized in August 1721. In 1735 Lucas Robbins, mariner, "a French Protestant of the City of Cork," took the Oaths at the General Assizes. In 1738 Peter Ferray, who was born in Havre, was naturalized and made a Cork citizen; and in 1764 John Baptist Langlois also obtained his naturalization at the

---

[1] *Vide* J.A.P.M.D., 1901.
[2] MS. notes to Smith's "Ancient and Present State of the Co. and City of Cork." Ed. Day & Coppinger.
[3] "Historical Notices of Cork."
[4] "History of the Refugees."
[5] "Histoire des Réfugiés."

Cork Assizes.[1] A Peter Boisseau was Warden of the Barber Chirurgeons' Guild in 1713,[2] and John Labarte is given as a merchant and freeman by Nixon in 1799.[3] His son, Edward, later removed to Clonmel.[4]

The name Lavitte is of especial interest since Lavit's Quay still exists, and more than one member of the family attained a place in the Corporation. The first to do so was Joseph Lavit, made free in 1696, who was appointed Sheriff in 1713 and Mayor in 1720.[5] His connection with the French Church has already been mentioned. Walter and Nathaniel Lavit, who served him as apprentices and may have been his sons, were made free in 1716. The former was Sheriff in 1733 and Mayor in 1745.[6] He was a churchwarden of Christ Church in 1737,[7] and a member in the same year of the first Market Jury sworn in Cork.

An interesting reference is made by two tourists who visited the city in 1746 to a " Mons. de Vitte, a French refugee merchant in Cork, who has acquired a large estate by traffic ";[8] since no mention occurs at any time in the Council Book of a M. de Vitte, and since a merchant of a " large estate " could scarcely escape notice therein, it is reasonable to connect this gentleman with the Walter or Nathaniel Lavit mentioned above. The " traffic " seems to have been in sugar, for in the Dublin newspaper, *Pue's Occurrences*, of December 1st, 1741, an advertisement is inserted to the effect that " Nathaniel Lavit at his Sugar House in Corke " will sell " all sorts of refined sugars, white sirrop, Mollosses and Spirits at reasonable Rates." A

[1] Hug. Soc. Pub., Vol. XXVII, p. 236.
[2] Court of D'Oyer Hundred Book.
[3] " Cork Almanack."
[4] Freemen's Register.
[5] Council Book.
[6] *Ibid.*
[7] Vestry Book.
[8] " A Tour Through Ireland," 1746 (Dublin).

Lieutenant Lavit is recorded by De Bostaquet[1] in the company of de Varengues under Schomberg in 1689, but any possible connection between him and the Cork family cannot now be traced.

Peter Dumas from Laroche "took the Oaths" as a Protestant Stranger in 1704,[2] and it was possibly his son, Peter, who was Sheriff of Cork in 1781, and his grandson, Peter William, who was Mayor in 1812.[3]

The first mention of an Allenette occurs in 1708, when the Council ordered that "John Allenet, merchant, and Sergnenoran Augée, gent.," [sic] be admitted free "on the act."[4] The spelling of the latter name represents a somewhat harassed attempt to indicate Lieutenant Seigneuron Augier, who was one of the Waterford Huguenots and will be further referred to in the chapter on that settlement. His fellow freeman seems to have been the father of Moses Allenet, whose eldest son, John, was admitted a freeman in 1761 and is recorded as carrying on a tanning industry in the City.[5]

Jacob Laulie, to whom Moses Allenet had been apprenticed, was made a freeman in 1718. Peter, his eldest son, was a churchwarden of Christ Church in 1748,[6] and one of the Market Jurymen in 1755. The efforts made to spell his name in the Church Records give an amusing example of the changes suffered by these French names. It is recorded as Laullie, sometimes as Lauke, rewritten always differently, and finally corrected into Laulie.

A David Cossort, merchant, from Rowen [sic] "took the Oaths" in November 1670,[7] and possibly settled in Cork,

---

1 "Mémoires Inédits."
2 Agnew, quoting Dublin Patent Rolls.
3 Council Book and Gibson's "Cork."
4 Council Book.
5 Freemen's Register.
6 Vestry Book.
7 Hug. Soc. Pub., Vol. XVIII, p. 343.

where in 1725 a Peter Cossart, merchant, obtains his Freedom[1] and appears as Cornet in a Regiment of Horse in the City Militia.[2] His son, John, was Sheriff in 1753, and another Peter Cossart held the same office in 1770.[3] John Cossart, son of the latter, removed to Dublin, and was established there as a merchant in 1813,[4] but the name seems to have been localized at a much earlier date in the capital, for an Anne Cossart was married there in 1693 to Pierre Goullin, the Portarlington settler.[5]

Many references to Daniel Perdriau (or Perdrian) occur in the Council Book. In 1695 he, in company with an Elias Perdriau, is admitted a freeman; both possibly as sons of Osea Perdriau who was made free ex gratia in 1683. In 1704 Daniel is Sheriff, and in 1712 Mayor. In 1716 it is ordered that "Alderman Perdrian take possession of the Castle of Black-rock, and the land thereto belonging in trust for the Corporation at six pence per annum." In 1719 he figures as one of the Governors of the Blue Coat School, and he was one of the petitioners in the request sent by the Corporation to the Duke of Bolton that the City Walls, which had suffered in the war of 1689-90, might be rebuilt.[6] His son, Daniel, seems to have removed to Cashel,[7] but other members of the family remained in Cork, and carried on trade as jewellers.[8]

The names Mathis and Jappie occur together in an Apprentice Indenture drawn up on November 14th, 1776, when John Peter, son of John Peter Mathis, deceased, was bound to John Jappie of Cork, master cooper.[9] This serves as a good

---

[1] Freemen's Register.
[2] C.H. & A.J., Vol. XXXII, No. 135. "Militia Commissions of the City of Cork." (Now destroyed in the Dublin Four Courts.)
[3] Council Book.
[4] Freemen's Register.
[5] *Vide* p. 167.
[6] Gibson, "Cork," Vol. II, p. 173.
[7] Freemen's Register.
[8] *Ibid.*
[9] Enrolment Book of Apprentices.

example of the close alliance preserved between the refugee families in the apprenticeship system. Peter Mathis, the elder, was Warden of the Skinners' Company in 1727,[1] but the family later entered the professions, for in 1787, Alexander Mathis, another son of John Peter, was bound to the Attorney, Richard Daunt,[2] and in 1823 "John Peter Mathis of Cork, gent.," was made a freeman.[3]

The master cooper must have been a man of resource and courage, for in September, 1772, "in testimony of his activity as one of the Parish Constables, in bringing to justice divers offenders at the hazard of his life," he is presented with the Freedom of the City.[4]   A stone in the Huguenot burial-ground marked the grave of another John Jappie, presumably his father, who died at the early age of thirty-eight in December 1737.[5]

The Plaincés were brewers, and in an Apprentice Indenture of 1751, Mathias Plaincé is bound to his father, John, in that trade.[6]   In 1713 Alexander Plance [sic] is Warden of the Whittawers, and in 1715 Master.[7] They may have been connected with the refugee family of Planché mentioned amongst the English Huguenots by Smiles, who states that its first representative escaped to that country concealed in a tub.[8]

Smiles also mentions the d'Altera family who removed to Cork from England, where they had fled in the sixteenth century from their estates near Nismes in Languedoc.[9]   The name appears first in Cork in 1707, when the Council ordered "that John Bombenan, James Verdille and James d'Alterie

---

[1] Court of D'Oyer Hundred Book.
[2] Enrolment Book of Apprentices.
[3] Freemen's Register.
[4] Ibid.
[5] J.A.P.M.D., 1901.
[6] Enrolment Book of Apprentices.
[7] Court of D'Oyer Hundred Book.
[8] "Huguenots in England," Appendix.
[9] Ibid.

[*sic*], Clothiers," be admitted free " upon the act." In July 1723, the names recur, when their owners are admitted free-men on the payment of £5.[1] This is difficult to explain, except by the supposition that a son of each, with the same name as his father, obtained his Freedom at that date.

In 1756 another James d'Altera, who must have been a grandson of the original settler, was bound apprentice to the merchant William Rickots, with whose family he must have formed a connection, for in 1825 a William Ricketts Daltera is made a freeman. This William Daltera, who was probably a son of James, was the proprietor of the Mail Coach Hotel in 1810, in company with Judas Daltera.[2] An attorney named James Daltera is mentioned by West at the same date. The family is now extinct in Cork, and Smiles states that the only surviving descendant was, when he wrote, a Surgeon-Major in the British Army.[3]

The Bonbonous family seem to have entered the profes-sions, for although in 1736 " Joseph, son of John Bonbonous deceased, clothier," is bound to John Hill of Cork " to frequent his spinning houses,"[4] his brother Peter, whose death is an-nounced in the *Freeman's Journal* on April 7th, 1767, was the first physician of the North Infirmary, established by Act of Parliament in 1751.[5] John Bonbonous, the original settler, made a considerable fortune as a woollen manufacturer, and on his death bequeathed a legacy to the poor of the French Church. The family is said to have been connected with the Bombomoux who distinguished himself in the Camisard wars. A colleague of Peter Bonbonous in the Infirmary was a Dr. Leplant, a surgeon,[6] who came of a family which is said to have escaped from Normandy in company with a certain

[1] Council Book.
[2] West, " Directory."
[3] " Huguenots in England," Appendix.
[4] Enrolment Book of Apprentices.
[5] Tuckey, " Cork Remembrancer."
[6] " Huguenots in England," Appendix. 1889 Edition.

Baroness De Soissan at the Revocation.[1] It is interesting to note as an example of the close alliance maintained between the Huguenot families in the City that the d'Altera and La Plante families were connected by intermarriage with that of Gollock, since a Thomas Gollock married Judith d'Altera, and his son, James, married a De La Plante.[2]

The Verdailles (or Verdilles) had become jewellers by 1754, and it would seem that they had previously had some connection with Dublin, for a James Verdaill died there in 1723.[3]

The Malet family is also found in Dublin. The first member to appear in Cork was "John Adam Malet, brewer, a Protestant Stranger," who was made free in September 1777.[4] The tombstone which still marks his grave in the Huguenot burial-ground states that he was born in 1769 and died in 1813. He had a son of the same name, who became a freeman in 1817,[5] and of his sons, Francis, James and John, one became a clergyman in Cork, and another a Fellow of Trinity College, Dublin.[6] It is believed that the family left France after the Massacre of St. Bartholomew. By 1729 they were established in Dublin and had intermarried with the Chaigneaus.[7]

Though the great majority of Huguenot settlers in Cork were business men, Monsieur Lawrence De La Main proved an exception to the rule. This gentleman, who had held considerable estates in France, set up in Cork as a dancing master, and purchased a small property called "Hop" Island near the City, dying there in 1762.[8] "The whole family," says West, "were

---

[1] Tuckey.
[2] Notes kindly submitted by a member of the Gollock family.
[3] Sir Charles Jackson, "English Goldsmiths."
[4] Freemen's Register.
[5] *Ibid.*
[6] Brady.
[7] J.A.P.M.D., 1912; also *vide infra* p. 73.
[8] Caulfield in *Gentleman's Magazine*, Sept. 1855.

particularly attached to music, dancing, and other polite arts. Some of its branches excelled in the former of these."[1]

This allusion points to Henry Delamain, son of the original settler, who was a composer and organist of the Cork Cathedral from 1781-1796. In 1788 an entry occurs in the Vestry Book of St. Ann's, Shandon, where it is stated that the vestry will accept a substitute organist supplied by Mr. Delamain as the latter is unable to accede to their request that he should hold that post. He died about 1798.

Another Huguenot exponent of the " polite arts " was the Rev. James Delacour, who wrote verse in imitation of Pope, his best known work being " A Prospect of Poetry," written in 1733, which won compliments from the poet Thompson. He was born at Killowen, near Cork, in 1709, graduated from Dublin University in 1727, and in 1744 was appointed Curate of Ballinaboy. He died insane in 1785, and is buried in the graveyard of St. Ann's, Shandon.[2]

The poet is said to have had as ancestor a Huguenot officer who settled at Portarlington, whence his descendants removed to Cork,[3] and if so he must have been a connection of the Captain André De La Cour who appears in the registers of the former colony from 1749 to 1797,[4] but as early as 1654 a John Delacourt was living in Ballinroe,[5] and a Robert Delacourt of Cork was attainted by the Parliament of 1689.[6] John Delacourt, the poet's father, had a second son, Robert, ancestor of the Mallow branch of the family.[7] He had two sons, Charles, apprenticed to a Cork attorney,[8] and Robert, of Bear Forest, Mallow, who was born in 1765. The latter played a

---

[1] " Directory."
[2] C.H. & A.J., Vol. XXXI, No. 134. Twiss, " Mallow and Some Mallow Men."
[3] *Ibid.*
[4] J.K.A.S., Vol. XI, No. 4. Le Fanu, " Portarlington."
[5] Brady.
[6] Gimlette, p. 259.
[7] Brady.
[8] Enrolment Book of Apprentices.

large part in the sporting and business life of the town; was one of the eight members of committee appointed to establish the Duhallow Hunt,[1] and founded "Delacour's" or the "Mallow Bank" in partnership with William Gallway in 1800. This bank issued notes for as small a sum as 1s. 1d., and thus supplied the want of a silver circulation. They were adorned with the crest and motto which indicated the family's noble origin, "Au ciel de la Cour." In 1823 the bank passed to the sole ownership of Delacour, but in 1835 it failed, like so many of the private banks of the day, and its owner died eleven years later.[2]

The Lamillières first settled in Dublin, where Cyrus and Henry Lamillière entered the University in 1701. They had been born in France but their father, Florence La Millière, joined William of Orange and fought as a Captain in Galway's Regiment of Horse.[3] Cyrus had a son, Alexander, born in Dublin in 1723. He graduated at Dublin University in 1744, entered the Ministry and eventually came to Cork, where from 1774 to 1782 he was Chancellor; from 1782 to 1796 Vicar of Holy Trinity; and from 1796 to 1800, when he died, Archdeacon. His son, Alexander, was ordained priest for the curacy of St. Nicholas in 1790, but his death seven years later cut short his career in the Church. Both are buried in St. Nicholas, with another son, Henry.[4]

It will be seen from the foregoing notes that most of the business and wealth of Cork in the eighteenth century lay in the hands of the Huguenots, and although their congregation had dwindled and their church services had ended by 1813, their influence continued in the Corporation and in commercial circles well into the nineteenth century.

As late as 1810 West's "Directory" gives many Huguenot

[1] C.H. & A.J., Vol. II, No. 14. "Minute Book of the Hunt."
[2] Tennison, "The Private Bankers of Cork and the South of Ireland." (Reprinted from the C.H. & A.J.)
[3] "Hiberniæ Notitia."
[4] Brady.

E*

names still existing amongst the leading citizens. Thus as members of the Corporation appear Besnard, Perrier, and Pick; as Attornies, Besnard, d'Altera, Jack and Quarry; as Merchants, Besnard, Cazalet, d'Altera, Fountaine, Hardy, Le Grand, Mazière, Perrier and Teulon; while a Lefebre appears as principal of one of the chief boarding schools.

Some representatives of these families still reside in the city which their ancestors benefited so materially, and " French Church Street " still remains to preserve the memory of this important settlement.

CHAPTER III

THE most important settlement in the County of Cork was one very unlike that of the City. While the refugees in the latter colony were interested almost solely in trade, those of Youghal were in most cases military men who made Ireland their home when the army of William of Orange was disbanded. Thus the Youghal settlers do not make their appearance until the Peace of Ryswick had put an end to the Williamite wars, and they never play a part in the corporate life of the town comparable with that of their fellow countrymen in the neighbouring city.

Four notable exceptions to this, however, are found in the careers of Richard Paradise and Samuel, his kinsman; of William Causabon and of Edward Gillett; all of whom either settled, or came of families which had settled, in Youghal before the Revolution of 1688, and all of whom figured amongst the leading citizens.

Richard Paradise, with his relative Samuel, fled from Limousin to settle in Ireland under the protection of the Earl of Cork. They became naturalized, and Richard was successively Bailiff (1679), Mayor (1683) and Alderman of Youghal, while Samuel was Bailiff in 1693. Richard Paradise married the daughter of Alderman Luther, Mayor in 1666, himself the descendant of a refugee from Germany, and their daughter,

Elizabeth, married Samuel Hayman, ancestor of the Rev. Canon Hayman, the historian of Youghal.[1]

The Causabons (or Casaubons) had been among the earliest of the French Huguenots to settle in England; the family had originally come from Bordeaux, whence Arnaud Casaubon fled at the Massacre of St. Bartholomew to Geneva. Here Isaac Causabon was born and eventually held a professorship. He returned to France and was appointed professor at Montpellier, but the assassination of Henry IV and the revival of the religious persecution caused him to emigrate once more, this time to England.[2] According to Fuller he was " fetched out of France by King James and preferred Prebendary of Canterbury," where he continued his numerous writings and where on July 1st, 1615, "Death stopped him in full speed."[3] His son, Florence Stephen, became a Prebendary of Canterbury, where he died in 1671, and in the following generation the family removed to Ireland and settled in the South. In 1672 Thomas Casaubon was Bailiff of Youghal, and in 1666 his son, William, appears in the baptismal register. This William was attainted by the Irish Parliament of James II in 1689.[4] He married Sarah, daughter of Arthur Hyde, M.P., and his son, William, was High Sheriff for County Cork in 1723 and M.P. for Doneraile from 1715-1727. The latter resided at Carrig, near Mallow, and married Arabella, daughter of the Rt. Hon. Sir John Rogerson, Chief Justice of the King's Bench.[5] His son, William, appears in a Militia Commission for County Cork as first Lieutenant-Colonel of Foot " in the room of his father, William Causabon, Esq., deceased, by Commission dated 27th February, 1743-4."[6]

---

[1] Gimlette, pp. 180, 195.
[2] " Huguenots in England," Appendix.
[3] Fuller's " Church History," Vol. III, Bk. X, p. 294.
[4] Gimlette, p. 259.
[5] C.H. & A.J., Vol. I (2nd series), No. 5. " Cork M.P.s."
[6] Ibid., Vol. XXXII, No. 135. " The Militia Commissions of Co. Cork."

The name Gillett occurs in Portarlington and Lisburn, and will be treated of in the latter settlement, but as early as 1660, a Richard Gillett figures in Youghal as Lieutenant of the first Foot Company of the four Companies of Militia to be raised there.[1] Edward Gillett, who was presumably his descendant, was a leading goldsmith in the early eighteenth century, and also one of the civic authorities of Youghal. In 1705 he obtained his Freedom, was elected a Common Councilman in 1712, and became Mayor in 1721. He was still living in 1740, and in 1749 a John Gillett, possibly his son, was continuing the trade of goldsmith.[2]

Another Frenchman, Gaspar Colline, is mentioned by Gimlette as settling in Youghal in the early seventeenth century. He appears in the Irish Chancery Rolls as having obtained a grant of land there soon after the fall of La Rochelle.[3]

The Youghal civic authorities were less generous in their treatment of these strangers than their brethren of Cork, for in 1664 it was laid down that " no foreigners were to be made free at large, only during his [sic] residence here,"[4] and in 1697, although it is ordered " that Protestant refugees might be enfranchised on payment of sixpence," it is also stressed that " they should not vote for seven years, nor be qualified 'till then to serve as Church-wardens."[5]

Later, however, when in 1753 a new group of refugees appeared from France, the Council relented, and it was ordered that " Whereas application has been made to the Corporation to consider of ways and means to encourage and assist the French Protestant Refugees now come and coming into this Kingdom, 20 li. a year, at least for three years, for

[1] Ormond MSS., Vol. II. Hist. MSS. Com. Rep., 1899.
[2] Sir Charles Jackson.
[3] Gimlette, p. 165.
[4] Cooke, " Memoirs of Youghal," 1749. Edited in C.H. & A.J., Vol. IX, No. 57.
[5] U.J.A., Vol. II. Art. " Youghal."

as many families as shall come and settle in this parish, be paid them yearly towards their support out of the Corporation rents,"[1] and in 1756 it is resolved "that all foreign Protestants, merchants and traders, that are willing to become inhabitants of this town, shall be admitted freemen during residence, and that the above byelaw be posted up and printed in the Dublin and Cork journals."[2]

The total number of refugees settled at Youghal did not exceed fifty, since no minister was provided for them. There is no record that they held a service in French, and no especial place of worship was set apart for them. The Rev. Arthur d'Anvers, who, with his brother Jacques, settled in Youghal about 1730, may have come as minister to them, but if so this must have been in a private capacity since, unlike the French clergy in Cork, he was not supported by any Government salary. The Huguenots were buried in the churchyard of St. Mary's, and it is from the register of this church that most of our knowledge of them may be gained.[3]

Besides that of the d'Anvers family, the Parish Registers contain the names Boisrond, Chaigneau, Coluon, DeHays, Delappe, Dezieres, Duclos, Falquière, Guin, Labatte, Legardere, Lampriere, Marvault, Mazière, Perdu, Ricard and Rouvière.

Théophile Boisrond was the son of Henry Boisrond de St. Leger, who was naturalized by Act of Parliament 2 Anne. It is stated that he was the son of Réné Boisrond de St. Leger by Benine his wife, born in the province of Saintonge in France,[4] and he was, therefore, a brother of Samuel Boisrond, Lieutenant-Colonel in Cambon's Regiment, who retired on pension in 1699, was naturalized in 1705, and settled in

[1] Council Book. Ed. Caulfield.
[2] *Ibid.*
[3] Canon Hayman in the U.J.A., Vol. II, has placed on record all that may be discovered from these registers with regard to the refugees.
[4] "Protestant Exiles," Vol. II, p. 317, and Hug. Soc. Pub., Vol. VII, p. 35.

Portarlington where he died in 1737.[1] The name Benin occurs again in the sister of Théophile, who married at Youghal a Monsieur Legardere, of whom no further record exists, in 1757.[2] A daughter Ann was born to Théophile Boisrond in 1755,[3] and it is possible that Hector Boisrond, who was a Lieutenant-Colonel in the British Army in 1760,[4] was a connection if not a descendant.

The first Chaigneau to settle in Youghal was, according to Agnew, Josias, who came from Labellonière in the Charante district of France, where his family held landed property. By his first wife, Jeanne Jennede, he had three sons, Lewis, Stephen and Isaac, and by a second wife, née Castin, a fourth son, John. Lewis became a successful merchant in Dublin, purchased the estate of Corkage, and married in 1688 Elizabeth Le Coudre. His daughter, Elizabeth, married Colonel David Renouard, and his son, David, sat for Gowran in the Irish Parliament, was High Sheriff of Dublin in 1717, and died in Youghal in 1753. He married Elizabeth, daughter of a Monsieur Maquarell, and of their four daughters, Elizabeth married James Digges La Touche, and Henrietta became Mrs. Hassard;[5] Mary Anne is stated by Hayman and Wagner to have married Mr. Simon Green in Youghal in the year of her father's death, but according to Agnew she became Mrs. Pratt.[6] The three sons of David Chaigneau were unmarried; one, the Rev. Peter Chaigneau, who died in 1776, was the first secretary of the Royal Dublin Society.

Stephen Chaigneau had two sons by his wife, one of the Mademoiselles Raboteau. The younger, Daniel, left no descendants, but Peter married in 1729 Marie Malet, the descendant of the refugee family which had left France in

---

[1] J.K.A.S., Vol. XI, No. 4. Art. "Portarlington."
[2] U.J.A., Vol. II. Art. "Youghal."
[3] *Ibid.*
[4] "Protestant Exiles."
[5] Wagner MSS.
[6] It is, of course, possible that she was twice married.

1572 and which has been mentioned in connection with the Cork Settlement,[1] and their sons, John and Abraham, were considerable merchants in Dublin. John was the father of Peter Chaigneau who purchased the estate of Benown in Westmeath, and was called to the Irish Bar in 1793 according to Smiles,[2] or in 1798 as stated by Agnew[3] and Wagner, and grandfather of John Chaigneau, buried in the Peter Street French Cemetery in Dublin in 1825.[4]

Isaac Chaigneau had a son David, who married Helena King and was probably that David Chaigneau minister of the French Church in Carlow in 1744, who will be dealt with in connection with that settlement.

John married in 1707 Margaret Martyn, and two of his surviving sons were Colonel William Chaigneau, Army Agent in Dublin, and John Chaigneau, Treasurer of the Ordnance. The latter married in 1745 Susannah Smith, and their son was the Rev. John Clement Chaigneau, Curate of St. Andrew's, Dublin.

As has been seen the Chaigneaus were one of the most widely distributed of the Huguenot families in Ireland. Their burial-places existed in Youghal, Carlow and Dublin, and their many alliances with other refugee families give them an added importance in the history of the settlements.

The Rev. Arthur d'Anvers, already mentioned, seems to have been educated at Kilkenny School,[5] and was Rector of Ardagh and Clonpriest in 1720 before settling in Youghal, where he was made a freeman and where he died in 1754.[6] His brother James, who died in 1740, must have had two sons, Thomas, whose baptism is recorded in 1737, and Arthur, who,

---

[1] *Vide* p. 65.
[2] " Huguenots in England," Appendix.
[3] Vol. II, p. 268.
[4] J.A.P.M.D., 1912.
[5] *Vide* p. 128.
[6] Brady, " Records of Cork, Cloyne and Ross," Vol. II, p. 22.

Brady states, was converted from Rome by the zeal of his uncle.

In June 1728 a record occurs in the Council Book of Youghal that Lieutenant James de Hays of the Five-place and South Green " have farther addition of the strand southwards towards the Poison Bush, the lease to be perfected to said Lieut. paying 3 Li. fine and 3 Li. yearly."[1] This the Lieutenant embanked and formed into the demesne now known as the Green Park. He and his brother seem to have been more wealthy than the average type of refugee, for in 1757 the latter bequeathed £100 to the Protestant poor of the town. The name continued in Youghal and was eventually corrupted into Hayes.[2] The family may have had some connection with the Jean Hays of Dublin, a merchant from Calais, whom Dumont de Bostaquet encountered during his visit to the City.[3]

The Duclos or Duclosse family emigrated to Ireland before the Revocation from Metz in the Department of the Moselle, where they had been seigneurs of Courcelles.[4] Paul Duclos was ordained priest at Cork and became Vicar of Ballymodan and later Prebendary of Island. Before his death, which occurred in 1717 or 1719, he removed to the King's County and is found as Chancellor of St. Canice, Ossory. In 1682 he married Francis Massiott of Shandon, Cork, and by her had five daughters, the eldest of whom married Robert Minnett of Annabeg, County Tipperary, in 1717.[5]

Perot Duclos, who settled in Youghal with his wife, a son Guillaume and a daughter Marguerite, may have been a relative of the minister. The daughter married William Parker in 1718, but the son died unmarried in 1753 and the name accordingly became extinct in Youghal. A second

[1] Council Book.
[2] U.J.A., Vol. II. Art. "Youghal."
[3] " Mémoires Inédits."
[4] Bull, "Protestant France" (1904), p. 271.
[5] Brady.

daughter, Hanna, was born there in 1710.[1] This surname affords a good example of the changes in spelling which the Huguenot names suffered at the pens of parish clerks; it is recorded in the registers as Deu Clos, Dewclose and Ducros, and the writer has been informed that the corrupted form of Dukelow is still existing in the west of Cork.

Another example is provided by the Ricard family, who settled in Youghal early in the eighteenth century. Robert Ricard may have been descended from that Andrew Ricard who was Mayor of Waterford in 1658,[2] or he may be connected with the Ricard who is given by Dumont de Bostaquet as *maréchal des logis* in the company of DeCussy under Schomberg in 1689.[3] His name, with those of his sisters, Jane (who married William Daly in 1728) and Hannah (who became the wife of James Mansfield in 1729), and his children, Alexandre (born 1727), Michael (who died in the same year) and John (who died in 1734), are all spelt correctly in the registers, but the marriage of his son Robert to Miss Anne Fortescue in 1744, and the baptisms and burials of their children, are recorded under the name Rickett. When Robert Ricard, senior, died in 1758 his name is written in the Burial Register as Riccard.[4] This family may also be connected with Cork, where in 1695 John Ricards is admitted freeman, and where William Rickots or Rickett figures as a merchant in 1756.[5] In 1708 a Joseph Rickards, mariner, is also admitted " free upon the Act." He seems to have left the sea and entered somewhat dishonestly into business, for in 1716 he is prosecuted for " making up and selling corrupt and unmerchantable tallow."[6]

The first representative of the Labat, or Labatt, family in

---

[1] U.J.A., Vol. II. Art. "Youghal."
[2] *Vide* p. 122.
[3] "Mémoires Inédits."
[4] U.J.A., Vol. II. Art. "Youghal."
[5] *Vide* p. 64.
[6] Council Book, Cork.

Ireland was a native of Claret, near Montpellier.[1] He served under William of Orange, obtained his commission as Lieutenant in November 1693, and was on the *Mountjoy* when it burst the boom across Lough Foyle and raised the siege of Derry. The family was, according to Smiles, connected with the Sabatiers and Chateauneufs,[2] which may have accounted for Monsieur André Labat's predilection for the Portarlington Settlement[3] where, as a Captain on pension from La Melonière's Regiment, he settled in 1699. He died in 1736 in Kilkenny, but he left a legacy of £3 to the Portarlington Church. Other members of the family settled in the North[4] and in Dublin, where the name exists to the present day, and those who came to Youghal may have been descendants of these, since the first mention of them in the South does not occur until 1740.

In that year an Isaac and Joseph Labatte were settled in Youghal as merchants in partnership. That they succeeded, at least temporarily, is proved by the fact that Joseph was Bailiff in 1750 and Mayor in 1751 and 1752; but by 1755 the business of the two brothers must have failed, for they are found petitioning the Irish House of Commons to insert a clause for their relief in an Act about to be passed for the relief of insolvent debtors, and in a list of Marshalsea prisoners for that date occur Maxwell Olive and Joseph Labatte, both of Youghal.[5]

In 1766 Isaac Labatte died, and his burial with those of his child John, and Joseph's son, Peter, are recorded in the Parish Register.[6]

One of the Williamite officers to settle in Youghal was Jean Rouvière, who fled from France at the Revocation and

---

[1] Hug. Soc. Pub., Vol. XVIII, p. 268.
[2] " Huguenots in England," Appendix.
[3] J.K.A.S., Vol. XI, No. 4. Art. " Portarlington."
[4] *Vide* Castleblayney Settlement.
[5] U.J.A., Vol. II. Art. " Youghal."
[6] *Ibid.*

eventually became a Lieutenant in Galway's Regiment of Horse.

It is said that his father, Antoine Rouvière, who remained in France, was condemned to the Galleys in May 1745, amongst others from the Des Arnoux district, by the Parliament of Grenoble. He would, however, have been a very old man at that time, and there is probably a confusion between two men of the same name.[1] The son married in 1722 Lucy Ann, daughter of Francis Marriott, Captain of Foot, and had a daughter, Susanna, baptized in Youghal in 1728,[2] which would prove that by that date her father had left Carlow where he had originally settled.[3]

Susanna Rouvière married, in 1745, Thomas Day of Ballyvergin, and thus became ancestress of the Day family of Cork, in whose possession many relics of the Rouvières existed until the death of Mr. Robert Day in 1914.[4]

The family must have owned ground at the south end of Youghal since the South Abbey site was entered on the Duke of Devonshire's leases as "Roviere's Holdings," and the Lieutenant held land in trust for James de Hays of Green Park already mentioned.[5]

Mr. Day gives Rouvière the rank of Captain but his daughter is baptized as the child of "Lieut. John Roviere," and he himself is buried in January 1735-6, as "Ensign John Roviere, a refugee."[6] Dumont de Bostaquet[7] gives a La Rouvière Cornette in Belcastel's Company, and a Rouvière Lieutenant in the Company of Varengues, both in Schomberg's Regiment of 1689, which became Galway's when the Marshal was killed at the Boyne, but only one Commissioned

[1] Hug. Soc. Pub., Vol. XVIII, p. 309, and XXVII, p. 119.
[2] Art. by Robert Day in C.H. & A.J., Vol. I (2nd series), No. 1, p. 34.
[3] Vide p. 132.
[4] Such as the wedding-ring of Lucy Ann Rouvière, and furniture brought by the Captain from France.
[5] Council Book.
[6] U.J.A., Vol. II. Art. " Youghal."
[7] " Mémoires Inédits."

Officer of this name appears on the Pension Lists, and since Jean Rouvière was retired as Lieutenant in 1702[1] and re-appears as Captain in the list of 1723 published in " Hiberniæ Notitia," it would seem that his rank and pension were raised after retirement.

There seems to have been some connection, which Mr. Day states but is unable to prove, between the families of Rouvière and Mazière. Amongst the Rouvière family papers in his possession was a Commission appointing David Mazière to be Lieutenant in the Portuguese Regiment of Foot under Anthony de Colombière, dated 1708, and signed by the Earl of Sunderland and the Queen; and the first child born to Thomas and Susanna Day in 1746 was named David Mazière Day.[2]

The de Mazières came from the Province of Aunis, north of Saintonge.[3] Peter fled at the Revocation and joined, like Rouvière, the army of William of Orange, where he served as Lieutenant in Casaubon's Company in the Regiment of Schomberg.[4] He settled in Youghal, where the birth and death in the same month of his son David are recorded in 1744. His own death occurred in March 1745-6, when "Lieut. Mazuere [sic] a French Refugee " is buried, and his wife followed him two years later.[5] Other members of the family settled in Cork, where the firm of Mazière and Sainthill flourished in the later nineteenth century.

A certain Peter Mazière was a wine merchant in the City in 1798 and he figures largely in the " Journal of Mr. Samuel Reily,"[6] who was his fellow traveller in the mail coach from Cork to Dublin in September 1798 when it was held up at Red Gap, twenty-four miles from Dublin, by the rebels. The

---

[1] Hug. Soc. Proc., Vol. VI, p. 303.
[2] C.H. & A.J., Vol. I (2nd series), No. 1, p. 34.
[3] " Huguenots in England," Appendix.
[4] Dumont de Bostaquet.
[5] U.J.A., Vol. II. Art. " Youghal."
[6] C.H. & A.J., Vol. II (2nd series), No. 22.

Journal gives an animated account of the adventure, which might have had unpleasant consequences for the merchant, who could not dispossess the insurgents of a fixed idea that he was an Orangeman, despite Reily's assurance to them that he was a merchant "who sold bottled porter in Cork."

This must be the Peter Mazière who was one of the original proprietors of the Cork Institution,[1] a proprietor of the St. George Steam Packet Company, and owner of the *Superb* steamship plying between Cork and Bristol.[2] He was a freeman of the City, as was George Mazière, who was one of the original members of the old Cork Library founded in 1820.[3]

The Mazières were also localized in Dublin, as their burial-places in the Merrion Row French Cemetery prove. The earliest tombstone of the family marked the grave of Samuel De La Mazière, who died in 1726, and that of his wife Jane de Valois and his children Paul, Jane and Margaret. Andrew De La Mazière, who died in 1788, seems to have married into the Le Blanc family, and a Magdalene and Louisa Mazière married respectively Pierre Galan and John Perrier earlier in the same century.[4] The name is now extinct in Cork and Youghal, and, as far as may be ascertained, also in Dublin.

Of the other Huguenot settlers in Youghal few data remain, and those mostly in the Burial Register of St. Mary's. Thus Cornet Daniel Coluon, "a refugee," is buried in July 1738; Captain James Dezières in January 1746-7; John Guin, "a Huguenot," in April 1733; his wife in 1752, and his son, Peter, in 1774; Clement Lampier in March 1761; Ann, "daughter of John Marvault, surveyor," in September 1766; and David Perdu in January 1734-5.[5]

[1] *Ibid.*, Vol. XII, No. 69, p. 44.
[2] *Ibid.*, Vol. XXIII, No. 113.
[3] *Ibid.*
[4] J.A.P.M.D., 1912, and *vide supra* p. 58.
[5] U.J.A., Vol. II. Art. "Youghal."

In 1699 a marriage between Isaac Falquière and Elizabeth Carey is recorded, and in 1731 the marriage of Elizabeth Falquière, possibly a daughter, to Thomas Banks.[1] She seems to have been the sole representative left of her family in Youghal at that date, and of the other families mentioned above all records seem to have perished.

Hayman states that a Marvault and a Perdu were living in humble circumstances in Youghal about 1854.[2] The latter name is connected also with the Lisburn Settlement, and Marvault with that of Waterford. A "Jno. Lamprie, Comber," is mentioned by Cooke in his list of Youghal Freemen before 1749,[3] and bearing in mind the many changes in spelling and pronunciation that these names underwent, it is remotely possible that he was connected with the Clement Lampier (or Lamprière) mentioned above. This name also occurs in Dublin and in Mallow.[4]

A Durant was a merchant and glazier in Youghal in 1622,[5] but in his case a Huguenot ancestry cannot be proved, although the name occurs in the Returns of Aliens as that of a Frenchman settled in London in the sixteenth century,[6] and is recorded by Smiles as among the Huguenots of Dauphiny.[7]

Another settler whose Huguenot origin is doubtful, although he is listed among the refugees by Hayman, was Michael, son of William Delappe, who was buried in St. Mary's churchyard in 1769.[8] This name, which also occurs in the north, is given a Scottish descent by Burke.

A few other names of possible French extraction occur in

---

[1] *Ibid.*
[2] U.J.A., Vol. II. Art. "Youghal."
[3] "Memoirs," 1749, C.H. & A.J., Vol. IX, No. 57.
[4] *Vide* p. 53.
[5] Westropp, p. 29.
[6] Hug. Soc. Proc., Vol. X, p. 45.
[7] *Vide* p. 118.
[8] U.J.A., Vol. II. Art. "Youghal."

the Burial Register about 1744, but these were in most cases those of French prisoners of war,[1] and as Youghal decreased in importance it is safe to assume that it lost its attraction for the Huguenots, who moved, as in the case of the Mazières, to Cork or other centres which offered greater advantages for trade and social intercourse.

On August 31st, 1765, the Red Head Galley, commanded by Captain Richard Neale, arrived in Cork harbour.[2] She had on board sixty Huguenot families who had come on the invitation of Thomas Adderley, the public-spirited Parliamentary representative of Bandon, to introduce the manufacture of silk to that neighbourhood.

He had already introduced the linen manufacture with marked success. The average output of his looms for the six years before 1755 was about 45,000 yards,[3] or, as Bennett states, 422 pieces, principally sheetings and diapers, in a little over a year,[4] and he now hoped to achieve the same results in the silk industry. He granted the French settlers leases for sixteen years at low or non-existent rents of the houses which he had constructed for them at Innishannon;[5] he planted mulberry trees, but he could not control the moist Irish climate which killed the silkworms and ruined the enterprise. The colonists left after about twenty years for Spitalfields and other weaving centres in England,[6] and all that remained in local memory of the sixty families who had come there was the title of " The Colony " given to the

---

[1] U.J.A., Vol. II. Art. " Youghal."

[2] Tuckey, " Cork Remembrancer," also Bennett, " History of Bandon," p. 320.

[3] Gill, p. 85.

[4] " History of Bandon," p. 315.

[5] Hug. Soc. Proc., Vol. VIII, p. 127. Caulfield, annoting Smith's " History of Cork," states that the leases were for twenty-one years at low rents, as does Bennett.

[6] " Projet de Colonisation." Hug. Soc. Proc., Vol. VI, pp. 370-432.

cluster of houses on the Bandon Road, a field for some years known as "The Mulberry Field,"[1] and the grave of one of the settlers, with that of the pastor who had accompanied them to Ireland.

In Faulkner's *Dublin Journal* of August 11-15th, 1752, a letter is printed which shows the high hopes entertained for the future of the Colony. Having given a glowing account of the linen manufacture, the writer concludes by expressing " the pleasing hopes we have that the same spirit of industry will display itself in different ways, as we hear that many families of the French Protestant Refugees will be settled here, for whom houses are to be built, and land granted to them in different proportions free from rent for five years."

That these hopes were realized at least for a time, is proved by a resolution passed by the Royal Dublin Society on January 23rd, 1766,[2] when it is ordered that "the sum of twenty-two pounds fifteen shillings be paid to Mrs. Elizabeth Cortey, of Innishannon, in the County of Corke, as a present from the Society in consideration of the large quantity of cocoons and raw silk from silk worms bred by her." " That the Assistant Secretary do write to Mr. Adderley to request that he will inquire of Mrs. Cortey upon what terms she is willing to instruct such persons as may be recommended to her in the management of silk worms and raw silk," and " that a gold medal be presented to Mr. Adderley for his large plantation of white mulberry trees at Innishannon."

Dublin seems to have greatly interested itself in the under-taking, and a charitable society, known as " La Société pour les Protestants Réfugiez," was formed to assist the refugees arriving there in 1751, and principally to promote the

---

[1] C.H. & A.J., Vol. III, No. 26. Alcock, "Innishannon." The author states that the last of the houses, though ruinous, was in existence in 1894.
[2] C.H. & A.J., Vol. III, No. 25. " Thomas Adderley."

Innishannon enterprise. When this failed the affairs of the Society were wound up.[1]

Before the failure of the Colony, carpets as well as silk seem to have been manufactured there. The *Gentleman's Magazine* for June 1770 states that " a manufacture of carpeting is established at Innishannon in the County of Cork, from whence a piece was finished for the presence chamber in the Castle [at Dublin] by order of His Excellency the Lord Lieutenant, who visited the factory on his tour through that quarter."

The Rev. Peter Cortez, who came with the settlers as their minister, must have visited Cork some years previously to his flock, for on February 20th, 1760, having taken the necessary Oaths, he was " licensed by the Bishop to read service in French, preach and administer the Sacraments (according to ye use of the Church of Ireland and no other) in ye parish Church of Innishannon, or wherever else may be appointed for the said French congregation to assemble."[2]

He was the nephew of Corteiz the companion of Antoine Court, and had studied at Lausanne. In 1744 he had been consecrated by a provincial Synod of Hautes-Cevennes, and, though often in danger of imprisonment or death, had carried on his ministry until 1752. In 1755 he was in Zurich,[3] but left Switzerland for Ireland, where he was granted a Civil List pension of £60 per annum from the ninth of January, 1760, until his death.[4] This occurred in 1802, when he was buried in Innishannon churchyard in the tomb of Matthew Belsaigne, a fellow refugee.

Mademoiselle Cortez, sister of the minister, came with him to Innishannon as a girl of fifteen. She, too, was buried in the Belsaigne tomb in the early nineteenth century.

[1] Hug. Soc. Proc., Vol. VIII, p. 127.
[2] Brady, quoting Diocesan Register.
[3] " Projet de Colonisation."
[4] Caulfield, " Annals of Kinsale."

Matthew Belsaigne was a native of Languedoc who, as was stated on his tomb, " sacrificed his fortune, country and all earthly considerations to his God and Religion."[1] He died in 1761 aged fifty-seven. His son, Matthew Hodder Belsaigne, who died in 1833, was made a freeman of Cork, and it is possible that the John Bellesaigne who had a glass shop on the Long Quay in that city in 1773 and one in Patrick Street in 1787[2] was a brother of the latter. All the more likely as Matthew Hodder's son, who died aged sixteen in 1824, was named John. His twin sister, Eliza Minton, did not long survive him, for she was buried in 1828[3] and the name is now extinct in Cork.

Bennett[4] states that the " Rev. M. Belsang " [sic] succeeded Cortez in his pastoral duties, but by 1802 there could have been few Huguenots remaining, and Brady makes no mention of a cleric of this name.

Another tomb recorded the name of a Howard, originally Howbard, said to be a fellow countryman of the Belsaignes,[5] but nothing further is known of this settler, and the name is not French.

Sir Richard Cox was, like Adderley, a believer in the value of foreign colonists, and at least forty families from Switzerland were settled on his estate by Lord Galway's agent, de Virazel.[6] Although no trace of them now remains, Bennett has preserved the names of three of the Bandon colonists, the Beaumonts, Willises and Barters, who, he states, came "all the way from the sunny banks of the Loire."[7] Another was Lieutenant-Colonel Chartres, the descendant of

[1] J.A.P.M.D., Vol. II.
[2] Westropp, p. 117.
[3] J.A.P.M.D., Vol. II, No. 1.
[4] " History of Bandon," p. 321 note.
[5] J.A.P.M.D., Vol. II, No. 1.
[6] Hug. Soc. Proc., Vol. XIV, p. 214.
[7] " History of Bandon," p. 280.

a Bourbon,[1] who served in the Williamite wars,[2] and later removed to Belfast. Both Alexander and Ralph Chartres from Cork were amongst those attainted by James II.[3]

The Beaumonts may possibly have come to Ireland from the Norwich Settlement, where the name also occurs, and they may have had some connection with that Giles Beaumont who, under Charles I, obtained a grant of denization in England, Ireland and Virginia on his offer to take thither a number of men and plant them at his own charge with the privilege of paying no more customs than the King's own subjects.[4] Or they may have been relatives of the Théophile Beaumon, an ex-Cornet of Dragoons, who died in Portarlington in 1749.[5] As for the Willises and Barters, Bennett gives no clues as to their strangely English names, and his statement cannot now be verified or disproved.

Other and more authentic French names are to be found in Bandon, but these are of French officers who were prisoners there in 1746 and 1747.[6]

It has been stated that the Barrys of Bandon and the Places of Kinsale were of Huguenot origin, with the original surnames of Du Barry and De La Place. A John Place had charge of the French prison at Kinsale, and his daughter, Ann, married the Rev. John Barry who was ordained in 1824 and sent as a Wesleyan missionary to Jamaica. Both families subsequently emigrated to America and are now extinct in the south of Ireland.[7]

Kinsale was not regarded as a place of settlement, but some Huguenot names are found there. Thus in the Council

[1] " Protestant Exiles," Vol. III, p. 240.
[2] U.J.A., Vol. IX, p. 142.
[3] Gimlette, p. 259.
[4] Ibid., p. 168.
[5] J.K.A.S., Vol. XI, No. 4. Art. " Portarlington."
[6] Bennett, p. 306.
[7] C.H. & A.J., Vol. XXXIII, No. 137. " Memoirs of the Barry-Place Family."

Book, under date October 1665, it is recorded that "John Choisin, a Frenchman, having taken the Oath of Supremacy before the Lord Chancellor of Ireland, as appeareth by certificate; and also taking same here again, in consideration of 15 li was admitted a freeman." He had "taken the Oath" in August of the same year, and was then described as a merchant from Paris.[1] In Kinsale he seems to have quickly become a trusted citizen, for in 1666 he is employed with others in auditing the Chamberlain's accounts.[2]

Jean Lecost is another French name that figures on the Freemen's Roll of Kinsale. He obtained the dignity in 1708 and more cheaply than Choisin for, possibly as a "Protestant Stranger," he was only required to pay twenty shillings. The name is also found in Portarlington, where a Lieutenant Hercules De La Coste retired on pension in 1699,[3] and in Dublin, where Peter Lacost, "son of Hercules Lacoste, Portarlington, Gent," was apprenticed in 1723 to the goldsmith Martin,[4] and where a Claud Lacoste "of the city of Dublin embroidere and Jane his wife who departed this life 8th Jan. 1762," were interred in Merrion graveyard.[5]

The name De La Croix is connected both with Cork and Kinsale. The Isaac and John De La Croix who have already been referred to as freemen of the former city, came originally from Calais, where the father carried on business as a merchant. He settled later in Dover and thence removed to Cork, where the sharp practices of both father and son aroused the indignation of other traders. The minister Fontaine, who suffered from the malignity of the elder de La Croix, records their transactions in a very unfavourable light, and according to him the son was forced to abscond.[6]

[1] Hug. Soc. Pub., Vol. XVIII, p. 339.
[2] Council Book. Ed. Caulfield.
[3] J.K.A.S., Vol. XI, No. 4. Art. "Portarlington."
[4] G.H. & A.J., Vol. VIII, No. 53. "Dublin Goldsmiths."
[5] J.A.P.M.D., 1902.
[6] "Memoirs," Ch. 13, p. 171.

A daughter married the merchant Ambrose Jackson, who became a freeman in 1713,[1] but apart from this no other record of them exists in the City.

In Kinsale, however, the name appears as early as 1695, when Mr. Francis Lacroix is summoned at the Grand Jury Presentments "for the great nuisance occasioned by the French Prisoners."[2] He was sworn a burgess in 1697 in company with Moses La Croix apothecary.[3] The latter was a man of influence on the Corporation, and his name appears constantly in the records until his death in 1734, at the age of eighty. He is buried in the Church of St. Multose in company with Mary Anne La Croix, probably his daughter, who died in 1787.

Brady[4] gives a Lewis Lacroix who was ordained deacon at Cork in 1700 and served as Vicar-Choral of the Cathedral until he obtained the living of Killanully in 1724. He seems to have been a somewhat unsatisfactory cleric, for he is twice warned to reside on his prebend on pain of suspension, and as Vicar-Choral is admonished by the Bishop in June 1720 "for neglecting to attend ye service some days this week."

The name Martel is also connected with Cork and Kinsale. It is mentioned by Gimlette as first occurring in Irish records during the reign of James I, and he instances Philip Martell,[5] Mayor of Cork in 1607, with William, a landholder in Duncormick, and David, a property owner in Fermoy, both under Charles I. Actually, however, a Thomas Martell was Provost of Kinsale in 1455, and an Edmund Martell was once Provost and held the office of Sovereign twice during the reign of Henry VII.[6] It can scarcely, therefore, be regarded as a

---

[1] Freemen's Register.
[2] Council Book.
[3] *Ibid.*
[4] "Records of Cork, Cloyne and Ross," Vol. I, pp. 151, 268.
[5] "Huguenot Settlers," pp. 151 and 165.
[6] O'Sullivan, "History of Kinsale," Appendix, p. 218. In the same way the REYNELL family of Cork and Kinsale appears in England as early as 1433, although a JAQUES and EDMOND REYNELL were naturalized in Ireland in 1693 who may have been Huguenots.

Huguenot name, and Christopher Martell of Kinsale, who petitions the Corporation as one of that City's "ancient natives" in 1660,[1] seems to prove a pre-Huguenot ancestry in Ireland. The fact remains, however, that a William Martell sought for his denization in 1619,[2] so that there may have been two distinct families of this name in the South, the second coming from abroad during the religious persecutions. Besides Philip Martell, Thomas of this name was Mayor of Cork in 1635, Stephen was Sheriff in 1626, and David, possibly the property owner, was Sheriff's Bailiff in 1691.[3] Others of the name held important positions in the Guilds of the City, for in 1694 Patrick Martell was Warden of the Barber Chirurgeons, and in 1700 James Martell is recorded as Master of the Cordwainers.[4] The name does not occur amongst the Sovereigns of Kinsale after Philip Martell's term of office in 1528, and it may be possible that the Kinsale Martells removed to Cork.

In addition to the Martells, Gimlette gives Daniel Hignette, Richard Covert, John Mascal (Clerk) and Charles Nicholette as landed proprietors of Huguenot ancestry in the County of Cork during the seventeenth century.

Daniel Hignette was Sheriff of Limerick in 1671,[5] and a Wetenhal Hignet Sheriff of Cork in 1730, and this name, with that of Covert, is given by Dr. De La Cherois Purdon amongst the Lisburn colonists.[6] Richard Covert, who was Sheriff of Cork in 1657 and Mayor in 1662 and 1682, was attainted by the Parliament of James II in company with a William Covert of Dublin.[7]

---

[1] Council Book.
[2] Patent Rolls. James I. Quoted Hug. Soc. Pub., Vol. XVIII.
[3] Council Book, Cork.
[4] Court of D'Oyer Hundred Book.
[5] *Vide* p. 206.
[6] *Vide* p. 190.
[7] Gimlette, p. 259, and Council Book, Cork.

The Rumley family of County Cork is supposed to descend from Huguenot settlers. One branch was resident at Bally-trasna, Cloyne; another in Ballinacurra. In 1774 Mary, daughter of Thomas Rumley of Ballydaniel, married at Aghada Jaspar Joly, great-grandfather of the Astronomer Royal.[1]   It is thought that the name was a corruption of Romilly, a family which came from Montpellier, and traced amongst its English descendants the famous lawyer and politician, but no mention of an Irish branch of this family is made by Smiles,[2] who bases his account on the Memoirs of Sir Samuel Romilly himself.

Amongst the colonies in the south of Ireland the Baronne de Chambrier[3] mentions that of Tallow, but no trace of this remains to-day.   Agnew,[4] writing in 1871, states that "there is still a family named Arnauld" descending from the original colony, and it is possible that the Stephen Arnault who was Warden of the Coopers Company in Cork in 1720 was one of these settlers.[5]   A John Arnauld, cousin of James Fontaine, the Huguenot minister of Cork and a co-operator with him in the Bearhaven fishing venture, was settled as a merchant in London at the end of the seventeenth century,[6] and it may be suggested that a branch of his family was attracted to the south of Ireland by Fontaine's connection with the district.

The lack of evidence as to the small County Cork settle-ments and their early dissolution is probably to be accounted for by the nearness of the City.   Possibly many of the Cork Huguenots were first connected with the surrounding colonies, and had been attracted thence to the larger settlement, and

---

[1] C.H. & A.J., Vol. VII, No. 50. "Notes on the Rumley Family."
[2] "Huguenots in England," p. 327.
[3] Hug. Soc. Proc., Vol. VI, pp. 370-432. In County Waterford, but included here owing to the probable connection of its settlers with Cork.
[4] "Protestant Exiles," Vol. III, p. 240.
[5] Court of D'Oyer Hundred Book.
[6] "Memoirs," p. 181.

a good reason for this may be found in Fontaine's remark that " Refugees came from various parts to settle in Cork when they heard that a French Church was established there."[1] The name Arnault mentioned above with that of Mazière and Belsaigne, found both in the City and the County settlements, is proof of this interconnection, and in a study of the history of the Huguenots in the City of Cork it is probable that some of the now unknown Tallow and Bandon colonists are also under review.

[1] *Ibid.*, p. 170.

CHAPTER IV

THE SETTLEMENTS IN WATERFORD AND WEXFORD

I

AMONGST the Irish seaports the City of Waterford was especially favoured by the Huguenots, and both traders and military men found refuge there and helped considerably towards its prosperity in the seventeenth and eighteenth centuries.

Gimlette assigns as a reason for this that Waterford had always been well known on the Continent; in the time of Henry VII for its Rhenish and Gascoigne wine trade, and in the sixteenth century through those Flemish merchants who preferred to reside there rather than on the Continent in order to watch over their trading interests. He points out also that after the 1641 Rebellion the Puritan followers of Cromwell who settled here in large numbers kept up a sympathetic intercourse with the Protestants of Holland, France and Geneva, and were the more ready to welcome them when they were driven abroad.[1]

It is obvious, too, that a city so favourable for trade, the seaport of a rich agricultural hinterland should have attracted the thrifty Frenchmen, even had no other inducement been

[1] *Vide* Art. "Waterford" in U.J.A., Vol. IV, 1856, where Gimlette instances the monument in the old Waterford Cathedral to a Flemish merchant who had died there in 1545.

offered them to settle there, but when the Waterford Corporation metaphorically held out open hands to these foreigners,
a large settlement in the locality was assured.

When the Act "for encouraging Protestant strangers to
inhabit Ireland," which had been passed by the Parliament of
1662, was re-enacted in 1692, Waterford was especially named
as a suitable place of settlement.[1] It had been chosen as such
by the Duke of Ormond,[2] and the civic fathers, who in 1682
had authorized a house to house collection in answer to the
order of the Lord-Lieutenant for the relief of the fugitive
French Protestants,[3] now in 1693 themselves offered a not
wholly disinterested invitation to these refugees. On March
27th of that year they passed a resolution "That this city
and liberties do provide habitations for fifty families of the
French Protestants to drive a trade of linen manufacture,
they bringing with them a stock of money and materials for
their subsistence till flax can be sown and produced on the
lands adjacent and that the freedom of the city be given to
them gratis, that Mr. Mayor and Mr. Recorder are desired
to acquaint the Lord Bishop of this diocese therewith."[4] The
Mayor of that date was Daniel Lloyde, the Recorder Minard
Christian, himself a "Protestant Stranger," though of Danish
descent,[5] and the Bishop was Dr. Foy who granted the
Huguenots the choir of the old Franciscan Abbey for their
worship. The congregation conformed and the church,
according to Ryland, "was endowed (by Government) with
£60 per annum as a stipend to the officiating clergyman."[6]
Gimlette states that £40 per annum was voted by the Corporation as salary for the first French minister, and this is attested

[1] *Ibid.*
[2] Hug. Soc. Proc., Vol. VI. "Projet de Colonisation."
[3] Downey, quoting Municipal Records in "The Story of Waterford,"
p. 191.
[4] Council Records. Quoted Gimlette.
[5] From Middleburg, Zealand.
[6] "History of the County and City of Waterford."

by the fact that he seems to have found difficulty in obtaining it, and in 1702 the Corporation agreed "upon reading the petition of David Gervais, French Minister," that "his salary of £40 per annum be continued and the arrear paid."[1] These conflicting statements can only be reconciled by the supposition that the Corporation supplemented the Government grant, although this presupposes an unusual generosity on the part of the civic authorities of Waterford, since in all the other settlements except that of Portarlington, where the church was a private endowment of the Earl of Galway, the French ministers were salaried from Government and not from local funds.

The Rev. David Gervais was succeeded as minister by:

> James Denis.
> Gédéon Richon.
> George Dobier (or Daubier).
> Daniel Sandoz.
> Josiah Franquefort.
> Augustus Desvories.
> Peter Augustus Franquefort.

That the church had a congregation large enough to necessitate the appointment of an assistant minister by 1731 is evinced by the Visitation Book of the diocese for that date, when "Anthony Frank, Literatus Ecclesiae Galliae," is recorded as assistant to "Jacobus Denis, Minister," and even before this an unofficial assistant seems to have been employed, for during the ministry of David Gervais the burial in 1714 of "Benigne Bellet, wife of Mr. Isaac Bellet of St. Johns" was performed by "Mr. William Denis in the French Church."[2]

The Gervais family came from Tournon in Guienne whence Pierre and Daniel, the sons of Jean Gervais and Anne

---

[1] Council Records. Quoted Gimlette, U.J.A., Vol. IV.
[2] Parochial Records. Quoted Gimlette, U.J.A., Vol. IV.

Fabre, fled as children with an uncle to England at the Revocation. In 1710 Daniel was naturalized and became a Captain in the British Army and Gentleman Usher to Queen Anne. He married Pauline Balaguier, daughter of the minister in the French Church of Peter Street, Dublin, but died without issue. His elder brother, Pierre, married in 1717 Marie Françoise Girard, and died in 1730 leaving three sons, the elder of whom, Peter, became Collector of Revenue in the north of Ireland. He died in 1800 leaving a son, the Rev. Francis Gervais, proprietor of the estate of Cecil in the County Tyrone, whose death occurred in 1849.[1] The name seems to have been localized in Ireland even before 1685, for a John Gervais held land in Queen's County under Ormond.[2] The connection of the Waterford minister with either branch cannot be traced, but the French origin of the name is assured. Another branch, probably of the Waterford Gervais family, settled in Lismore, where in 1708 the Rev. Isaac Gervais was appointed Vicar-Choral, and where he was buried in 1756. In 1743 he became Dean of Tuam, and was succeeded by his son, Henry, in the Vicar-Choralship of Lismore.[3] The latter, who was priested in Cloyne in 1728 and became Curate of St. Paul's, Cork, in 1742, was appointed Vicar of Templebodan by Letters Patent from the Crown in 1755. He became Treasurer of Cashel in 1768 and Archdeacon in 1772, a post which he held until his death in 1790. His daughter married the only son of Bishop Chevenix of Waterford, and their daughter, Melesina, married Richard Trench, whose family will be dealt with amongst the Huguenots of the West.[4]

The connection of this Gervais family with the Huguenots of Waterford is proved by a burial entry quoted by Gimlette

[1] Burke, "Landed Gentry."
[2] Gimlette, "Huguenot Settlers," p. 194.
[3] U.J.A., Vol. IV. Art. "Waterford."
[4] Brady. For the Trench family *vide infra* p. 209.

from the Waterford Register under date September 15th, 1714, when "Will, son of the Rev. Isaac Gervais and Catherine, his wife, of Lismore" was buried in the French Church.[1]

As has already been stated, David Gervais experienced some difficulty in drawing his salary from the Corporation. He seems to have had more than one passage of arms with that august body, for in 1714 he makes the complaint that Alderman David Lewis had stored hay and stones in the old abbey, thus blocking the passage of the congregation who attended the French Church. He won his point and the Alderman was ordered by the Council to find storage for his goods elsewhere.[2]

By 1714 Gervais had been appointed a Prebendary of Lismore Cathedral and so in financial matters must have been more independent of the Council. He died two years later and was buried in Christ Church, his widow continuing to draw the grant made to him by the Crown.[3]

The Rev. James Denis does not seem to have fared even as well as his predecessor at the hands of the Corporation, for in January 1718 he petitions for a pension "setting forth that he has a great family of a wife and eight children," and £5 is granted to him "during the pleasure of this Board." Four years later it is ordered by Council "that Mr. Denis' salary, minister of the French Church, be suspended."[4] He cannot, however, have been by any means destitute, for he was in receipt of an annual Government grant of £40 from at least 1717 to 1727[5] and, like Gervais, obtained the Prebend of Donoughmore. In 1720 he became a beneficiary, to the extent of £50, under the will of the Earl of Galway.[6]

---

[1] U.J.A., Vol. IV. Art. "Waterford."
[2] Municipal Records. Quoted Downey, p. 272.
[3] U.J.A., Vol. IV. Art. "Waterford."
[4] Municipal Records. Quoted Gimlette.
[5] "Hiberniæ Notitia," and notes from MS. copy of the Pension Lists, in Nat. Mus., Ire.
[6] Agnew, "Henri de Ruvigny," Appendix.

A Stephen Dennis, merchant from France, from whom the minister may have descended, was naturalized in Ireland during the reign of Charles I.[1] The name also occurs amongst the Cromwellian settlers established in Kilkenny and Tipperary,[2] and is found in Kinsale in the person of Captain James Dennis, who held the chief office in the Corporation in 1710, 1711 and 1713, and again under George I.[3]

The will of the Rev. Gideon Richon, recorded in 1768, shows that he, too, held other livings besides that of the French Church. He is described as Rector of Fenoagh, and he leaves £5 "to the poor of the Parish of Desert of which I am Vicar" and "£5 to the poor of Clonmel where many years curate." All the rest he leaves to his sister, "Mrs. Anne Jourdan of the City of Dublin,"[4] whose husband was perhaps connected with the Huguenot family settled in the north of Ireland in 1703.[5]

Another Huguenot will of interest is that made in 1749 by Mrs. Martha Sandoz, mother of the Rev. Daniel Sandoz, who succeeded Dobier in the ministry of the French Church. She seems to have been a lady of property for she leaves to "Beverly Usher and Rev. Josiah Franquefort the houses, lands and orchards of Ballytrucklemore, without St. John's Gate,"[6] presumably in trust for her son and daughters, Martha and Catherine, or for the poor French of Waterford, to whom a bequest of £5 had been made by her husband, Abraham Sandoz, in 1732.[7]

Of Dobier and Desvories nothing seems to be known save that the latter may have some connection with the Portarling-

---

[1] Hug. Soc. Pub., Vol. XVIII, p. 332.
[2] *Vide* p. 122.
[3] O'Sullivan, "History of Kinsale," Appendix.
[4] J.W.S.E.I.A.S., 1914. "Old Wills of the Diocese of Waterford and Lismore."
[5] *Vide* p. 199.
[6] J.W.S.E.I.A.S., 1914.
[7] Will in Prerogative Office, Dublin. Quoted Smith, "Ancient and Present State of the Co. and City of Waterford."

G

ton minister of this name; but the Franqueforts were a notable Huguenot family whose history may be studied in Portarlington as well as Waterford.

In 1699 Pierre, son of Jacques de Francquefort of Soulignonne in Saintonge, leased a holding in the former town. At that period he was serving in a Foot Regiment and from 1709-1713 he again took service as a Captain of Marines, but he played an important part in the colony and, with his brother Jacques, was an elder of the church. He married a Mademoiselle de Bonnefoy and had four sons and three daughters. Of his sons, François and Henry both entered the Army, and Josias, born in 1710, took Holy Orders, and, after officiating for Monsieur Desvories at Portarlington from 1736-7, became Curate of St. Olave's in Waterford and minister of the French Church. He died in 1759, four years after his father. Henri de Franquefort married Esther, daughter of Jean de Fontanier, a Captain in Galway's Horse, who was lamed during the Irish Campaign and retired on pension to Portarlington in 1692, where he died in 1720, and where his daughter's grave with that of other members of her husband's family may still be seen. François married Angelique de Coutiers, daughter of another Portarlington settler, and, with daughters, had one son, Pierre Auguste, born in 1732, who, like his uncle, took Holy Orders in order to serve the French Church.[1] He was appointed minister at Waterford and resided there from 1762, when he succeeded Desvories until his death in 1819,[2] but a gravestone to his wife, Elizabeth, who predeceased him by twenty-five years, was placed in the Portarlington churchyard and serves to show that the Waterford branch of the family was never wholly separated from their first place of settlement. One member of this family was a very late comer to Ireland. This was James Paul Defranquefort, who obtained his certificate of naturalization in March 1800 as " a French nobleman

[1] J.K.A.S., Vol. XI, No. 4. Art. " Portarlington."
[2] U.J.A., Vol. IV. Art. " Waterford."

and formerly Lieut.-Colonel of a Regiment of Horse in the service of the King of France, now of the City of Waterford, Ireland."[1]

The Rev. Peter Augustus was the last minister to officiate in the French Church. He was licensed, as his uncle had been, for the curacy of St. Olave's, and, as in the case of the Rev. Daniel Sandoz who held the Prebend of Mora, is not recorded as French minister in the Visitation Records. In 1803 he visited his relatives in France and suffered the indignity of two imprisonments, the one on the Continent on the renewal of war, and the other in England as a French spy when he was at last permitted to return to that country. During his ministry the roof of the French Church collapsed and the services were for a short time afterwards conducted in the vestry. Later they were transferred to St. Olave's, but by then the congregation had almost disappeared and with his death the French service was allowed to lapse.[2]

The Huguenots seem to have been greatly attracted to the clerical profession and many French names are found amongst the clergy of the diocese, owing, perhaps, to the encouragement afforded to them by Bishops Foy and Mills and the fact that their successor, Bishop Chevenix, was himself the descendant of a Huguenot.

He came of a distinguished Lorraine family which fled at the Revocation. One branch settled in Brandenburg, the other, represented by the Rev. Philippe Le Chevenix, who had been pastor of the Church of Limay, near Mantes, in England.[3] Philippe Le Chevenix was naturalized in 1682, removed to Ireland and settled at Portarlington. He had one son of the same name, who became a Major in the 2nd Carabineers and fell at Blenheim. One of his three sons was Richard, born 1698,[4] who rose to eminence in the Church,

[1] Hug. Soc. Pub., Vol. XXVII, Appendix V.
[2] U.J.A., Vol. IV. Art. "Waterford."
[3] Smiles, "Huguenots in England," Appendix.
[4] Hug. Soc. Proc., Vol. VIII, p. 366.

G*

obtaining the bishopric of Killaloe and later that of Waterford and Lismore in 1745. He had been chaplain to Philip, Earl of Chesterfield, at the Hague, and when the latter became Viceroy the Bishop interested him in establishing a branch of the linen trade in Waterford. His public spirit was further proved at his death in 1779, when he left £1,600 to the Waterford diocese and £1,000 to that of Lismore.[1] His only son, as has already been stated, married into the Gervais family and was the grandfather of Richard Chevenix Trench, Archbishop of Dublin.

John Jaumard, Archdeacon of Lismore; William Grueber, Chancellor, Treasurer and Precentor of Lismore; James and Arthur Grueber, successively Prebendaries for Kilrosantie; all are given by Gimlette as being of Huguenot stock, and the Venerable George Louis Fleury, Archdeacon of Waterford for fifty-two years, was a cousin of Bishop Chevenix and had originally come to the diocese as his chaplain.

The Grueber family, whose founder was Daniel Grueber of Lyons who was naturalized in 1685, was connected with Dublin as well as Waterford, and mention is made of some of its members in the Registers of the French Conformist Churches of the Capital from 1703. Not all of these were clerics, and a Lieutenant John Grueber was Adjutant of the Louth Militia in 1796. His first wife was Isabella Bonafous, who was buried in Portarlington, the home of her family,[2] in 1798.

The Fleurys were descended from the French nobility. Shortly before the Revocation Louis Fleury, the Protestant Pastor of Tours, fled, with his wife Esther, his son born 1671, and two daughters, to England where they were all naturalized in 1679.[3] He came to Ireland as one of the private

[1] U.J.A., Vol. IV. Art. "Waterford." Hug. Soc. Proc., Vol. VIII, p. 368. Art. on the Trench Family.
[2] J.K.A.S., Vol. XI, No. 4. Art. "Portarlington."
[3] Hug. Soc. Proc., Vol. VIII, p. 122.

chaplains of William of Orange and was present with the army at the Boyne. Later he became pastor at Leyden where his son, Philip Amuret (or Amaury), was educated and ordained "to preach the Gospel to the French in Ireland."[1] Philip Fleury was appointed chaplain to Colonel La Bouchetière's Regiment of Dragoons, but as he is also stated to have officiated in the French Church of La Patente from 1704-1706 he cannot have accompanied the regiment abroad. From 1716 till his death in 1734 he served in the French Church of St. Patrick's, Dublin,[2] but he seems to have kept his connection with his regiment for in 1719, when they were quartered in Ardee, he was instrumental in suppressing a mutiny in their ranks, "Not without danger of losing his life which on that occasion he did very freely expose."[3] He was the father of the Rev. Antoine Fleury, also educated at Leyden and ordained there in 1728. In 1730 the latter was licensed to the French Church of St. Patrick's, a post which he resigned on his appointment to Coolbanagher in 1736. He was appointed Vicar-Choral of Lismore in 1761,[4] and died in 1801, being buried in the French Cemetery in Portarlington.[5] By his wife, Marie Julie, daughter of Colonel Paul Brunet de Rochbrune, he had a son George Louis, educated in Trinity College and ordained for the ministry, who, as has already been stated, came to Waterford with Dr. Chevenix.[6] He was appointed Prebendary and Treasurer of Kilgobinet and in 1773 was made Archdeacon of Waterford, a position which had not been filled since 1667. His daughter married the Rev. Richard Ryland, author of the "History of Waterford."[7] Three of his sons entered the ministry and a fourth was

---

[1] U.J.A., Vol. IV. Art. "Waterford."
[2] Hug. Soc. Proc., Vol. VIII, p. 122.
[3] Letter, Lord Galway to Duke of Bolton, 1719. Quoted Cole, "Records of Cork, Cloyne and Ross."
[4] Hug. Soc. Proc., Vol. VIII, p. 122.
[5] *Vide* p. 171.
[6] Cole.
[7] U.J.A., Vol. IV. Art. "Waterford."

Captain J. Franquefort Fleury of the 36th Regiment.[1]

Another branch of the Fleury family seems to have settled in Cork, for in Doneraile·churchyard a monument existed to the memory of David Fleury, son of James Fleury and Louise Le Marchand, who was born in the parish of Torchand in Lower Normandy in 1667 and died in 1720.[2] He seems to have become attached to his place of settlement for he bequeathed the interest on £50 a year in perpetuity to the poor of the parish.[3] A certain T. C. Fleury, who graduated in medicine at the University of Edinburgh in 1760, may also have had some connection with the family. He settled in, Dublin, where he became the first systematic Lecturer on Midwifery, and where he died in 1797.[4]

The refugees of Waterford represented other professions besides that of the Church.

A Huguenot physician, Peter de Rante, was employed as doctor to the poor and paid a salary of £10 per annum by the Corporation for his work. He had married into the Alcock family and possibly owed his appointment to this connection with the leaders of the Council, but in 1722 he suffered, as the minister James Denis had done, from their economizing zeal, and lost his post. In the next year, however, he was restored and continued to serve the Council until his death in 1756. His first wife died in 1716 and he married secondly a Miss Anne Pyke, but he was buried beside Mary Alcock in the French Church.[5] His will, drawn up in 1753, shows that he must have had a son and daughter. It states that he leaves all his possessions to his daughter, Mrs. Ann Fortin, widow, save for £10 per annum to his granddaughter, Anne Derante. If his daughter Mrs. Jane Derante's child is born alive it, too,

---

[1] Cole.
[2] J.A.P.M.D., Vol. III, and Smith, "Ancient and Present State of the Co. and City of Cork."
[3] Smith. *Ibid.*
[4] Cameron, "History of the College of Surgeons, Dublin."
[5] U.J.A., Vol. IV. Art. "Waterford."

is to receive £10 yearly.[1] The daughter Ann may have married that Thomas Fortin who was a merchant in Waterford in 1725.[2] Her will was made in January 1782, and by it she leaves her sister-in-law, Martha Fortin, "my watch and two silver spoons, plate, pepper-box and punch-ladle and the use of my plate candle sticks for her life and then to the Rev. Peter Augustus Franquefort," also her "Interest in the lands of Bally-truckle under Alexr. Boyd, deceased, for life, and after to reduced Protestant Gentlewomen and not to be sold." Susanna Vashon is left £5 yearly and the wife of Simon Bonige £5. She wishes to be "interred in the French Church near the remains of my father Mr. Peter Derant."[3]

Martha Fortin does not seem to have obtained her legacy, for both ladies must have died in the same year. On March 4th, 1786, probate of Martha Fortin's will is granted to Elizabeth, widow of Josias Franquefort, her executrix, and in October administration of Anne Fortin's to the Rev. George Fleury and the Rev. Richard Ryland.[4]

Jacques Reynette was another Huguenot doctor who practised in Waterford during the eighteenth century. His daughter married Captain John Ramsay, and their son was the originator of the *Waterford Chronicle*, one of the earliest of provincial newspapers in Ireland.[5] Gimlette states that Reynette died in 1720, but his will was proved in 1730 and mentioned marriage articles with Frances France of Waterford in 1723. One of his executors was the Rev. Nathaniel France of Youghal, presumably a relative of the lady, and Abraham Sandoz, the father of the French minister, was a witness to the will.[6]

The Reynet or de Reynet family held estates in Vivarais,

[1] W. & S.E.I.A.J., 1914. " Old Waterford Wills."
[2] C.H. & A.J., Vol. VIII, No. 53. " Dublin Goldsmiths."
[3] W. & S.E.I.A.J., 1915. " Waterford Wills."
[4] *Ibid.*
[5] U.J.A., Vol. IV. Art. " Waterford."
[6] W. & S.E.I.A.J., 1914. " Waterford Wills."

from which they fled at the Revocation. Henri de Reynet settled at Waterford, but only two of his sons remained in Ireland, the youngest returning to France, and, on professing the Roman Catholic religion, regaining the property. The Freedom of Waterford was conferred on the descendants of Henri de Reynet, who played an important part in the civic life of the city.[1] In 1755 James Henry Reynette held office as Sheriff and was later appointed Mayor. He seems to have worshipped not at the French Church but at St. Olave's, where his name appears amongst the churchwardens and vestrymen.[2] The name is also localized in the north of Ireland, where Henry Reynett, son of Lieutenant Henry Reynett, was curate of Annahilt in 1761, and Vicar of Magheragall in 1765. He was born in Sandhills, County Monaghan, in February 1736 (old style) and graduated in Dublin University. In 1777 he was J.P. for Antrim, and from 1782-1790 Vicar of Billy in that county. He appears also amongst the Lisburn Huguenots since, there being no Vicarage at Magheragall, he resided in the former town while officiating there.[3] General Sir James Henry Reynet was a notable descendant of this family.[4]

Waterford, like Portarlington, Youghal and Dublin, attracted some of the officers who were disbanded after the Irish Campaign. The names of these settlers, quoted by Gimlette from the return of pensions that had fallen in and been granted in 1719,[5] are as follows:

Lieut. James d'Augier.
Capt. Louis Belafaye.
Peter Chelar.

---

[1] "Huguenots in England," Appendix.
[2] U.J.A., Vol. IV. Art. "Waterford."
[3] Hug. Soc. Proc., Vol. XIV, No. 2, p. 257.
[4] "Huguenots in England," Appendix.
[5] H.C.J., Appendix, 1719.

Captain Du Chesne.
Lieut. Emmanuel Toupelin Delize.
Capt. Franquefort.
Lieut. Besard de Lemaindre.
Capt. John Vaury.
Major Sautelle, who came to Waterford at a later date
    than his brother officers.

Lieutenant James d'Augier is given as having died in
Waterford on September 11th, 1718, so that he cannot have
been that Lieutenant Seigneuron Jacques Augier who has
already been referred to as a freeman of Cork.[1] The latter
was the son of Peter Augier of Castel Jaloux in Guienne.[2]
He served in Portugal and Spain under Lord Rivers and
Ruvigny, and was apparently pensioned with other officers
on their return to England in 1713. He must be the
" Centurion Augier " mentioned as having come from Piedmont in the Pension Returns of 1719, and he was still enjoy-
ing this grant in 1727.[3] Gimlette conjectures that the James
d'Augier of Waterford had an earlier pension, on the supposition that he served under Ruvigny in Ireland, but little else
can be discovered about him. The name occurs in Ireland
as early as 1628, when Réné Augier was made a " denizen."
He was actively engaged as a Parliamentary agent during
the Commonwealth war, and in this capacity was sent to
Paris.[4] A Robinson Augier, who was apprenticed to the
Dublin goldsmith, Daniel Pineau, in 1714, may have been
connected with the Lieutenant,[5] but by that date the name
was widespread throughout the country.

The Sautelle family originally fled from Tours, and once
founded in Waterford played an important part in that city's

[1] *Vide* p. 61.
[2] Hug. Soc. Pub., Vol. VII, p. 115, and XXVII, p. 21.
[3] MS. copy of Pension List, in Nat. Mus., Ire.
[4] Gimlette, " Huguenot Settlers," p. 185.
[5] C.H. & A.J., Vol. VIII, No. 53. " Dublin Goldsmiths."

history. In 1729 Francis Sautell was Alderman, and the granddaughter of the Major married John Roberts, the leading architect of the city. Of their twenty-four children one became the Rector of Kill, and his grandson was Field-Marshal Lord Roberts.

Of the other officers little can be recorded. In the Cathedral Registry under date April 12th, 1714, it is noted that " Lieut. Peter Besard Delamaindre and Mrs. Jane Dubay were married by Mr. David Gervais in the French Church." In 1708 Thomas, the son of Captain Louis Duschenne [sic] and Catherine his wife, was buried there, and in the same year the burial is also recorded of Susannah, wife of Lieutenant Emmanuel Toupelin Delize.[1] Captain Franquefort of the Piedmont army has been already mentioned as the father of Josias Franquefort, the Waterford minister. Captain John Vaury later removed to Portarlington, but he did not forget Waterford, for on his death in 1719 he bequeathed £10 to the French Church there, as did Peter Chelar, the ex-Quartermaster of Lord Galway's Horse, in 1738.[2]

" During the period from 1693-1815," writes Egan,[3] " the old Franciscan Monastery presented a most singular spectacle. That portion of it repaired for the French Church, viz. the Choir and Chancel, were used for the Protestant Church service, whilst Mass was said in the upper portion for the inmates of the Holy Ghost Hospital. Later on, as if all religious forms of Christianity were destined to share the ground, the Methodist congregation built a neat church upon the site of the northern aisle." Egan, however, does not mention the fact that the cellars adjoining the abbey were utilized as storehouses by the Waterford Huguenot merchants, and that even the abbey itself was sometimes put to

---

[1] U.J.A., Vol. IV. Art. " Waterford."
[2] Will in Prerogative Office, Dublin. Quoted Smith, "Ancient and Present State of Co. and City of Waterford."
[3] " History, Guide and Directory of the Co. and City of Waterford."

this additional use. Gervais's petition against Alderman Lewis for blocking the entry to the Huguenot Church has already been noticed, and in a report on a petition sent up in 1737 by " the merchants and traders, inhabitants of Waterford,"[1] against a proclamation from the Crown which ordered that the value of French gold coin should be reduced to standard, reference is made to the locale of the traders and the goods in the cellars adjoining the church.

The wine trade greatly interested the Huguenots, many of whom had their own ships, and it was these traders in especial who petitioned against the restrictions on foreign coin; but many other industries also occupied them. Thus Sir William Brereton records in 1635 that at Waterford there dwelt "a judicious apothecary who hath been bred at Antwerp, and is a traveller; his name is (as I take it) Mr. Jarvis Billiard by whose directions and good advice I found much good,"[2] and Peter de Pienne, who was a printer in Cork in 1649, seems to have removed his business to Waterford in 1652. With the change of locality he seems also to have changed his political views, for while in Cork he printed a copy of the " Eikon Basilike," in Waterford his press is found producing Cook's " Monarchy no creature of Gods making —in which is proved that Monarchial Government is against the mind of God."[3]

Another Waterford business man of Huguenot origin was Simon Bonique (or Bonigue), who has already been mentioned in connection with the will of Anne Fortin. He was a man of enterprise, for in the *Dublin Daily Post* of January 16th, 1739, an advertisement appeared in which it was stated that " a sugar refining house had lately been established in Waterford by Messrs. Boyd and Bonique."[4]

[1] H.C.J., Ireland, Appendix.
[2] " Travels in Ireland," 1635. Printed in C. Litton Falkiner's " Illustrations of Irish History."
[3] C.H. & A.J., Vol. VI, No. 47. " List of Cork Printed Books."
[4] W. & S.E.I.A.J., 1915.

He seems to have held some position in civic matters, for at the Spring Assizes in 1741, in company with Peter Vashon and Charles Grandrie, he signs a presentment as a member of the City Grand Jury.[1]

The Corporation of Waterford was more interested in the linen trade than in any other industry, but it was not until Louis Crommelin had established himself in Lisburn, and had visited Waterford on his tour, that the desire evinced in the petition of 1693, already quoted, was fulfilled. Jean La Trobe, one of his assistants, was sent to Waterford, and by Crommelin's energies and the enterprise of English manufacturers, like John Radburne and Jonathan Ever in 1721, or Abraham Fairbrother and Thomas White in 1744, assisted by the Linen Board and Corporation,[2] the manufacture of linen and sailcloth was carried on for a time with some success. Nevertheless, Smith, writing in 1746,[3] states that " the Linen and Hempen Manufacture is not as yet carried on in this part of the Kingdom to any tolerable degree of perfection. The methods of hiring here are very different from those of the north which these people will not comply with. If colonies of the Northern inhabitants are to be invited into these parts which it is presumed is the best method of spreading the Linen manufacture hither, they must have land set them at a cheaper rate than our cottagers pay for it."

Smith's reflection on the linen trade must have been caused by a scheme set on foot in the same year by Dr. Chevenix, who, owing to his influence with the Lord-Lieutenant, persuaded the Linen Board to place a substantial grant at the disposal of the Smith family of Belfast, who were induced to remove to Waterford and there set up a manufactory. Two Dutch families were imported to teach the

[1] *Ibid.*
[2] Downey, p. 327.
[3] " Ancient and Present State of the Co. and City of Waterford."

manufacture of tapes and bobbins, and fifty Protestant households, some of them descendants of the Huguenots of Lisburn and Dundalk, were brought from the north of Ireland to work for the Smiths.[1]

That the undertaking was for a time most successful is proved by the report made on the petition sent up by this family in 1761. This stated " That there were not more than 300 hanks of yarn to be bought when they first came to Waterford which would not make more than five pieces of linen," but that " near 5,000 pieces of cloth have been made this last year to the value of between £10,000 and £12,000." " If all the machines were constantly at work," it was added, "upwards of 1,400 persons might be usefully employed."[2] " This manufacture may equal all the rest of the Kingdom in quantity and surpasses in quality," was Stephenson's[3] glowing tribute to their work in 1755.

The linen trade of the South, however, was doomed to a chequered career. The work of La Trobe had failed in 1746, possibly owing to " the sloth and idleness " to which, according to the Smiths, the poor of Waterford "were inured,"[4] and with the invention of the power loom the manufactory of the Smiths met the fate of all small local enterprise in England and Ireland. The Linen Guild, which had once been the most important in the city, sank into insignificance, and when Gimlette wrote in 1856 nothing was left of this once flourishing industry save the manufacture of a coarse tarpaulin cloth and bacon wrapping carried on in the cloister of the old Franciscan Abbey.[5]

Of the Waterford Huguenots engaged in this industry, Jean La Trobe and the Vashon Brothers were the most

[1] Downey, p. 332.
[2] H.C.J., Nov. 9th, 1761.
[3] " Journal of a Tour of Inspection," 1755. He was an Inspector for the Linen Board.
[4] H.C.J. Petition to Hse. of Com. by Smiths, Nov. 3rd, 1761.
[5] Gimlette, U.J.A., Vol. IV. Art. " Waterford."

important. The former was the descendant of a noble family from Languedoc. He fled at the Revocation to Holland and thence to Ireland as the close friend and fellow worker of Louis Crommelin. As has been stated he was appointed one of the assistants of the latter, and besides the linen trade of Waterford he was responsible for encouraging manufactories throughout Leinster.[1] He settled in Dublin before his death, and Smiles states that his descendants emigrated to Pennsylvania, although the name La Trobe was still extant in Waterford when Gimlette wrote.[2]

In 1733 the two brothers Vashon proposed to convert " the Bridewell and garden " into a factory for the linen and hempen industry. The Corporation granted them the land on a lease for ninety-nine years at a " pepper corn " rent, provided that they kept the looms at work and would agree to manufacture 10,000 yards of sailcloth yearly. Simon Vashon was entrusted with the charge of the waterworks in 1719, and in 1726 was appointed Mayor. His brother, Peter, was Sheriff in 1735, and in 1738-9 Simon Vashon, junior, was elected Mayor twice in succession.

In 1740, however, a serious charge was brought by Alderman Barker, then Mayor, against Peter and Simon Vashon. It was alleged that they had fraudulently dealt with certain money orders of the city in order to charge the city with them a second time. It would appear that Peter put forward the excuse that the late Alderman Congreve had given him certain " City Orders " which had been previously passed, but this was declared " false, scandalous and malitious as appears by undoubted proof this day laid before us." The Vashons denied the allegations, but when the inquiry was finally held in March 1742 neither of them appeared at the Guildhall nor submitted any defence. The charges were therefore taken as proved, and the Vashons removed from the

---

[1] " Huguenots in England," Appendix.
[2] U.J.A., Vol. IV. Art. " Waterford."

Municipal Board and disfranchised. In 1745 the Recorder was paid a fee of twenty guineas " for his trouble in coming from Dublin in term time upon the Disfranchising of the two Messrs. Vashon." Despite this unfortunate affair the Corporation granted in 1750 £10 a year to Elizabeth Vashon and Susanna Vashon, the widow and daughter of Simon Vashon the elder deceased.[1]

Amongst other French names in the Corporation Records appear those of Chaigneau and Ayrault, who were Common Council-men; John Espaignet who was Sheriff in 1757, and Jeremy Gayott who held the same office in 1709.

Although the Huguenots possessed their own place of worship, many of them may be found amongst the church-wardens and vestrymen of the other Waterford churches. Gimlette has traced in the records of St. Patrick's the names Blanche, de Maison, Oderoft, Hagerein, Boisrond, Luné and Guillard; in those of St. Peter's and St. John's: Le Maistre, Sprusson, Ducla, Shelmadine, Sautelle and Spurrier; in those of St. Olave's: Reynette, Latrobe and Vinson; and in those of the Cathedral, Gayott.[2]

Other names, as Coquin, Dermozan and Marcel, occur, in addition to those already mentioned, in the registers; with those of Souberment, who was clerk to the Rev. Peter Augustus Franquefort, Legrediere, Ponseaux, Petipres, Roquet, Latour, Tournere, de Landre, Martel, Bessonet, Dubourdieu and Perrin.

The Boisronds, like the Chaigneaus, are connected with the Youghal Settlement, and the dubiously Huguenot name Martel occurs in Cork and Kinsale. The Tourneres came from the North, the Le Maistres are connected with the Carlow colony, and the Dubourdieus and Perrins will be dealt with amongst the Huguenots of Lisburn.

The names of other Waterford Huguenots occur in a

[1] Downey, quoting from Municipal Records.
[2] U.J.A., Vol. IV. Art. "Waterford."

will made by John Galtier in 1729, and one of Paul de Soulas de Mereux in 1726-7,[1] which are worth quoting.

Galtier bequeaths his estate to Simon Vashon, Francis Sautelle and Henry Duffan as his trustees and executors. He leaves £20 "to my relative Francis Bernard," and £20 to his daughter Jane "for marrying"; £20 to Stephen Brunell; £20 to Marie Sautelle (daughter of Francis); £10 to the "sone of Peter Languedoe [sic] at Mr. Marvaults"; £10 to the French Church of the city. "The trustees to put at interest £200 to pay half yearly to Francis Bernard and Jane and their survivors interest thereon, and after their death £100 to the treasurer of the two French Churches by name St. Patrick and Mary Abbey; and other £100 to the two French Churches, by name St. Peter and Lucy Lane."[2] The will was witnessed by John Lacombe and Alexander and John Demaison.

The earlier will, that of de Soulas de Mereux, is written in French. It is "signe, scedliet et delivré en presence de John Bigos, L. Duffan and Moses Vernous." "The sone of Peter Languedoe" seems to have been a special care of the Huguenots, for he again comes in for a legacy. "Trente shillings" are left "au fils de la veufe de Languedoe." The testator must have been a relative of the Marvault in whose house the boy lived or worked, for he gives "à ma cousine Gabrielle Marvauld la somme de dix livres sterling." It is tempting to connect this Marvauld with the "surveyor" of the same name in Youghal whose daughter, Ann, died there in 1766.

To "Mademoiselle Espaignet" de Mereux leaves "la somme de quarante shillings" and "aux pauvres de l'Eglise française de cette ville la somme de trois livres sterling." He makes "ma chère bonne et bien amiée Belle soeur, Lusanne [sic] Dastory, Dame de Campernet," his heiress and

---

[1] W. & S.E.I.A.J., 1914. "Old Waterford Wills."
[2] Not Lady Lane as corrected by the annotator in the W. & S.E.I.A.J. *Vide* chapter on Dublin, p. 222.

cuts his nephew off with a shilling; " Je laisse et donne Paul de Soulas Mereux, mon neveu, qui est en Moscovie un shilling." Finally he leaves " a ma d'heritière le soin de la sepulture de mon corps comme elle trouvera convenable."

Towards the end of the eighteenth century the Huguenot population in Waterford had so far declined that the extraordinary expedient of the New Geneva Settlement was hit upon. It is not necessary here to trace the costly failure of this scheme,[1] since it lies outside the history of the Huguenots. It brought a few new French residents, such as Monsieur Clavière, into Waterford, but left no mark on the history of the city. Clavière, who had been one of the leaders of the Genevese, finally removed to France, where he was created Minister of Finance by the Jacobins, and shared, with most of the Revolutionary leaders, the reward of the Guillotine, and the factories which had been built for the Geneva workmen became barracks for recruits for the Peninsular War, and soon fell into ruin.

In 1803 the Huguenot colony was still further thinned by the return of many of the descendants of the original settlers to France.[2] Death and intermarriage removed other names, and, as Ryland wrote in 1824, " The Congregation is now entirely broken up by the death of the late respectable and venerated minister, who, in early life, officiated to a large congregation of his countrymen, scarcely one of whom remained to follow him to the grave."[3]

Nevertheless some Huguenot families still remained in Waterford, and even as late as 1856 Gimlette could write: " Louis Perrin is judge of one of Her Majesty's Courts. The Assistant-Barrister of the County is a Bessonet; the Stipendiary Magistrate here is a Tabiteau;[4] the late Clerk of the Peace, a

[1] Which has been admirably told in "Notes on New Geneva." W. & S.E.I.A.J., 1915. See also Gimlette, U.J.A., Vol. IV.
[2] U.J.A., Vol. IV. Art. "Waterford."
[3] "History of Waterford."
[4] *Vide* p. 136.

Delandre; the Governor of the City Prison is one of the Latrobes; the last officer of the Constabulary was a Dubourdieu."[1]

II

Not very many settlers seem to have made Wexford their home, and all trace of those who did so has gone. That there must have been a Huguenot colony there is evinced by the fact that in 1684 the then Bishop of Ferns and Leighlin, who was afterwards the famous Archbishop Marsh, was directed by the Privy Council to find a place of worship for the French Huguenots in Wexford, then numbering forty-two families.[2] He allowed them to hold service in St. Mary's Church, and Pierre Bouquet de St. Paul, minister of the French Church in St. Patrick's in 1715, was one of their pastors before taking office in Dublin.[3] He later became Rector of Carlingford, County Louth, and will be dealt with amongst the Huguenots of the North.[4]

Despite the fact that few made a permanent settlement there, Wexford was known to foreign refugees at a very early date. Thus in 1551 Protestant refugees from the Low Countries were brought over to work the silver and lead mines sunk at Clonmines. As has already been shown,[5] the foreigners, under the leadership of Joachim Gundelfinger, made themselves unpopular and the mines eventually failed and were suspended.

Under Ormond, foreigners were employed near Enniscorthy in ore smelting and iron manufacture. The chief of

---

[1] U.J.A., Vol. IV. Art. "Waterford."

[2] Registry Book, Diocese Ferns and Leighlin, quoted Le Fanu. Hug. Soc. Proc., Vol. XII, p. 245.

[3] Hug. Soc. Proc., Vol. VIII, p. 119. "The French Churches of Dublin."

[4] *Vide* p. 201.

[5] *Vide* p. 4.

these was Didier Fouchant, who, according to Gimlette, in May 1664 petitioned that he and some others had " expended £30,000 upon iron works on lands formerly belonging to Dudley Colclough, an Irish rebel, who procured the King's letter for these lands for life, with remainder to his son, Patrick,"[1] and prayed that a saving clause might be introduced into the " Act of Explanation " which was then before the Irish Parliament in order to settle the vexed question of the distribution of land after the Commonwealth evictions and grants. The Earl of Cork supported Fouchant, but the work fell into decay.

Earlier than this, after La Rochelle had fallen in 1628, a Jean Louis and Jean Gerard were enrolled in the Irish Chancery Rolls as tenants of Adam Colclough of Tintern, County Wexford.[2] Gimlette speaks of the Chambrés as a Huguenot family also settled there, but Burke[3] states that Calcot Chambré, the founder of the name in Ireland, came from Wales. John Jerones had a burgage in the town under Ormond, and an Abel Guilliams held 1,591 acres in County Wexford at the same period.[4] The latter may have been connected with the Thomas Guyllyms who was a landowner in Cavan,[5] or with the John Guilliams who married Ann Rittoud in Youghal in 1668.

But the most important of the Wexford settlers was Matthew de Renzie, who obtained first a grant of land in the King's County and then the Clobemon estate in Wexford. The son of French refugees who fled to Bohemia, he had been born in Cologne,[6] and seems to have come from Antwerp

---

[1] H.C.J. Quoted Gimlette, " Huguenot Settlers," p. 195. As this Act was in consideration only during November and December 1665, and no Parliament met in 1664, the given date seems questionable, and probably 1665 is intended.

[2] " Huguenot Settlers," p. 165.

[3] " Landed Gentry."

[4] Gimlette, p. 194.

[5] Ibid.

[6] Ibid., p. 212.

to Ireland, where he was naturalized in 1605.[1] He later entered the service of Charles I, was knighted by that monarch, and in 1622 obtained a grant of the property in King's County. He died in Athlone in August 1635, but his estates passed to his descendants, and though in the redistribution of the forfeited lands under Ormond 115 acres of his land in Garvally were forfeited to the King, the rights of the de Renzie family were reserved.[2] One of his lineal descendants was a minister in Bonmahon, County Waterford, when Gimlette wrote. De Renzie himself claimed descent from "that famous and renowned warrior, Goerge Castriot, alias Scandeberg," as stated on his monument in Athlone.[3]

No trace of the Wexford colony existed into the early nineteenth century. De Latocnaye[4] found a French family there, it is true, but these were refugees who had fled from the Revolution of 1789. As in Youghal or Kinsale, the earlier refugees had died out or left the district, and of the southern seaports Waterford and Cork alone preserved a memory of the Huguenot settlements.

[1] Smiles, p. 292.
[2] Gimlette, p. 193.
[3] *Ibid.*, pp. 170 and 212 note.
[4] "A Frenchman's Walk through Ireland," 1796-1797.

CHAPTER V

THE Huguenot settlers of the seaport towns were the masters of their fate in that, at their own discretion, they might choose such places of residence as seemed to them best; but the midland colonies were of a more artificial origin, the fruit of the Duke of Ormond's desire to encourage Protestant Strangers, and of Ruvigny's efforts to establish the ex-officers of his army in a congenial environment.

When Sir Peter Pett, the Member for Askeaton, memorialized the Duke of Ormond as to the desirability of "the setting up of a cloth manufacture and the manufacture of fine worsted stockings and Norwich stuff in all parts of the Nation for making the best advantage of their wool and employing the poor,"[1] the Viceroy lent a ready ear to a scheme that echoed his own aspirations and determined to prove the efficacy of such a policy in his towns of Clonmel and Carrick. Hence he employed Captain Grant[2] as agent to establish artisans in Clonmel, and in 1667 five hundred families of Walloons and French were invited from Canterbury and given houses at nominal rents and long leases. Some of these settled later in Carrick-on-Suir, where half the dwellings in the town

---

[1] Carte, "Life of Ormond," Bk. VI, p. 342.
[2] "A man well known by his observations on the Bills of Mortality." Carte, "Life of Ormond."

were put at their disposal with five hundred acres contiguous to the walls at a "pepper corn" rent for three lives.[1]

A Monsieur de Fountisne seems to have come with the settlers as minister, and Gimlette states that such French names as Descarpentries, De Durand, De La Mere, De La Roche, Du Four, Du Pont, Farange, Gast, Jourdan, La Febure, Le Froy and Legard are found amongst the refugees in Canterbury, and suggests that these names in Ireland may have originated in the Clonmel colony.[2] This, however, must be disproved in some instances; thus the LeFroys seem to have settled first in Limerick, and Lieutenant-Colonel Anthony LeFroy, who made his home there, although descended from a Canterbury weaver, did not come to Ireland until the latter half of the eighteenth century,[3] while the name Gast only occurs in Ireland after the Peace of Utrecht, when Daniel Gast settled in Dublin.[4] A De La Mere and a De La Roche were landholders in Galway and Meath respectively[5] when Ormond was called upon to revise the Cromwellian grants; and a John and Robert Durant, the former from Canterbury, were appointed by Cromwell as chaplains to the Irish Garrisons.[6] Both forms of the name Durant and Durand are found amongst the English Huguenots. Smiles[7] states that they originated in Dauphiny and were of noble rank. A François Durand, a Protestant minister of Languedoc, fled to Geneva at the Revocation, where he recruited the Dragoon Regiment of Baltasar and part of the Regiment of Colonel Blosset de Loche for King William.[8]

---

[1] *Ibid.*, Bk. VI, p. 342.

[2] "Huguenot Settlers," p. 197. Some of the names listed by Gimlette are not French, such as Noble which is that of a Scottish sept, and have therefore been omitted.

[3] *Vide* p. 204.

[4] *Vide* p. 151.

[5] *Vide* pp. 199, 214.

[6] Gimlette, p. 186.

[7] "Huguenots in England," Appendix.

[8] *Ibid.*, and Hug. Soc. Proc., Vol. IX.

In Ireland the name was localized in Youghal as has already been stated.

The name DuFour occurs in Lisburn; while in 1727 a John Venaac Dufour appears as Ensign in a Foot Regiment of the Cork Militia.[1] It is also connected with Dublin, where Isaac Dufour was at one time master in the school for Huguenot children and where his son was apprenticed to the goldsmith James Vidouze.[2] The Jourdans (or Jourdains), too, belong to the north of Ireland, where a member of this family was Rector of Dunshaughlin in 1703,[3] and to Dublin where Mrs. Anne Jourdan, sister of the Rev. Gideon Richon, French minister of Waterford, was residing in 1768.[4]

Le Febure (or Le Fevre, or Le Febre) is also found amongst the Dublin and Lisburn colonists, while, with Legrand and Dupont, it is later localized in Cork, where a Mr. Le Febure maintained a French Academy at the Lough in 1799.[5] In Dublin a Jacob Lefebure was a merchant in 1725, and his son, Anthony, was apprenticed to a goldsmith and was himself taking apprentices by 1732.[6] The family seems originally to have come from Rouen and was established in Dublin when De Bostaquet visited the City,[7] probably having removed there from the Wicklow Settlement.[8]

Le Grand occurs in Kilkenny, where, as will be seen, William, son of Captain Le Grand, was entered at the college in 1753, and in Cork where a tombstone in the French churchyard laconically stated, " This is the burying place of Jonathan Le Grand."[9] No other trace of this settler may be

[1] C.H. & A.J., Vol. XXXII, No. 135. " Militia Commissions for Cork."
[2] *Vide* p. 189.
[3] *Vide* p. 199.
[4] *Vide* p. 97.
[5] Nixon's " Cork Almanack," 1799.
[6] C.H. & A.J., Vol. VIII, No. 53.
[7] " Mémoires Inédits."
[8] *Vide* p. 219.
[9] J.A.P.M.D., 1901.

found in the City, but a cabinet-maker of this name is given in West's " Cork Directory " of 1810.

In 1699 Andrew Dupond, " Dr. of Physick," was admitted a freeman by the Corporation of Cork as a French refugee,[1] and in 1701 James Dupont also obtained this privilege.[2] They may have been connected with David Dupont, merchant of Dublin and native of Bordeaux, who obtained Letters of Denization in 1704.[3] The name seems to have died out in Cork City, but in the Mallow Register of Burials a Margaret Dupont and a St. John Dupont are entered in 1789 and 1798 respectively.[4]

Of the remaining names in Dr. Gimlette's list no further record occurs, and none of them is now existent in Clonmel. No trace of the minister De Fountisne remains, and the only other Huguenot cleric who may have held office in the settlement was Charles De La Roche, minister of the French Church in St. Patrick's from 1700 to 1702 and chaplain to Colonel Fontjulian of Lord River's Brigade in 1706, who, it has been suggested, served in Clonmel in 1699.[5]

Another name that has been suggested as connected with the Clonmel colony is that of Guerin. Jacob Guerin, the original refugee, came to England in 1563 from Normandy and settled in Canterbury. Other members of the family later followed him, of whom Samuel and Daniel were naturalized in 1682 and Francis in 1688,[6] and it was possibly one of these who served under Lord Galway from 1691 to 1699 and was granted a pension of four shillings a day on the Irish Establishment although the identity of the pensioner cannot be established. A Solomon de Guerin with his wife Anne was naturalized in 1697, and his son Charles was baptized at

---

[1] Freemen's Register.
[2] *Ibid.*
[3] Hug. Soc. Proc., Vol. XXVII, p. 235.
[4] C.H. & A.J., Vol. XXX, No. 131. "Mallow and Some Mallow Men."
[5] Hug. Soc. Proc., Vol. VIII, p. 114.
[6] " Huguenots in England," Appendix. 1889 Edition.

Westminster in 1698. This family later removed to Dublin, where the father died in 1709 and where the son entered Trinity College with a brother or cousin, Maynard Guerin. A Pierre Guerin appears as an elder of the French Church in St. Patrick's Cathedral from 1693 to 1710 who may have been connected with the family although he came from Macon in Burgundy. The will of a Gaspar Guerin was registered in Charleville in 1670, so that many Huguenots of this name seem to have settled in Ireland, and the writer has been informed that it was in existence in County Tipperary in the nineteenth century, although by then its bearers had become Roman Catholics.[1]

Even before the establishment of the weavers from Canter-bury, one or two French names are connected with the latter county. Thus Paul Amiraut (or Amyrault, or Emerott as he is called in the State Papers) was Independent Minister in Carrick under Henry Cromwell. He was a Frenchman although he emigrated from the Palatinate. In England he obtained a benefice, holding the Vicarage of East Dereham, Norfolk, in 1648. During the Civil War he took the side of the Puritans and, like the Durants, was appointed to the Cromwellian garrisons in Ireland. He returned to England shortly before the Restoration, but on that event lost his living there owing to his nonconformity and retired again to Ireland. Here he changed his opinions once more, for in 1665 he was Archdeacon of Kilfenora, in 1666 Provost of Tuam and in 1667 Chancellor of the diocese of Killaloe.[2] In 1690 a Joseph Amyrault, probably his son, was Archdeacon of the same diocese,[3] and from 1695-1713 Rector of Finnoe, County Tipperary.

Other settlers of Flemish and French origin came to

---

[1] Notes submitted by a descendant.
[2] Gimlette, p. 185.
[3] *Ibid.*, p. 186.

Ireland in the regiments of Cromwell, and in the re-distribution of Irish land obtained grants for their services. Amongst the foreign exiles who were recruited chiefly from the eastern counties of England and are later localized in Kilkenny and Tipperary, appear Thomas Dennis, Colonel William Rosville, Louis Dyck, Peter Chavenie, John Amyos, Thomas Valentine, John Curtoise, Daniel Waldoe and Joseph Jacques.[1] Andrew Ricard held 3,435 acres in Waterford and Tipperary and John Paris 995 acres in Tipperary.[2]

The latter may have been a son of that Lieutenant-Colonel Henry Paris who was one of the Commissioners of Revenue at Clonmel in 1654 and was instrumental in replanting the country after the native Irish had been dispatched across the Shannon.[3] The family seem also to have taken to trade, for in 1697 Thomas, son of Lieutenant-Colonel Paris, was apprenticed to Francis Cuthbert, a Dublin goldsmith.[4]

Andrew Ricard was Mayor of Waterford in 1658 and again in 1666.[5] In 1695 a John Ricards is admitted freeman of Cork and in 1758 a Robert Ricard died in Youghal having established a family in that town.[6]

The name Denis, as has been seen, is found also at Waterford, where the Rev. James Denis was a minister of the French Church.

That of Jaques belongs to Cork. A Lieutenant Jacques was an officer of the army in Ireland in 1659, but, if he was a relative of Joseph Jacques mentioned above, he could not have shared the latter's politics, for Gimlette[7] states that " he was most active in aiding Lord Broghill and Sir Charles Coote in their exertions on behalf of their monarch," and his was

[1] *Ibid.*, p. 182.
[2] *Ibid.*, p. 194.
[3] *Ibid.*, p. 182.
[4] C.H. & A.J., Vol. VIII, No. 53. "Dublin Goldsmiths."
[5] Smith, "Ancient and Present State of the Co. and City of Waterford."
[6] *Vide* p. 76.
[7] " Huguenot Settlers," p. 187.

one of the signatures on the Declaration for the re-establishment of the orthodox ministry. The Jacques of Cork are thought to have been silk weavers, but very little reference to them can be found in the City records. What is stated is unfortunate, for, under date 1736, it is placed on record that "Henry Jacques was pilloried for perjury" since "he suborned Daniel Connel to swear false examinations against John Breade for being a papist carrying arms."[1] The name in its corrupted form of Jaikes or Jack continued until recent years and was existing in Limerick into the present century. One of the last tradesmen of the name in Cork was a wood carver, and in Dublin this trade has also been carried on by a Jacques until the present day.

A Jacob Jacques, innkeeper, of Roscommon, was attainted by the Irish Parliament of James II in 1689 in company with the Tipperary settler Thomas Valentine.[2] This name also occurs in Lisburn, and it is possible that it may be connected with the de Vallentins who fled to England after the Revocation and established themselves in London,[3] but if so the Irish settler must have decided to emigrate a considerable time before his relatives.

The manufactures at Clonmel and Carrick, like those in the kindred colony of Chapelizod, which will be dealt with in the chapter on the Dublin Settlement, flourished at first, but in the eighteenth century fell into decay.

Smith,[4] writing in 1746, says of Carrick that it "has been for many years famous for the making of ratteens, a woollen manufacture which that town has brought to great perfection, so as to make them equal to the finest cloth. They have them of various colours worth from 3s. to 30s. a yard. It is incredible what numbers are employed in that little town in this

---

[1] " Cork Remembrancer."
[2] Gimlette, p. 259.
[3] " Huguenots in England," Appendix.
[4] " Ancient and Present State of Co. and City of Waterford."

manufactory, men, women and children finding sufficient work." But the prohibitory statutes passed against the wool trade did much to ruin this industry, which after 1699 could only have been carried on for home consumption. Professor Gill[1] states, "I have been unable to find any sign of manufacturing activity in Chapelizod or Carrick in the early years of the eighteenth century," and when Lewis compiled his Topographical Dictionary in 1837 the manufacture was " nearly extinct," with only " a very limited trade in ratteens " at Carrick. He attributes the failure of the woollen industry to the fraudulent practice of "stretching the cloths to augment the measurement until the Dublin merchants refused to buy them."

Another Huguenot colony was established at a later date at Kilkenny, which had already been chosen by Piers Butler in the sixteenth century for the introduction of a tapestry manufacture in the hands of Flemish artisans. This, says the Baronne de Chambrier, "was a colony of the Duke of Ormond. It was Conformist and composed of nobles, merchants and artisans. The pastors there were Messieurs David and Renoult and the names of Gillot and Balaguier are found there in 1694 and 1698."[2] It is somewhat extraordinary that the settlement should have assumed such large proportions since no trace of church or people remains to-day. Even more extraordinary is an entry made by Luttrell in his Diary of State Affairs under date March 23rd, 1693. "Major General Ruvigny," he writes, "hath settled a French University at Kilkenny in Ireland and several French divines are come thither. Mr. Dallions is by the King made first professor of divinity and colleges are erecting with all possible speed."[3] This is the only reference to be found to any such undertaking in Kilkenny. If a " University " had

[1] " Rise of the Irish Linen Industry," p. 9 note.
[2] " Projet de Colonisation," Hug. Soc. Proc., Vol. VI, p. 428.
[3] " A Brief Historical Relation of State Affairs."

been erected some trace would remain to-day, and no record exists of even a church. Kilkenny College, founded by Piers Butler and chartered in 1684, can scarcely have been confused by Luttrell with a "French University" although some Huguenot children appear in its register.[1] The "first professor of divinity" seems to be that Monsieur Benjamin Daillon who officiated in Portarlington from 1698-1702 and then in Carlow. As will be seen in dealing with his history in Portarlington, he served as minister of the Church of La Patente in Spitalfields before coming to Ireland; no mention is anywhere made of his having held a post at Kilkenny, and if such a responsible position had been his it seems unlikely that he would have quitted it for an ordinary ministry in one of the French Churches. The scheme may have been planned, but it can scarcely have been carried out.

There seems, however, to have been a large congregation of Huguenots in Kilkenny, and it is possible that, if they lacked a church, they had at least a definite place of meeting for worship. Messieurs Gillot and Balaguier can only have visited this settlement as they each had churches of their own, Monsieur Gillot (or Gillet) serving in Portarlington from 1694-1698 and Monsieur Balaguier in the Nonconformist Church in Dublin from 1693-1724.[2]

The David family came from Rochelle[3] and the Kilkenny minister was at one time chaplain to the Duchesse De La Force. Renoult was a Franciscan of Norman birth who abjured in London in 1696. He was Rector of Timahoe, County Kildare, from 1706 to 1719 and was living in Dublin in 1728.[4] Both appear in the registers of the French Churches in Dublin.

---

[1] James II endeavoured to establish it as a Royal College. It is just possible that William and Ruvigny intended to continue this on behalf of the Huguenots.
[2] *Vide* pp. 150, 229.
[3] Smiles, "Huguenots in England," Appendix.
[4] From information kindly supplied by Mr. T. P. Le Fanu.

When Crommelin was invited to Ireland it was suggested that he should establish himself at Kilkenny in order to further the linen manufacture there which the Ormonds were so anxious to achieve. He agreed to do so if he obtained an extension of his patent and £2,500. This the country considered itself too poor to supply, but his patent was extended,[1] and William Crommelin, his brother, who was also one of his assistants, settled in Kilkenny, married into the Ormond family, and carried on the manufacture of linen for a time at least with success. The linen trade in the South, however, was doomed to failure. This Professor Gill states was largely due to the slump in the trade after the Seven Years War.[2] The southern manufactures were chiefly concerned with coarse cloths, and this branch of the trade was particularly severely affected. Young[3] considered the southern industry " too insignificant to merit a particular attention," and when Besnard in 1816 made his survey as Inspector for the Linen Board he reported that no trade was then carried on in Kilkenny.[4]

Apart from the Huguenots engaged in this industry some property holders in the County Kilkenny were Frenchmen. The earliest is perhaps one Nicholaus de Rochelle, who is enrolled in the Irish Chancery Rolls under date August 2nd, 1630, as owner of " Le Black Friars," Kilkenny,[5] which must have been purchased by him from the Corporation, to which the site and precincts of the Monastery of the Black Friars had been granted by Henry VIII.[6] Another fugitive, who called himself Jacobus de Rochell, obtained property in Tallow at the same period.[7]

---

[1] Lecky, " History of Ireland," Vol. I, p. 182.
[2] " Rise of the Irish Linen Industry," p. 123.
[3] " Tour in Ireland."
[4] Gill, pp. 125, 128.
[5] Gimlette, p. 165.
[6] Lewis, " Topographical Dictionary."
[7] Gimlette, p. 165.

The d'Espard family early established itself in the County Kilkenny, the first of that name to settle there being Philip d'Espard, who fled to England at the Massacre of St. Bartholomew and became a Civil Servant and the holder of landed property in the Queen's County and County Kilkenny under Elizabeth. His grandson, William, was Colonel of Engineers under William III, and his great-grandson represented County Kilkenny in the Irish Parliament of 1715. Other members of the family were High Sheriffs of the Queen's County and magistrates there and elsewhere.[1]

Another Huguenot officer who served in the Irish Campaign and later appeared in Kilkenny was Monsieur Jean La Rive of St. Antonin in Rouerge, who according to one statement escaped with his wife disguised as an orange seller to Holland at the Revocation. There he entered the service of William and campaigned in Portugal. He later settled in County Kilkenny as agent to Sir Christopher Wandesforde of Castlecomer, where a tombstone to his memory existed in the churchyard. La Rive had two brothers, St. Martin and William Maret. The former, who served in the French Navy, is said to have aided their escape. William obtained the command of an English gunboat and served later in Canada, but, like his brother, he retired to Ireland, dying in Dublin in his eightieth year.[2]

As has already been stated, the Register of Kilkenny College affords some indication of the French names occurring in the district. Amongst the scholars appear:

Boursiquot, Isaac, entered	June 1708
Danvers, Arthur, entered	April 1697
Debat, Theophilus, son of Surgeon Debat, entered	June 1746
De La Rue, —, entered	June 1711
Delaune, William, entered	June 1704
Desroy, Abraham, entered	April 1702

[1] Smiles, "Huguenots in England," Appendix.
[2] *Ibid.*

127

Doucett, John, entered   July 1697
Doucett, James, entered   Jan. 1704/5
Fontjulian, Charles, entered   May 1709
Jaques, Gideon, entered   June 1696
Labord, John, son of Lieut.-Col., entered   Oct. 1757
Larive, John, son of Henry, Esq., of Castlecomer,
    entered   Feb. 1769
Larive, Thomas, son of Henry, entered   July 1769
Larive, William Forward, son of Henry, entered   April 1769
Le Grand, William Henry, son of Capt. Le Grand
    (deceased), entered   April 1753
Meheux, James, entered   July 1711
Mercier, Charles, son of Claud M., Capt. of Horse,
    entered   Aug. 1707
Metge, James, son of Baron M. of the city of Dublin,
    entered   Oct. 1798
Trench, Michael, Frederick, son of the Rev. Frederick
    Trench, entered   Jan. 1753
Winthuysen, Henry, son of Mr. W., merchant in
    Bordeaux, entered   June 1749[1]

The Larive children were probably the grandsons of the original Kilkenny settler, and Desroy and Boursiquot were sons of those Kilkenny merchants, John Deseroy and James Bouriquott [sic], who were naturalized in 1698;[2] but as boys came to this famous school from all over Ireland it is not safe in every case to assume that their parents belonged to the county. Thus the Metge family settled in the North, the Trenches in the West, and the Merciers and Labords in Portarlington and Dublin, while the Arthur Danvers who entered there in 1697 must be that clergyman who died in Youghal in 1754.[3] Charles Fontjulian must have been the son of Colonel Fontjulian of Lord River's Brigade, and the names Jaques and Le Grand are both, as has already been mentioned, connected with Cork. William Delaune possibly

---

[1] *Vide* Article on the Register of Kilkenny School in J.R.S.A.I., Vol. LIV. Parts I and II.
[2] Hug. Soc. Pub., Vol. XVIII, p. 347.
[3] *Vide* p. 74.

became a Dublin goldsmith, for, in 1733, William, son of "Gideon de Laune, deceased, gent. of Dublin," was bound apprentice to Arthur Weldon in this trade.[1] He may have descended from that Henry de Laune, native of France, who received his denization during the reign of Charles I[2] and addressed the King with improvements for commerce in Ireland, or from the Richard Delaune who obtained the Freedom of Cork "by special Grace" in 1666.[3] Gideon de Laune was one of the Dublin Protestants attainted by the Parliament of James II.[4]

No other means of tracing the Kilkenny settlers seem now to exist. The colony, like those at Clonmel and Carrick, must have lost its individuality very much earlier than most of the other settlements in Ireland, and with the failure of the southern linen trade the last link with the Huguenot manufacturers disappeared.

Amongst the midland colonies that of Carlow had some importance, but here again little trace of the settlers remains, and it is completely ignored by both Smiles and Weiss. "Every kind of Church Register in Carlow prior to the year 1744 has been lost," writes Agnew.[5] "There is therefore no vestige of a French Church there." There is, however, sufficient evidence that there was a congregation of French worshippers, since, in the estimates called the "Establishment for Ireland," occurs the item, "To a French Minister at Caterlough £30 per annum." Another proof of this is found in a Memorial in the State Paper Office, drawn up in January 1696, by "The French Churches which observe the discipline of the Churches of France and Geneva." In this a list of ministers and their congregations is given, and

---

[1] C.H. & A.J., Vol. VIII, No. 53. "Dublin Goldsmiths."
[2] Hug. Soc. Pub., Vol. XVIII, p. 332.
[3] Freemen's Register.
[4] Gimlette, p. 259.
[5] "Protestant Exiles," Vol. II.

amongst them a minister is attributed to " Caterlow " with a salary of £50 a year.[1]

In order to have obtained this grant the congregation must have numbered over fifty, and must have conformed to the Established Church. The Baronne de Chambrier[2] states that Carlow had a French minister as early as 1693, but the first that can be definitely traced is the Rev. Benjamin Daillon who left Portarlington for this settlement in 1702 according to Agnew,[3] in 1708 according to Mr. Le Fanu,[4] and served the latter congregation until his death in 1710 (new style). With his wife, Pauline, he is buried in the churchyard of the parish.[5]

Another minister at Carlow was the Rev. Charles Louis de Villette, who served the French Church there from 1723-1737 before being licensed to the French Church of St. Patrick's, Dublin. He was the son of a refugee from Burgundy and was born in Lausanne in 1688. As well as obtaining the ministry to the French refugees at Carlow, he was appointed Rector of Kilruane in the diocese of Killaloe. According to Smiles he was famed for his writings on religious matters. He married twice, his first wife being Margaret Besnardon and his second Jane Blosset. He died in 1783.[6]

A third pastor of importance in Carlow was David Chaigneau, son of Isaac Chaigneau, the Dublin merchant, whose family settled first in Youghal, where their history has been recorded.[7] Chaigneau served in Carlow about 1744, and died there in 1747. He is buried as " Minister of the

---

[1] Quoted Reid, " History of the Presbyterian Church in Ireland," Vol. II, p. 465.

[2] " Projet de Colonisation."

[3] " Protestant Exiles," Vol. III, p. 107.

[4] Hug. Soc. Proc., Vol. XIV, p. 223.

[5] For the inscription on his tomb *vide* J.A.P.M.D., Vol. 1, p. 139. *Vide* also p. 152.

[6] Hug. Soc. Proc., Vol. VIII, p. 128.

[7] *Vide* p. 73.

French Church and Curate of Carlow."[1] He was a graduate of the University of Dublin, which he entered in 1724. In 1730 he was priested at Cloyne. He died intestate, and his children, David, William, John and Elizabeth, with his wife, are named in the Letters of Administration.[2]

Even before the Revocation Carlow must have been known to French settlers, for as early as 1680 a French name, that of John Davellier, appears in the list of vestrymen of the church,[3] and the family of Blancheville settled there as tenants of Sir Edward Butler during the reign of James I.[4]

A branch of the Lemaistre family seems to have established itself there as well as at Waterford and Dublin, for a " Michael Lemaistre, son of Elizabeth Lemaistre, Widow of Carlow," is apprenticed to Charles Lemaistre, a Dublin goldsmith in 1739,[5] and a Matthew Le Maitre died there in 1782.[6]

The La Chapelle family also seem to have some connection with Carlow, for in 1758 a Mrs. Mary La Chapelle was buried there.[7] An Armand Boisbelau De La Chapelle was sent to minister to the French Church in Ireland after the Revocation; he seems to have assisted Bartholomew Balaguier in the ministry of the Dublin Nonconformist Church in 1694,[8] but according to Smiles left after two years for Wandesworth, although he may have established a family in Ireland, or later returned there. The name, however, was fairly widespread. About 1723 a contractor named Daniel Chappel set up a large concern for linen printing at Balls-

---

[1] J.A.P.M.D., Vol. V, p. 6.
[2] Brady, " Records of Cork, Cloyne and Ross."
[3] J.A.P.M.D., 1902.
[4] Gimlette, p. 148.
[5] C.H. & A.J., Vol. VIII, No. 53. " Dublin Goldsmiths."
[6] Agnew, Vol. II, p. 316.
[7] Ibid.
[8] Hug. Soc. Proc., Vol. VIII, p. 105, and Smiles, " Huguenots in England," Appendix.

bridge,[1] and a Thomas Chapel was apprenticed in 1715 to the Dublin Huguenot goldsmith, John Paturel.[2] Either may have descended from the Chapelle whom Dumont de Bostaquet lists as *maréchal des Logis* in the Company of de Varengues under Schomberg.[3] The important Dublin family of Raboteau has also a place among the Huguenots of Carlow, for John Charles Raboteau was born there during his parents' journey to their place of settlement in Dublin, and it is possible that the James Rabbittoe whose burial, according to Agnew, figured in the Carlow Registers,[4] was a brother of the Dublin merchant.

Two officers of Lord Galway's Regiment settled here after the Irish Campaign; these were Jean Rouvière, who moved later to Youghal,[5] and Lieutenant La Boulay, who obtained ten acres in Carlow parish, granted by the Trustees of Forfeited Estates on June 17th, 1703, to " Charles La Bouleey of Carlow, Gent.," and later called " Labully's Fields." He had three sons, Henry, Thomas and James, and a younger brother, Jean, also a Lieutenant on pension, who had escaped from France in 1685, entered the service of Holland two years later, and served through the war in Ireland, finally settling in Portarlington where he died in 1708.[6]

In connection with these pensioned officers who established themselves as landed proprietors, an interesting tombstone existed in Castle Dermot churchyard, County Kildare, to record the burial of " Captain Beter [*sic*] Balandrie who dyed 29th May, 1735, aged 75." The Parish Register noted that Captain Peter Ballandrie was " an Ancient French gentle-

[1] Gill, p. 77.
[2] C.H. & A.J., Vol. VIII, No. 52. " Dublin Goldsmiths."
[3] " Mémoires Inédits."
[4] Vol. II, p. 267.
[5] *Vide* p. 77.
[6] Agnew, Vol. II, p. 182; Hug. Soc. Proc., Vol. IX, p. 584; and J.K.A.S., Vol. XI, No. 4. " French Veterans at Portarlington."

man of Mirmont's Regiment,"[1] and his name may further be traced in the Pension Lists.

The greater number of these officers, however, were attracted to the settlement at Portarlington which had been especially prepared for their occupation. This was the most characteristic, if not the most important, of the Irish colonies, and though it forms part of the midland group, it must be treated of in a separate chapter.

[1] J.A.P.M.D., 1901.

CHAPTER VI

IT is a strange jest of history that of all the counties in Ireland those dedicated to Mary Tudor and Philip of Spain may be said to play the most important part in the annals of the Huguenot settlements, for beside the Barrow River, half in King's County, half in Queen's, lay the refugees' own town, granted to a French Protestant, sublet by him to other Frenchmen; planned, built and adorned by Frenchmen; with its French Church, its French Parochial Registers, its French school and even its French pear trees. That strange corner of France in a foreign land where the Huguenot officers of William's army found a home and planned their gardens and built their houses as nearly as possible in the style that they had known before their exile. Where the manners, habits and customs of the French nobility long existed, and the graceful speech of the period of Louis XIV might still be heard generations after the original settlers had been laid in the cemetery behind the French Church.

"The high-pitched roof with its oaken beams and pur-lines; the dormer windows and the tall and massive chimney stacks," says Sir Erasmus Borrowes in speaking of the Portarlington houses, "clearly intimate that the Huguenot tradesmen had brought with them reminiscences of the Chateaux of Garonne and Charente and that La Borde, the mason; Capel the smith; and Gautier the carpenter had lent the foreign handicraft that characterised their construction."[1] With such architectural features to point to its origin, and a population almost exclusively French until the eighteenth century, Portarlington preserved its characteristics as a Huguenot settlement for longer than any other of the colonies in Ireland.

Before tracing its history, however, that of the few settlers scattered throughout the King's and Queen's Counties may be reviewed.

Gimlette states that under Charles I Beauville Predieux was granted an enclosure of forty acres in Moneyclare, Queen's County,[2] and Matthew de Renzie was also a land-owner at this time, since in 1622 he received a grant of land in the King's County, before obtaining the Clobemon estate in County Wexford.[3]

Under the Commonwealth John Marriott and Mary Fountain held land in King's County with John Gaick, Philip Bigoe and Thomas Franke. In Queen's County the names Gervais and Levellis occur.[4]

Philip Bigoe (or de Bigault as the name was originally spelt) is of especial interest, for he was one of the foreign manufacturers who established glassworks in Ireland. His family had originally come from Lorraine and had settled in England about the latter half of the sixteenth century, when the original settler obtained grants of land in the King's County from Queen Elizabeth. In 1623 Abraham Bigo obtained a lease of the Castle town and part of the plough-land of Clonoghill (near Birr) " with all the woods there to be spent and employed on the premises " from Sir Lawrence Parsons of Birr Castle, on the understanding that he was " not to set up any glass house or glasswork on any other

---

[1] U.J.A., Vol. III. Art. "Portarlington."
[2] " Huguenot Settlers," p. 168.
[3] *Vide* p. 115.
[4] Gimlette, p. 194.

land, or to buy wood of any other for his glasswork." He surrendered the lease in 1627, but his relative, Philip Bigoe, obtained his Letters of Denization in Ireland from Charles I, and established himself in Birr, where he, too, set up a glass manufacture. Amongst the glassworks referred to in Boate and Molyneux's " Natural History of Ireland," appears that of Birr with the statement that " from this place Dublin was furnished with all sorts of window and drinking glasses and such other as are in common use,"[1] but no trace of this remains to-day. Bigoe died in 1668, but he was followed in the glass manufacture by Ananias Henzie (or de Hennezel), whom his daughter, Katherine, had married, and who, by 1670, had established a glass-house in Portarlington. This manufacturer also came from Lorraine, and the two families seem always to have been connected, for the de Hennezels appeared in England at the same time as the de Bigaults, having been brought there by John Carré (or Carye), the glass manufacturer who has been mentioned in connection with Cork.[2] A Peter Bigot, described as a native of Bloys in his Letter of Denization, was a merchant in Dublin in 1704,[3] who may have had some connection with the glass manufacturer. The de Hennezel family later intermarried with that of Armstrong in King's County and of Eyre in County Galway.[4]

Another Huguenot family to settle in the King's County was that of Tabuteau. Peter Tabuteau fled from France to Holland in 1685, where he died in 1691. He married Elizabeth Flanc and left a son, Stephen, born 1669, who married Renée, daughter of Gidéon Bion. They had two sons, Gidéon and Augustus, and a daughter, Anne Renée, who married Daniel Olivier of London and Rotterdam. The younger son was naturalized in 1721, married Henrietta

---

[1] " Huguenots in England," Appendix. 1889 Edition.
[2] Westropp, " Irish Glass," pp. 32-6, and *vide* p. 29.
[3] Hug. Soc. Pub., Vol. XXVII, p. 127.
[4] " Huguenots in England," Appendix. 1889 Edition.

Brions, and died in Bengal, leaving a son, Gideon, who established himself first in Southampton and then in Tullamore, King's County. His sister, Henrietta, who died there in 1805, seems to have accompanied him to Ireland. Gideon married, in 1753, Mary Butin, and had a son and a daughter. The latter married Anthony Molière of Amsterdam, and the former, Joseph Brions Tabuteau, M.D., of Tullamore, married Eleanor, daughter of Benjamin Batt, and had a family of three sons and a daughter. One of the sons was J.P. for King's County, another a Resident Magistrate, and the third was appointed Consul for the Netherlands in Dublin. All of them married and left descendants,[1] and members of the family have resided in Portarlington to the present day, where a memorial in the church records their motto, " Toujours sans tâche."

One of the few officers who preferred to settle outside Portarlington was Stephen Cassan, a native of Montpellier, who was born in 1659, fled to Holland at the Revocation and entered William's army. He served under Schomberg in the Irish Campaign, and married Elizabeth, heiress of General Joseph Sheffield of Essex and Cappoly, Queen's County. Here he settled, and his only son, Matthew, born 1693, built the family mansion of Sheffield. The latter's eldest son, Stephen, barrister-at-law, was High Sheriff of the County in 1763, and died ten years later, leaving two sons and a daughter. The eldest son was High Sheriff in 1783 and a Major in the Queen's County Militia, and his son, Matthew, married a daughter of the Earl of Portarlington.[2]

In the short period from 1660 to the end of the century this town had suffered many changes. It, or rather the village near the castle of Lea which formed its nucleus, had originally belonged to the O'Dempseys, but Charles II granted it to Sir Henry Bennet, first Baron Arlington, who changed

---

[1] Burke, " Landed Gentry."
[2] *Ibid.*

its name from Port-na-hinch to Portarlington. In 1688 the estate was purchased by Sir Patrick Trant, an officer and keen supporter of James II.[1] He shared the fate of the O'Dempseys when William came to power, and on June 26th, 1696, the estate was granted by that monarch to his general, Henri de Massue Marquis de Ruvigny, who had already held a custodian grant for three years of the property and had granted a lease, dated 1692, to the first Huguenot settler.[2]

The career of this remarkable man illustrates how important a part the Huguenots played in both English and Irish history.[3] His father, who had been a general in the French Army, Councillor of State, Deputy General of the Reformed Church in France, and Ambassador at the Court of Charles II, left Versailles for Greenwich at the Revocation and there founded a French Church, formed a nucleus for French Society in England, and raised, in 1689, regiments for William's Irish Campaign. The old Marquis died in 1689, and his son, Pierre, styled La Caillemotte, met his death at the Boyne. The surviving son, now second Marquis of Ruvigny, joined the Irish Army after his brother's death, was made Major-General and Colonel of Schomberg's Horse, aided Ginkell in the Siege of Athlone, and commanded the Cavalry at Aughrim. In 1691 he was created Baron of Portarlington, and in 1697 Earl of Galway. In 1693 he joined William in Flanders, where he distinguished himself at Neerwinden. Later he was sent as Envoy Extraordinary to the Duke of Savoy, and was appointed Commander in Chief of the forces in Portugal. During his career in Ireland he was a Lord of the Privy Council, and three times Lord Justice, but the jealousy shown by the English Parliament towards William's Dutch and Huguenot allies caused the removal of Ruvigny

---

[1] Lewis, " Topographical Dictionary," and U.J.A., Vol. III. Art. " Portarlington."

[2] U.J.A., Vol. III.

[3] For his history see Smiles, " Huguenots in England and Ireland," Crossley's " Irish Peerage," and Agnew's Biography, " Henri de Ruvigny."

from his Irish appointments, and the Act of Resumption took from him his Portarlington grant. " I went," writes Evelyn,[1] on June 22nd, 1701, " to congratulate the arrival of that worthy and excellent person, my Lord Galway, newly come out of Ireland, where he had behav'd himselfe so honestly and to the exceeding satisfaction of the people; but he was remov'd thence for being a Frenchman tho' they had not a more worthy, valiant, discreet, and trusty person in the two Kingdoms on whom they could have relied for his conduct and fitnesse. He was one who had deeply suffer'd as well as the Marquiss his father, for being Protestants." He died in England in September 1720, and was buried in Micheldever churchyard near East Stratton where he had made his home during his last years. His will is of great interest since he did not forget his refugee friends, and in the list of legacies appear some half-dozen names of French settlers in Ireland.

Sir Erasmus Borrowes states that the total number of acres granted to Ruvigny in the Portarlington estate reached 16,500 English.[2] On this the disbanded officers of the regiments of La Melonière, La Caillemotte and Du Cambon, with those from Ruvigny's own Regiment of Horse, were invited to take out leases at rents ranging from about two shillings and sixpence an Irish acre. These were renewable for ever, subject to a small renewal fine. The settlers were scattered in the surrounding villages until accommodation could be provided for them in their own town, but by 1694 the Consistory of the Refugees was in existence, and by 1696 they had succeeded in erecting their church.[3]

This does not seem to have been effected without difficulty. The settlers had been led to hope for help from the Government, but the money had been devoted to other

---

[1] " Diary " Ed. William Bray.
[2] U.J.A., Vol. III. Art. " Portarlington." He held grants of land also in Kerry and elsewhere.
[3] Ibid.

purposes, and the Charitable Fund collected for the refugees in Ireland had been exhausted. In April 1694 they addressed the Consistory of the French Church in St. Patrick's, begging its members to appeal to the Lord's Justices to allow to the Portarlington colonists the same advantages as enjoyed by those on the lands of Lord Blayney and Sir Richard Cox. A year and a half later another petition to the House of Commons on behalf of the refugees in Ireland stated that, owing to its poverty, the colony in Portarlington had not yet been able to build a church or obtain a schoolmaster or a surgeon.[1]

Galway, however, provided both a French Church and an English one. They were both endowed with a rent charge bringing in £40 per annum for the minister's salary,[2] but since by 1701 the English families only numbered five in comparison with the sixty-four French households, this latter church, St. Michael's, was the smaller of the two.[3]

The Earl's many absences from Ireland necessitated the appointments of agents for the settlement. These were Jacques Belrieu, Baron de Virazel and Charles de Sailly, who was later sent abroad to arrange for the refugee colony in Virginia. An account has already been given of their activities with regard to the proposed settlement in Ireland of Huguenots from the overcrowded Swiss cantons.[4] This scheme fell through, but Weiss states that " the Marquis de Ruvigny invited thither (to Portarlington) about 400 French,"[5] and when he returned to Ireland as Lord Justice in 1697, he actively engaged in promoting the settlement. He appointed an old officer, Jean David Boyer, described in the registers

---

[1] Hug. Soc. Pub., Vol. XIX. Introduction to "The Portarlington Registers."

[2] U.J.A., Vol. III. Art. "Portarlington."

[3] Agnew, "Henri de Ruvigny." Sir Erasmus Borrowes states that a hundred and fifty families of English and French were living in the town and immediate neighbourhood in this year.

[4] *Vide* p. 20.

[5] " Histoire des Réfugiés," Bk. III, p. 281.

as his "Steward," to act with de Virazel, and, besides the churches, he built two schools and endowed them with £32 per annum in perpetuity as salaries for the teachers.[1] The settlers, who were of varied origin, coming from Normandy, Languedoc, Saintonge and Dauphiny, were mainly military in profession, and were nearly all aristocratic in rank. During de Bostaquet's sojourn there, however, a physician, a surgeon, six shopkeepers, four shoemakers, three blacksmiths, two weavers, two tailors, two masons, one butcher, one locksmith, one carpenter, one gardener, and eleven labourers appear in the registers as exceptions to this rule among the 267 refugees then residing in Portarlington. Galway, too, cared especially for the corporals and troopers of his own regiment, and four settled in his colony. These were Gaspard and Louis Pajon, Jean Bessière, Corporal of Horse, and Jacques Beauchant,[2] who, with his son Samuel, became a leading shopkeeper and elder of the French Church,[3] and was chosen to sign the petition from the congregation to the Duke of Dorset in 1733.

The Earl's first idea in founding the settlement would seem to have been a commercial one. "M. Ruvigny is establishing a French Colony in Ireland to carry on a manufacture to trade there with England and Holland," reports Luttrell on February 9th, 1671-2;[4] but if Portarlington were the colony mentioned, this scheme was singularly unproductive, for the only industry engaged in there was that necessary for the consumption of the inhabitants, save for the linen manufacture carried on in a very small scale by the Foubert family, and the glassworks already mentioned of de Hennezel.

The Fouberts were descended from Abraham Favert, who served as Chief Magistrate of Metz in the reign of Henry IV.

[1] U.J.A., Vol. III. Art. "Portarlington."
[2] Hug. Soc. Proc., Vol. XIV, p. 214.
[3] J.K.A.S., Vol. IX, No. 4. Le Fanu, "French Veterans at Portarlington."
[4] Luttrell, "A Brief Historical Relation of State Affairs."

His sons Francis and Abraham entered the Army, and the latter was created a Marshal of France by Louis XIV— although his three sons had adopted the reformed faith. They fled from France and took service under William of Orange,[1] who appointed Major Henry Foubert his aide-de-camp. This officer fought at the Boyne and subsequently settled at Portarlington, where his descendants, as already stated, engaged in the manufacture of linen.[2] The name is still in existence in Cork at the present day.

After the Peace of Ryswick the Portarlington colony received a substantial addition from a new band of officers on pension who settled there,[3] but it suffered a corresponding loss from those who joined up for the wars of Anne and never returned.[4]

The principal proprietors of land under the Earl of Galway were the Baron de Virazel and Jean Nicolas, "cy-devant Lieutenant de Cavalerie dans le regiment de Galwai." The latter held 2,000 acres around Lea Castle at the modest rent of £60 per annum. Rents in Portarlington were surprisingly cheap. One John Hillen held from a refugee a house, garden and upwards of two acres at five pounds per annum, which might be commuted into a labour rent at five-pence per day.[5]

Lieutenant Nicolas, who came from Jonsac in Saintonge and served throughout the campaigns in Ireland, Piedmont and Flanders, seems to have been closely connected with the founder of the colony. In 1699 a baptismal entry records that the Earl stood sponsor for the child of Jean Grosvenor, Cornet of Dragoons in the Regiment of Essex, but that in his absence the infant was presented by Jean Nicolas, "envoyé exprès de son excellence my lord Comte de Galuuai." His

---

[1] "Huguenots in England," Appendix. 1889 Edition.
[2] U.J.A., Vol. VI. Art. "Portarlington."
[3] Weiss, Bk. III, Ch. 1, p. 280.
[4] Hug. Soc. Proc., Vol. XIV, p. 214.
[5] U.J.A., Vol. VI. Art. "Portarlington."

sister Pauline, " femme de M. de Daillon notre Pasteur," also presented the child, who was the grandson of the minister through his mother, Anne de Daillon. Nicolas must later have removed to Dublin, for in the will of Ruvigny £200 is left to Captain John Nicolas of Dublin,[1] and the marriage of his son Charles to Charlotte des Vignoles, daughter of a refugee officer of Nîmes, and of his daughter Henriette to Paul du Clousy, were solemnized respectively in the French Churches of St. Mary's and St. Patrick's in that city.[2]

When the Act of Resumption of the Forfeited Estates granted by William was passed in the English Parliament in November 1699, the leaseholders of Portarlington were gravely alarmed. The author of a pamphlet, published in 1701,[3] is eloquent on their behalf. " I can't but take notice of the deplorable condition of the poor French Protestants at Portarlington, which is part of the Lord Galway's grant. Those poor people by the encouragement they had from the compassion and goodness of that Lord built about 130 neat tenements in that place which must now become the habitations of Irish Papists. It must seem a very extraordinary hardship to people who have any bowels of compassion to see such a number of miserable people who were a long time afflicted with severe persecution in their own country find such treatment in a country to which they fled for refuge."

A more reasoned defence was put forward by the Trustees for the sale of the forfeited estates, who laid before Parliament " The case of the distressed refugees settled in and near Portarlington in the Queen's Co. Ireland."[4] They stated that " there are about 150 families, English and French Protestants planted in the lands of Portarlington, who have laid out their whole substance in purchasing small leases "; that " the lands

---

[1] Agnew, " Henri de Ruvigny."
[2] J.K.A.S., Vol. XI, No. 4.
[3] " Jus Regium," or " The King's Right to Grant Forfeitures." Pamphlet. London, 1701.
[4] Quoted U.J.A., Vol. III. Art. " Portarlington."

were part of a grant of the Right Honourable, the Earl of Galway, who hath thereon erected an English and French Church and two schools, and endowed them with pensions amounting to £100 per annum "; but that " the whole value of all is not above £500 that would come to the publick."

The Huguenots themselves besought that a clause might be added to some Bill confirming their leases, and, in the first year of Anne, this was effected by Act of Parliament,[1] and the churches and school houses with their endowments were vested in trust in the Bishops of Kildare. The property, however, comprising some 8,312 acres, passed by purchase in 1703 to the " Hollow Sword Blade " Company of London; but that the leaseholders and their new landlords were on the best of terms is evinced by the presence at a baptism in the French Church of the Commissioners of the Company, who stood sponsors for the infant.[2]

From the Hollow Sword Blade Company the estate passed by purchase to Ephraim Dawson, ancestor of Lord Portarlington; but the leases were not interfered with and Agnew states in 1864 that " there is still a family (in Portarlington) by the name of Champ who have held land uninterruptedly on a lease from Lord Galway."[3]

These leases are of the greatest interest since they serve as a guide not only to the names of the original settlers but to the position of their houses and lands. As an example, the author has been permitted to quote " parcels " out of a lease for lives renewable for ever granted by Ephraim Dawson to Judith Magdalen de Tuigny dated August 21st, 1718, and renewing an older lease. By it the lessee obtains:

" All that and those the tenement in the suburbs in Portarlington whereon Le Sire David de Proissy, Signeur Chastelain Deppé's late dwelling house was built; and another

[1] Quoted at length in Introduction to the Portarlington Registers, Hug. Soc. Pub., Vol. XIX.
[2] U.J.A., Vol. VI. Art. " Portarlington."
[3] " Henri de Ruvigny."

plot thereunto adjoining westward by the said house and garden ranging with the street of Portarlington aforesaid and the lane that leads to the common, commonly called Smith Street and westwardly mearing with Alex. Saint Arnoule's plot and tenement; and another plot confronting the said plot and ranging with the street aforesaid to the little bridge and the channel or Watercourse from the said little Bridge to the big river or Barrow, and on the east side with Colonel Du Petit Boe's park; and 14 acres of land in the Deer Park as the same hath been trod out to the said Messire de Proisey mearing on the one side with the great Road, on the other side with Monsieur Lavelle's Lands, and on the other side with Mr. Andrew Preston's land and on the South side with Isaac Piozett's land; and also six acres of meadow as the same has been likewise trode out and mearing on one side with Mr. Daniel Perrett's land in Kildare and with Monsieur Lavell's land in the Park. . . ."

David de Proisy, Seigneur Chastelain d'Eppe, mentioned in the lease, was a Captain of Cavalry in de Tuigny's Company under Schomberg.[1] He took an important place amongst the Portarlington settlers and became an *ancien* of the church. His death occurred in 1712 and he was predeceased by his wife Magdalaine De La Barge and by his five sons, who served in the armies of England, Holland and Brandenberg.[2]

Daniel Le Grand Chevalier Seigneur Du Petit Bosc had been a Lieutenant-Colonel in the Regiment of La Melonière. Born in 1642, a native of the Pays Du Caux, he had escaped to Holland in 1687 and settled at the Hague. There he entered William's service and campaigned until 1692, when he retired on pension to Portarlington, where he died in 1737. He married Anne de Vivefoy and had five children, three of whom died in infancy. His daughter Elizabeth married Jacques de Crosat, who had served as an Ensign in Cambon's

---

[1] Dumont de Bostaquet, " Mémoires."
[2] J.K.A.S., Vol. XI, No. 4.

Regiment and who became Sovereign of the Borough of Portarlington from 1740 till his death in the following year. Her brother, Charles Gaspard, was also Sovereign in 1743 and again in 1747, and an elder of the French Church. He left two sons, Daniel and Jean Gilbert.[1]

"Monsieur Lavelle" may be Henri Robert d'Ully Vicomte de Laval who was one of the most influential of the Portarlington colonists. He had possessed large estates at Gourlencour in Picardy, but in 1688 had been imprisoned in Verneuil while his wife, Madelaine de Schelandre, was removed to Sedan and his eldest son to imprisonment in Laon. The parents had been liberated and had settled in Portarlington by 1695 when "Gabrielle d'Ully fille de M. Vicomte de Laval" represented Catherine de La Goupillere as "Maraine" at the baptism of a son of the Seigneur Du Petit Bosc, and where the baptism of Daniel David de Laval, son of the Vicomte, is recorded. Another daughter, Marianne, was married at the French Church in St. Patrick's Cathedral, Dublin, in the previous year to Captain Abraham de Courtelle Ardesoif of Alençon in Normandy who had served with La Melonière's Regiment and had been pensioned in 1692, when he leased a house and farm from Lord Galway in Portarlington.[2] The elder brother was not freed until 1705. Five sons of the Vicomte fought in the wars of Anne; of these Louis Fontaine (who took his name from an estate of the family in Picardy) embarked with his brother, Joseph, and Lieutenant Pierre de Bette, also a Portarlington refugee who had served in Belcastel's Regiment in Ireland and Flanders, from Cork for the war in Portugal. A letter from him to his sister in Portarlington, quoted by Sir Erasmus Borrowes, describes the death of his brother and friend in an engagement with a French squadron *en route*. He served under Captain Nicolas, already mentioned.[3]

[1] *Ibid.*
[2] *Ibid.*
[3] U.J.A., Vol. III. Art. "Portarlington."

Gabrielle d'Ully de Laval, the godmother mentioned above, married John Villeneuve, brother of Bermon Villeneuve, a merchant of Dublin. His will is extant dated July 2nd, 1716. In it, having left £5 to the poor of the French Church in Portarlington and a legacy of £50 to his brother, with £50 to be divided amongst the latter's children present and to come, he bequeathes " my rideing horse and pistolls to my brother-in-law David Dully de Laval and my red cloak and a pair of boots to Mr. John de Boyer." Finally he leaves " the remaining part of my estates and worldly substance in this kingdom of Ireland to my beloved wife Gabrielle Dully de Laval." Amongst the witnesses to the will are Jean Faure, Antoine Lasalle and Marc Antoine Mezerac. It is signed also by James Dunn, who must have been an attorney in Portarlington at the time, for his signature is also attached to the will of Pierre Duron, another Huguenot resident, dated July 27th, 1725.

The recipient of the red military cloak and boots was evidently Jean David Boyer, the " steward " of Lord Galway, previously mentioned, who came from Civray in Poitou. He had been a Lieutenant of Infantry in the French Army but fled to Holland in 1686, where he joined that of William. He was wounded at the first siege of Limerick, and on his retirement settled at Portarlington as agent for Ruvigny. He was made Sovereign of the Borough in 1726 and 1735, and he died there in 1744. Of his two children, Jean died in 1692 and Jeanne married Marc Vulson de St. Maurice, also of Portarlington, and left descendants.[1]

Jean Fauré, Lasalle and Mezerac were also officers on pension in Portarlington. Lasalle, who was born at Camarès in Rovergne, served as a Cornet in Galway's Horse and seems to have fought during the war in Spain. Fauré was pensioned in 1692 and Mezerac in 1699. The former died two years

[1] J.K.A.S., Vol. XI, No. 4.

after signing the will and the latter in 1748.[1] All three names, Boyer, La Fauré and Lasalle, are also connected with Dublin where an Andrew Boyer, merchant from Montpellier, took the Oaths in January 1670,[2] and where a Peter Faure and a James Lasalles, "son of Mark Lasalle, gent," were apprenticed as goldsmiths in 1726 and 1717 respectively.[3]

The Registers of St. Paul's, the French Church of Portarlington, were kept in French until September 20th, 1816. They are still treasured in Portarlington and consist of two complete volumes, and the first entry, on Sunday, June 3rd, 1694, records the happy augury for the new settlement of the birth of a son to François César Meray and his wife. They have been edited by Mr. T. P. Le Fanu and published *in extenso* by the Huguenot Society of London,[4] and though it is not possible to quote more than one or two of the entries in the course of this chapter, they form an indispensable background for the study of the Huguenot families of the settlement.

The church remained Calvinistic until the ministry of de Bonneval, despite the efforts of William Moreton, the High Church Bishop of Kildare, who in 1701 stated his intention of consecrating the two churches.[5] He was determined that the French congregation should conform to Episcopacy, and in 1702 a "Formulaire de la Consecration et Dédicace des Eglises et Chapelles, selon l'usage de l'Eglise d'Irelande. Traduit de l'Anglois par l'orde de My Lord Evêque de Kildare et en faveur des Protestans François Réfugiés habitans à Portarlington Comté de la Reine" was printed in Dublin.

He seems to have found as much difficulty in dealing with the minister Daillon as the Bishop of Cork had in the case

---

[1] *Ibid.*
[2] Hug. Soc. Pub., Vols. XVIII and XXVII, Appendix.
[3] C.H. & A.J., Vol. VIII, No. 53. "The Goldsmiths Company of Dublin."
[4] Hug. Soc. Pub., Vol. XIX.
[5] U.J.A., Vol. III, and Hug. Soc. Proc., Vol. XIV, p. 223.

of Fontaine.[1] The Portarlington minister stated "qu'il n'était pas un homme à faire son ministère par moitié,"[2] held to his consistorial authority, and refused to part with it on any terms.

Though Daillon resigned, and the ministers eventually came under the jurisdiction of the Church of Ireland, they were not paid by Government until 1733, for in this year the congregation are found petitioning the Duke of Dorset, then Lord-Lieutenant, to increase the salary of their minister. They state that the Rev. M. Anthony Ligonier de Bonneval had a pension of three or four pence per day as Military Chaplain which ceased on his death, and that now they have to contribute to the support of the present clergyman, Monsieur Théodore Desvories, which they cannot afford, "having nothing to maintain themselves and numerous families but the small pensions and half-pay allowed them by His Majesty." They add that theirs is the only conforming French Church in the kingdom without an allowance from Government, and that the colony is the most considerable, save for Dublin, in Ireland. In answer to this plea they were granted an additional £50 per annum, which brought the minister's salary to £90 per annum, at which figure it remained into the nineteenth century.[3] The church, however, had not been altogether neglected by the State, for in 1715 the congregation received a mark of royal favour when the Princess of Wales presented to them Communion and other church plate, which is still preserved in Portarlington.[4]

The service was continued in French until the ministry

[1] Vide p. 35.
[2] Hug. Soc. Proc., Vol. XIV, p. 223.
[3] U.J.A., Vol. VI. Art. "Portarlington."
[4] By the kindness of the present rector the writer has been enabled to examine the registers and plate. The latter bears the following inscription: "Donné par son Altesse Royale Madame Wilhelmina Carolina Princesse de Galles en Faveur de L'Eglise Française Conformiste de Portarlington. Le 1 Mars 1714/15."

of Charles de Vignoles, and he maintained it in English until 1841. A list of the pastors, compiled by de Vignoles, with the dates of their ministries, appears in the older of the two registers and is as follows:[1]

	1694–1696.	J. Gillet.
	1696.	Bellaguier.
	1696–1698.	J. Gillet.
(May)	1698.	Darassus.
	——	Ducasse.
(June)	1698–1702.	Benj. Daillon.
	1702–1729.	Ant. Ligonier de Bonneval.
	1729–1739.	Théodore Desvories.
	1739–1767.	Gaspard Caillard.
	1767–1793.	Antoine Vinchon Des Voeux.
	1793–1817.	De Vignoles, Père.
	1817–1841.	Charles de Vignoles, fils.

Messrs. Balaguier, Darassus and Ducasse, however, are not described in the registers as ministers of the Church and were only visiting preachers from the churches in Dublin. It is interesting to note that Balaguier and Darassus were Nonconformist ministers while Ducasse belonged to the Conformed Church of St. Mary's. At the time of his visit to Portarlington he was chaplain to Colonel Echlin's Regiment in Dublin. All these ministers will be dealt with in the chapter on the settlement in that city.

In 1736 Josias de Franquefort assisted Monsieur Desvories for a year before taking up his duties in Waterford,[2] and from 1803-1817 a Swiss clergyman, Jean Rebillet, was assistant chaplain to de Vignoles and at the same time master in the French school.[3]

---

[1] "Registers," Hug. Soc. Pub., Vol. XIX.
[2] *Vide* p. 98.
[3] Hug. Soc. Pub., Vol. XIX. "Registers."

Smiles states that, at one time, John Gast, son of Daniel Gast, who settled in Dublin after the Peace of Utrecht,[1] was pastor of the French Church. He later became Rector of Arklow and Archdeacon of Glendalough, and was well known for his " History of Greece,"[2] but he was never minister of the church in Portarlington and only acted for a time as " lecteur."[3]

Monsieur Jacques Gillet, before serving in Portarlington, had officiated in the Chapel de La Tremblade and in the church in Crispin Street, London. He came from Bergerac, and although he had escaped to Holland returned to his native place about 1691 before his flight to England.[4] When he left Portarlington in 1698 he seems to have resumed his ministry in England until 1715.[5] In 1701 he was in London, for he married Jeanne Mestre in that year in his old church in Crispin Street.[6] The first two entries in the register of the Nonconformist Church in Wood Street, Dublin, are signed by him as "Pasteur," but he does not seem to have been a minister in this church and possibly only visited it *en route* to London.[7]

There were numerous families in England and Ireland at this time of Gilletts and Gillots. The name will be further dealt with in Lisburn, where it is also localized.

The Rev. Benjamin Daillon, Sieur De La Levrie, came of the noble family of Du Lude. He was born in 1630, was educated at Saumur for the Church and, as minister of the church at La Rochefoucauld in Angoumois, was fined and banished by the " Lieutenant Criminel " when the church was demolished and its Consistory suppressed. In 1684 he was a

---

[1] Introduction to the "History of Greece."
[2] "Huguenots in England," Appendix.
[3] Hug. Soc. Pub., Vol. XIX.
[4] U.J.A., Vol. III. Art. "Portarlington."
[5] Hug. Soc. Proc., Vol. VIII, p. 107.
[6] Hug. Soc. Pub., Vol. XXXII, p. 84.
[7] Hug. Soc. Proc., Vol. VIII, p. 107.

prisoner in the Conciergerie of Paris, but in the following year he arrived in England, and three years later he appears as minister of the church of La Patente in Spitalfields,[1] a post which he held until 1697. In 1693 he accompanied Lord Galway to Ireland and was mentioned as "professor of divinity" in the abortive scheme for the establishment of a French University in Kilkenny. From March 1695 Galway employed him "on important and confidential business," and in the spring of 1698 recommended him as minister to the Consistory of Portarlington. In 1702 he resigned this post, probably owing to his quarrel with the Bishop of Kildare. Sir Erasmus Borrowes states that he then removed to Carlow, as does Agnew,[2] but Mr. Le Fanu has proved that in 1708 Daillon sold his house in Portarlington to Josias de Champagné and believes that he did not leave for his last ministry till then.[3] He served the French Church in Carlow, as has already been stated, until his death on January 3rd, 1709-10.[4] He married Pauline Nicolas and had two daughters, Pauline and Anne. Pauline married Jean Paquet, Sieur De La Boissiere from Roche Riquié in Angoumois, who retired as an Ensign from Belcastel's Regiment,[5] and had four children, Charles, Susanne, Marie and Anne, all born at Portarlington. Anne married Jean Grosvenor and their son Henri was the godson of Lord Galway, previously mentioned.

Marie Paquet married François Mercier, also of Huguenot stock, who was a Lieutenant in the Royal Warwickshire Regiment in 1733 and died on active service in the West Indies in 1742.[6] Gimlette gives a Robert Mercier as a landholder in Waterford and Kerry under Ormond,[7] and a Claud

[1] U.J.A., Vol. III, Art. "Portarlington," and Hug. Soc. Proc., Vol. XIV, p. 223.
[2] "Protestant Exiles," Vol. II, p. 107.
[3] Hug. Soc. Proc., Vol. XIV, p. 223.
[4] *Vide* p. 130.
[5] J.K.A.S., Vol. XI, No. 4.
[6] *Ibid.*
[7] "Huguenot Settlers," p. 194.

Mercier was a Captain of Horse in 1707 when his son Charles is entered at Kilkenny School.[1] There was more than one officer of this name in the Irish Campaign, and Dumont de Bostaquet's list[2] contains a Mercier " l'ainé " and a Mercier " cadet," both Lieutenants of Infantry. Branches of the family seem to have settled both in Portarlington and Dublin, and Richard Edward Mercier of the latter city had some fame in 1793 as the publisher of " Anthologia Hibernica " and of a periodical entitled *The Flapper* in 1796.[3] A Peter Mercier was an apothecary in Portarlington at the end of the eighteenth century, and on the tombstone in the French burial-ground, erected to his memory by his daughter, Paulina Dumoulin, it was stated with obvious inaccuracy that his ancestor Benjamin Daillon had been " the first Minister of this Church."[4]

Daillon must have been a man of obstinate character. He was the author of an " Examen du Principal prétexté de l'oppression des réformés en France," which he published at Amsterdam,[5] and, as has been seen, he did not scruple to stand out against the Church of Ireland, even at the risk of losing its favour towards the refugees.

His successor, Antoine Ligonier de Bonneval, was the eldest son of Antoine de Ligonier, Sieur de Vignals, who was a descendant of that Antoine Ligonier who had been Consul at Castres in 1569. The minister's mother was Marie de Rotolp De La Devèse, and Dr. Wagner states that " there were several alliances between Ligonier, de Rotolp, De La Devèse, d'Esperandieu, d'Aiguefonde, de Falguerolles and de Terson, all of which families' latest representatives are among the refugees of Ireland."[6] Before leaving France de Bonneval

---

[1] *Vide* p. 128.
[2] " Mémoires Inédits."
[3] Gilbert, " History of Dublin," Vol. II, p. 334.
[4] J.A.P.M.D., Vol. VI.
[5] U.J.A., Vol. III. Art. " Portarlington."
[6] Hug. Soc. Proc., Vol. VIII, p. 380.

had been minister in the churches of Sablayrolles and Pont de Camarès, and that he was forced to fly from the latter community is proved by a Certificate given to him by it in which it is stated that he was " menacé d'un décret." His congregation also state that " il a vescue parmi nous avec toute sorte de bénédiction; nous ayons esté en singulière édification par la pureté de ses moeurs, par la sagesse de sa conduite, et par tout l'exercice de sa charge."[1] He became connected with the de Bostaquet family in Portarlington by his marriage with Judith Julie, widow of De La Blachière, some time before March 1713. They had one daughter, Anne Marie, born 1716, who married in 1737 Jacques Louis de Vignoles, and her son, Jean de Vignoles, born October 1740, became minister of the French Church in 1793. After her death her husband married Marie Anne d'Aultier de Bonvillette, daughter of the Dublin merchant.

Of Louis Théodore Desvories very little information seems to exist. He married in 1717 Caroline, daughter of Auguste Le Goux de Laspois, described as a Captain in the regiment of Montjoye, who died in Dublin in 1709, and had nine children, of whom a son, Jean, settled in Devon. His wife's mother, who was buried in Portarlington in January 1737-8, was a daughter of Amos de Ferre De La Chapelle, naturalized in 1706, granddaughter of Nicholas Grignon, a Paris merchant who obtained his denization in 1682, and a descendant of Jean Petitot, the artist.[2] The name Desvories also occurs in Waterford, where, as has been stated, the Rev. Augustus Desvories succeeded Josiah Franquefort as minister.

Gaspard or Gaspar Caillard served the Peter Street Church in Dublin from 1720-1739, when he was appointed by King's Letter to Portarlington. Like Des Voeux he also held a living in the Church of Ireland, for he was Rector of

[1] Dumont de Bostaquet, " Mémoires Inédits," p. 374.
[2] See Petitot Pedigree. Hug. Soc. Proc., Vol. VIII, p. 348.

Moyglare and Canon of Kildare.[1] He seems to have been an able preacher. In 1728 he published a book of sermons, and Wesley, who heard him deliver one, remarks on his "eloquent action."[2] He married Marie Anne, widow of David d'Arripe, born de Coutiers and therefore a granddaughter of de Bostaquet, whose chief claim to fame seems to be that she had so excellent a second husband. She died in 1772 and was buried with d'Arripe, but her tombstone stated, " Here lies Mary Caillard, born in Portarlington June 30th, 1705. Her second husband was the Rev. Gas. Caillard, Minister of the French Church, well known in the Literary world by his excellent productions, greatly tending to advance the cause of true religion," and almost in the nature of an afterthought was added, " She was a dutiful daughter, an affectionate wife and a tender mother."[3]

Antoine Vinchon Des Voeux was the second son of Monsieur de Bacquencourt, President of the Parliament of Rouen and a Roman Catholic. He became a member of the Reformed Church and fled to Holland, whence he was called to minister to the Nonconformist congregation of Lucy Lanc in Dublin in 1735. He succeeded the Rev. Jean Pierre Droz in 1751 in the publication of the first literary journal to appear in Ireland, which he continued under the title of the *Compendious Library or Literary Journal Revived*, and he obtained the M.A. Degree of Dublin University for his translation and Commentary on the Book of Ecclesiastes. As well as his ministry in the French Church Des Voeux held a chaplaincy to the regiment of Lord George Sackville, and in 1760 he left Dublin to join his regiment.[4] In 1767 he was back in Ireland and took up duty at Portarlington,

---

[1] Hug. Soc. Proc., Vol. VIII, p. 134. Mr. Le Fanu believes that he came from Cork, though no reference to him occurs there.

[2] " Wesley's Journal," June 1750.

[3] J.A.P.M.D., Vol. VI, p. 131.

[4] " Huguenots in England," Appendix; U.J.A., Vol. VI, and Hug. Soc. Proc., Vol. VIII, p. 87.

where he continued until his death in 1792. He married three times, his first wife being Marie Louise Quergroode de Challais; his second, Charlotte d'Exoudun, daughter of Captain Josué de Fay d'Exoudun, a native of Niort in Poitou and Captain in Miremont's Dragoons; and his third, Hannah Pain.[1] One of his sons was Sir Charles Des Voeux, Bart., who married Marianne Champagné, the descendant of another refugee.[2]

His gravestone in the French churchyard at Portarlington recorded that, as well as being French minister there he was Rector of Mansfieldstown in the County of Louth,[3] and he was also for a time French minister in Dundalk. In Dublin he had proved so difficult a colleague that on his departure no minister would accept a call to the Nonconformist Churches until it was definitely ascertained that he would not return.[4] In Portarlington, however, he seems to have been successful and popular, and he died in his eighty-third year " beloved, respected and regretted."[5]

The de Vignoles family came from Languedoc, where they possessed large estates. An Estienne de Vignoles fought in the wars of Charles VII. His descendant, Charles, fourth son of Jacques de Vignoles, Seigneur of Prades, near Nismes, born 1645, fled at the Revocation to Holland, where he joined William of Orange.[6] He followed that monarch to England, fought as a Major in the Irish Campaign, and finally settled in Dublin. In 1684 he married Marthe Des Bonneaux Du Roure.[7] Their only surviving child, Margaret, married her cousin, Scipio Duroure, and died in Dublin in 1721. In 1694, having become a widower, Vignoles married Gabrielle

---

[1] Hug. Soc. Proc., Vol. VIII, p. 87.
[2] Burke's " Peerage."
[3] J.A.P.M.D., Vol. VI.
[4] Hug. Soc. Proc., Vol. VIII, p. 135.
[5] J.A.P.M.D., Vol. VI, p. 131. Inscription on his tombstone.
[6] Agnew, Vol. II, p. 258.
[7] Hug. Soc. Pub., Vol. VII, p. 120, and Hug. Soc. Proc., Vol. X, p. 399.

d'Esperandieu, daughter of Jacques Sieur d'Aiguesfondes. Of his sixteen children, Charlotte married Cornet Charles Nicolas and emigrated to America; Marie married Josué de Fay d'Exoudun, the refugee from Poitou who settled in Dublin; the heir, Colonel Charles Vignoles, did not found a family; and it was left to the thirteenth child, Major James Louis Vignoles, of the 31st Regiment, to establish the name. He was born in Dublin in 1702, and married in Portarlington in 1737 Anne Marie de Bonneval as already stated. Their child, John, rose to be a Major in the Army, but after his father's death in 1779 entered the Church and officiated as minister in Portarlington. His son, Charles, born 1788, followed him in the ministry and was made chaplain to the Lord-Lieutenant. He continued to hold the office of minister of the French Church until 1841, when he resigned, and was shortly afterwards appointed Dean of Ossory.[1] In addition both he and his father held the post of minister to the French Church in Dundalk, though, as will be seen, this office could have entailed no duties.[2]

The refugee ancestor of the family died in Dublin in 1721 aged seventy-seven. His three sisters also came to Ireland and one became Madame Boileau of Dublin. An interesting declaration was submitted by him to the Auditor-General in 1714, when sworn declarations were obtained from 281 French pensioners on the civil list.[3]

Vignoles stated " Qu'il a servi pendant quinze années en France ou il a été Capitaine d'Infanterie; qu'il se refugia en Holande pour la cause de la Religion Protestante; qu'il passa en Angleterre avec plusiers autres officiers françois par les ordres de feu Roy Guillaume; qu'il fut fait Capitaine dans le Regiment d'Infanterie du Colonel Ducambon où il servit pendant la guerre d'Irlande." He adds that he is " frequem-

[1] Hug. Soc. Pub., Vol. XIX, p. 18.
[2] *Vide* p. 192.
[3] 18th Report Deputy Keeper of the Records, Appendix V, 1886.

ment incommodé de violentes douleurs de la goute et menacé d'une fluxion sur la poitrine . . . il est agé de 69 ans . . . il a une femme et huit enfants vivans auxquels avec la pention et 300 livres qui luy restent après ses dettes payées il peut à grande peine fournir ce qui leur est necessaire pour leur vie et leur vêtement." He possesses " ny terre, ny ferme, ny aucun negoce " and " il espère de la bonté de la Reyne qu'elle voudra bien lui continuer ladite pention " (of 3 shillings 6 sols a day, reduced after the Peace of Ryswick to 2 shillings 6 sols) " pendant le reste de sa vie, qui," he concludes hopefully, " apparament ne scauroit être longe."

Many of the most influential of the Portarlington settlers signed the Petition, already mentioned, made to the Duke of Dorset in 1733. On this such names occur as de Champagné, Guion, Du Petit Bosc, Francquefort, Claverie, Labrosse, Boyer, Beauchant Buliod, de Meschinet, Tirel, Cassel, Micheau, Dorval, Bainsereau, d'Arripe, Clausade, Foubert, Pilot, Quinsac, Terson, Camlin, Belliard and Labat.[1]

The last-named family is also connected with Youghal and Dublin, and has been dealt with in the former colony, and the Francqueforts are recorded amongst the Waterford settlers. Others, such as Du Petit Bosc, Boyer and Beauchant, have already been mentioned.

The de Champagnés were descended from the noble family of de Robillard of Torcé in Saintonge, whence the Chevalier Josias de Robillard, Seigneur de Champagné, fled at the Revocation. He became a Captain in Scravemore's Regiment of Dragoons, and was deputed by the Huguenot officers of William's army to act as their spokesman to Government. He remained in England in this capacity after his companions left for Ireland, and is said to have died of fatigue in Belfast in 1689 while hastening to rejoin his regiment. He married Marie De La Rochefoucauld, who was buried at Portarlington, and had four sons and four

---

[1] U.J.A., Vol. VI. Art. " Portarlington."

daughters. One of the latter, Susanne, married Baron Tonnay Boutonne de St. Surin, and had a son, Henri, Baron De La Motte Fouquet, the famous General of Frederick the Great.[1] Brady states that the youngest son escaped with his father, but Madame Champagné, in her graphic account of the flight, states, "on the tenth of April 1687 my four daughters and my two youngest sons, with my cousin, de Mascriée, left La Rochelle at night." The head of a wine cask was knocked out; the wine was emptied into the sea and they were put inside the cask. . . . "We set sail and arrived at Falmouth eight days after—not," she adds, "sans peur et bien de risque."[2]

Josias, the eldest son, who had left France with his father, fought as an Ensign in La Melonière's Regiment at the Boyne. He so distinguished himself in his army career that he was made aide-de-camp to the Lord-Lieutenant, and later Major of the 14th Foot. He eventually settled in Portarlington, married Jane, eldest daughter of Arthur Forbes, second Earl of Granard, and had an only son, Arthur, born in 1714. Champagné made many influential friends in Ireland, Dean Swift among the number,[3] and held considerable property round Portarlington. He played an important part in the life of the settlement and was Sovereign of the Borough from 1730-1732, and treasurer of the charity school founded by Lord Galway. He seems to have attended the Parish Church at Lea, and presumably was churchwarden there in 1730. In 1721 he visited Holland, where his mother was then living, and brought her back to his home in Portarlington. She died there in 1730, leaving a legacy to Théodore Desvories for the poor and one to Captain Pierre Franquefort.

[1] Brady, "Records of Cork, Cloyne and Ross."

[2] "Journal of Mme. de Champagné" in the possession of the Borrowes family, pub. in Hug. Soc. Proc., Vol. XIII, pp. 454-73. For a full account of the family see this article by Mr. Le Fanu and that on p. 560.

[3] "Letters of Dean Swift." Ed. Hill, pp. 51 and 61. Letters July 7th and Aug. 2nd, 1715.

Arthur Champagné was educated in Trinity College and took Holy Orders, becoming Vicar of Mullingar in 1746 and Dean of Clonmacnoise in 1761 as well as minister of the English Chapel in Portarlington.[1] He died in August 1800 and is buried in the French burial-ground.[2] In Mallow churchyard a tombstone was erected by him to the memory of his wife, who predeceased him in 1784.[3] She was Marianne, daughter of Major Isaac Hamon, also a refugee.

Of their children, Arthur became Rector of Cloncah, Derry; married in 1788 Mary, daughter of the Rev. Philip Homan of Westmeath, and died in 1790 leaving a son, Arthur, Vicar of Castlelyons. George became a Canon of Windsor, Forbes a Major-General, and Josias was knighted as a General. Jane became Countess of Uxbridge, Henrietta married Sir Erasmus Borrowes, and Marianne, as has already been stated, became the wife of Sir Charles des Voeux.[4] The family therefore provides a good example both of the inter-marriage which occurred even in modern times amongst the descendants of the refugees, and of the eminent positions these Frenchmen filled in the professions and society in the British Isles.

The Guion who signed the Petition must have been William de Guyon de Geis, son of the Sieur de Pampelonne who fled at the Revocation, joined William of Orange, campaigned in Piedmont and Germany, and, when pensioned, settled at Portarlington, where he became an elder and treasurer of the French Church, and where he died in 1740. He married Isabeau, sister of Captains Estienne and Noé Cadroy and daughter of Joseph Cadroy, a native of Bordeaux who joined the Portarlington colony in 1699. They had, besides four daughters, two sons, Joseph and Noé Etienne,

---

[1] Brady.
[2] J.A.P.M.D., Vol. VI.
[3] Ibid.
[4] Brady, and Hug. Soc. Proc., Vol. XIII, p. 560.

and several of their descendants, states Smiles, entered the British Army.[1] The signature " Labrosse " would seem to indicate Captain Jean Poisson De La Brousse of Cambon's Regiment, who took the Oaths in Dublin in 1698 and thence removed to Portarlington, where he became an elder of the French Church, and where he married and had three sons and a daughter. He died the year following the presentation of the Petition.

The name Cassel, like those of Buliod and Terson, is connected with the Portarlington schools. The Cassels escaped from France to Holland, bringing with them Lucy La Motte Grandore,[2] the heiress of estates in Languedoc. She married John Laborde, who fought at the Boyne and was perhaps an ancestor of the John, son of Lieutenant-Colonel Labord, who was entered in Kilkenny School in 1757,[3] and came to Ireland with him, and their daughter Anne married Isaac Cassel. Abel Cassel, a son of this marriage, was baptized in 1736; he died at the age of seventy, and his grave may still be seen in the French portion of the churchyard. Both Isaac and an elder Abel Cassel signed the Petition.[4] The name, however, does not originate in Portarlington, for even before the Revocation it had appeared in Ireland, and a Colonel Cassel, who is stated by Gimlette to have been a Protestant refugee, led the assault on Drogheda under Cromwell.[5]

The Micheaus were tenant-farmers on the French estates of the Robillards in the Seigneury of Berneré in Saintonge. They followed their lords to Ireland, and when the Champagnés had established themselves in Portarlington they

---

[1] " Huguenots in England," Appendix, and J.K.A.S., Vol. XI, No. 4.
[2] She signs herself " Anne Grindor " in the Portarlington Register, so there would seem to be some confusion about her Christian name.
[3] *Vide* p. 128.
[4] U.J.A., Vol. VI. Art. " Portarlington."
[5] " Huguenot Settlers," p. 180.

again held land from them there, and were Portreeves of the Borough when the Champagnés were Sovereigns. When Sir Erasmus Borrowes wrote in 1855 a descendant of the Micheaus was sexton in the church.[1]

Captain David d'Arripe, as reported on his tombstone, was " born in France which he left young on account of Religion. He served long as an officer in the English force with credit to himself and usefully for the State."[2] He was reduced after the Peace of Utrecht and retired on half-pay to Portarlington, where he died in November 1737 at the age of sixty-six, leaving two sons, Isaac, a Captain in the Army, who died in Dublin in 1800, and Pierre who remained in Portarlington.[3] His widow, as has previously been mentioned, married the minister Caillard.

Jean, son of Etienne Clausade of Caraman in Languedoc, served with Miremont's Dragoons in Piedmont and subsequently in the war in Spain. On his return in 1713 he was naturalized and pensioned as Lieutenant, and appears first in Portarlington in 1729, a later date than most of the other settlers. He was treasurer of the church from 1738 till his death in 1754.[4]

The Pilot who signed the Petition must have been the son of Josué Pilot who fled to Ireland from Poitou and commanded an independent company at the Siege of Derry. The son, who settled in Portarlington, was a surgeon in Battereau's Foot and later served under the Duke of Cumberland in the '45 Campaign. He married Esther Judith, daughter of Lieutenant Pierre de Bette already mentioned, and his descendants intermarried with the Hamons, Champagnés, Bouhéreaus and Des Voeux,[5] and thus provide a

---

[1] U.J.A., Vol. III. Art. "Portarlington."
[2] J.A.P.M.D., Vol. VI.
[3] J.K.A.S., Vol. XI, No. 4.
[4] *Ibid.*
[5] " Huguenots in England," Appendix.

good example of the close alliances maintained by the Huguenots in their exile.

The Hamons, with whom they allied, are said to have been of Dutch not French extraction, and a certain Hector Hamon fled from the persecutions of Alva to England, and was minister of Rye in 1569 and of the Crypt Church in Canterbury in 1574,[1] but Smiles gives the family a Norman origin, and the Colonels Isaac and Hector Hamon, who settled in Portarlington after the Irish Campaign, were both born in Paris. Hector Hamon served with General Primrose's Foot, while Isaac fought at Malplaquet and was Lieutenant-Colonel in the Queen's Regiment before his retirement in 1746. He died in Portarlington in 1755, leaving a daughter, Marianne Champagné. Both brothers seem to have settled for a time in Dublin before coming to Portarlington, and the three children of Hector Hamon and Marie Mazik were all born in the capital. Hector Hamon predeceased his brother by fourteen years, but another settler of the same name, who may have been his son, was buried in Portarlington in 1769.[2] Pierre Hamon, one of the children born in Dublin, took Holy Orders and also settled in Portarlington, where a tombstone records his death in 1798.

Captain Charles de Quinsac, like Jean Clausade, was a comparatively late comer to the settlement. Like him also he served in Piedmont, and he seems to have resided at first in Dublin, where his two sons, Charles and Jean, were born in 1724 and 1725. He appears for the first time in the Portarlington Registers in 1729 and he died sixteen years later.[3]

In a work which purposes to survey the Irish Settlements as a whole, it is not possible to mention the name and trace

[1] U.J.A., Vol. VI. Art. "Portarlington."
[2] J.K.A.S., Vol. XI, No. 4.
[3] *Ibid.*

the history of every settler in the very large Portarlington colony. A list of the military colonists will be found in Vol. XIV of the Proceedings of the Huguenot Society of London,[1] and in the admirable paper which has been so often quoted above, which includes a map showing their holdings and reconstructing Portarlington in the late seventeenth and early eighteenth centuries contributed by Mr. T. P. Le Fanu to the Journal of the County Kildare Archæological Society.[2] Here it is only possible to indicate briefly the history of the most important amongst the early residents of the Huguenot town.

Of these, the Sieur De La Hauteville, Lieutenant on pension; Charles de Ponthieu; Gédeon de Castelfranc; Pierre d'Aulnis, Captain; d'Aulnis de Lalande; Ruben De La Rochefoucauld; Guy De La Blachière; La Baume, and Pierre Goullin, " Cornette de cavalerie à la pension," are names which have been quoted by the editors of de Bostaquet's Memoirs, amongst some others which have already been dealt with, as characteristic of the settlement.[3] To these may be added Pierre Le Maignan; Charles de Bures Sieur de Bethen-court; Le Blanc; Pelissier; Sabatier, Duron and the author of the famous " Mémoires " himself.

Jacques De La Hauteville was a native of Dieppe who came to Ireland with William, served from 1689 in La Caillemotte's Regiment, and, having been wounded at the Siege of Limerick, was pensioned as an Ensign in 1691. He married the widow of Major Guillaume La Baume.[4]

Charles de Ponthieu, who settled in Portarlington as a Captain on pension, was born in Taillebourg in Saintonge.

---

[1] Vol. XIV, No. 2, p. 217.
[2] Vol. XI, No. 4, July 1933.
[3] " Mémoires." Introduction, pp. 41-2. The list from which the above names have been quoted does not always agree with the registers, and only those which have been capable of correction and proof by reference to the latter have been mentioned.
[4] J.K.A.S., Vol. XI, No. 4.

He left France in 1687, joined the Army in Holland, and came to Ireland with the King, where he was severely wounded as a Lieutenant of Grenadiers during the crossing of the Boyne. While in England he had married Marguerite, sister of Ruben De La Rochefoucauld, and had, among other children, two sons, Henri and Josias, and a daughter, Elizabeth, who married Jean Cavalier, the famous leader of the Camisard Insurrection in the Cevennes. She was thus connected with the Champagnés through Marie De La Rochefoucauld, who married the Chevalier Josias de Robillard, and this may account for the interest taken in her affairs by Major Champagné. Despite his old wound de Ponthieu enlisted for the war in Spain, and on his return he seems to have left Portarlington to settle in England, where he died in 1730.[1]

Gédéon de Castelfranc was the grandson of Philippe de Nautonier, Seigneur de Castelfranc in L'Albigeos and pastor of Montredon in Le Castrais.[2] The pastor married Marguerite Chamier, and had, with three daughters, two sons, Jacques, a minister at Angers, and Adrien, who became the Lord of Castelfranc and was forced to fly to England. His children were enslaved in the Caribbee Islands, but they were later liberated by order of the King[3] and also sought safety in England. Three sons fought in the wars in Flanders. Of these Gédéon, who became a Cornet in Miremont's Dragoons, survived and retired to Portarlington, where he established a malthouse and carried on farming on a moderate scale. The father, sailing from London to Holland, was captured by Algerines and died in slavery.[4]

Francis d'Aulnis de Lalande was a friend and school-

---

[1] Agnew, Vol. II, p. 128. Hug. Soc. Proc., Vol. IX, p. 584. J.K.A.S., Vol. XI, No. 4.
[2] Bull, "Protestant France," pp. 387, 402.
[3] Agnew. Smiles states that they were rescued by English seamen.
[4] Agnew, Vol. II.

fellow of Fontaine, the pastor of Cork, and is mentioned by him in his " Memoirs ": " Monsieur De La Lande who now (1722) lives at Portarlington in Ireland was at Rochelle in Mr. Arnauld's School at the same time I was there " (i.e. from 1644-1666). " We became the greatest friends."[1] He was the second son of Pierre d'Aulnis, who served as a doctor in Portarlington until his death in 1709. In 1685 he left the French Army, and, taking service with William, became a Captain in Belcastel's Regiment. In 1699 he retired to Portarlington, where he died in the year that saw the completion of his friend's " Memoirs." He married his cousin, Angelique, daughter of Captain Pierre d'Aulnis Du Caillard, a refugee in Holland.

His elder brother, Henri, settled on half pay in Dublin and had a daughter, Anne Henriette, who married Colonel Paul Mangin.[2]

The Ruben De La Rochefoucauld who settled in Portarlington was the son of François De La Rochefoucauld, Seigneur of Pardachet, of a junior branch of the great La Rochefoucauld family, and was a cousin of Josias de Champagné already mentioned.[3] He was also a distant connection of Frederick William De La Rochefoucauld, Comte de Marton, who was commonly styled Earl of Lifford, although he never received the Patent and the title remained a courtesy one.[4] He was the son of Frederick Charles de Rochefoucauld, Count de Roye, who was a General under Turenne and fled to Denmark and thence to England at the Revocation, where he died in 1690. The Comte de Marton served at the Boyne and was made Colonel of Cambon's Regiment after the latter's death until it was disbanded after the Peace of Ryswick, and later was Colonel of one of the

[1] " Memoirs," p. 43. Lart, Vol. II, pp. 1 and 2.
[2] J.K.A.S., Vol. XI, No. 4, and *vide* p. 181.
[3] *Vide* p. 159. Hug. Soc. Proc., Vol. XIII, p. 457, and Lart, " Huguenot Pedigrees," Vol. I, pp. 72-3.
[4] Agnew, Vol. II, p. 121.

six French regiments sent to Portugal. He died in London in 1749. A Francis De La Rochefoucauld, son of the Baron de Montandre, also fled to England. He served as Lieutenant-Colonel in Cambon's Regiment and was pensioned on the Irish Establishment. He, too, campaigned in Portugal, was raised to the rank of Field-Marshal and died in London in 1739.[1]

Pierre Goullin, who came from Lourmarin in Provence, served in Brandenburg in 1685 and thence accompanied William in the Irish Campaign. He settled first in Dublin, where he married as his second wife Anne Cossart, perhaps a connection of the Dublin and Cork families of that name, and then in Monasterevan, but he seems to have been closely connected with the Portarlington Settlement and he appears frequently in the registers of the French Church. The settler of the same name who died in the colony in 1770 was probably one of his numerous children.[2]

Pierre La Maignan is described in the registers as " Maréchal des Logis au Regiment de Galway filz de feu Pierre Le Maignan, Marchand, drappier demeurant à Condé sur-pays de Normandie." He married in September 1694 Demoiselle Jeanne Jacqueau " fille du Sieur Isaac Jacqueau, officer de Marine, demeurant en l'Isle d'Oleron, Province de Saintonge en France,"[3] and died in Portarlington in 1705.

Captain Charles de Bures de Bethencourt, a native of the Pays de Caux in Normandy, was an old friend and brother officer of Dumont de Bostaquet, but he was dead before the writer of the " Mémoires " had reached Portarlington.[4] He married Dame Anne Miffant, who was buried in Portarlington

---

[1] " Huguenots in England," Appendix, and Agnew, Vol. II, p. 118.
[2] J.K.A.S., Vol. XI, No. 4.
[3] Marriage Register.
[4] Hug. Soc. Proc., Vol. XIV, p. 218.   De Bostaquet (" Mémoires ") states that he died in 1697.

in 1694, and his brother, Michel de Bures Sailly, was also of the settlement.

There were two families of Le Blanc in Portarlington about 1699, that of "Le Noble Homme Louys [*sic*] Le Blanc, Sieur de Perce, Capitaine pensionné," and Claud Le Blanc "boucher." The latter family were still existing under the name of "Blong" when Sir Erasmus Borrowes wrote.[1] This change in name seems to have been early effected, for Peter "Blang" placed a tombstone to mark the burial-place of his family in 1756, and was laid there himself three years later. Elizabeth Phelan, his daughter, was also buried there, from which it would seem that they, unlike most of the early colonists, married outside the French stock. Théodore Le Blanc, minister of La Rochelle, who was attainted in 1685 for having received a "relapse" into his Church, and fled to Denmark, was, Sir Erasmus Borrowes states, probably of the same family as Le Blanc "the gentleman." The name, however, seems to have been localized elsewhere in Ireland at the same time, for an Andrew and a Mark Le Blanc, merchants from Alès, took the Oaths and received their naturalization in Dublin in 1704.[2] It is still extant in Portarlington.

In December 1698 the register records the marriage of Abel Pelissier (described in a later entry as "cy-devant mareschal des logis et aide maior du Regt. de Galuuai") and "Marie de Choisy fille de César de Choisy et de feu Marie Gilbert de Chef Boutonne, province de Poitou." The bridegroom was the son of Abel Pelissier and Anne Nicolas of Castres, who may have been a relative of the Captain Jean Nicolas already mentioned. In 1700 Abel, the eldest child, was born, and in the next year Alexander, who became a merchant in Dublin, where he died in 1777.[3] Jean, Jacques, Angelique, Marie and Marianne were other children of the

---

[1] U.J.A., Vol. III. Art. "Portarlington."
[2] Hug. Soc. Pub., Vol. XXVII, p. 235.
[3] *Vide* p. 243.

marriage.[1] Two of the sons took Holy Orders, and some of their descendants were officers in the English Army.[2] The family seems to have left Portarlington before the birth of Marianne, and Pelissier died in Dublin in 1727.

Even before Portarlington was ready to receive the refugees a Jean Sabatier had taken up his residence at Lea. He could not, however, have made Portarlington his permanent home, for he died at Mount Mellick in 1740. He, like the Le Blancs, seems to have found a wife of different nationality, for her name was Elizabeth Freeman. François Sabatier, a relative, was condemned to the Galleys and then incarcerated in the Chateau D'If, and his sufferings are recorded by Jean Bion.[3]

Pierre Duron has already been mentioned as a Portarlington settler whose will was dated 1725. He married Anne Viger and had a son, Isaac, and he seems to have died about 1728, when the will was proved. Isaac Duron married Marie Magdalen Bailard or Beliard,[4] whose ancestor, Jean, fled from Dieppe and died in Portarlington about 1695, and of their children, Mary, who died in 1839, married into the Powell family and was the ancestress of the late Archdeacon Dacre Powell of Cork, and Henrietta into that of Booth.[5]

Perhaps the most famous of the Portarlington Huguenots was Captain Isaac Dumont, Seigneur de Bostaquet, whose "Mémoires" throw such light on the affairs of the refugees and on the Irish Campaign. He came of the landed gentry of Normandy, and was born in 1632 at the Manor of Bostaquet near Dieppe. After the Revocation he fled to Holland where he obtained a commission in the Dutch Army, and whence he sailed with William's troops for England. There he settled at Greenwich, but on the reassembling of the

---

[1] U.J.A., Vol. III, et seq. Art. "Portarlington."
[2] "Huguenots in England," Appendix.
[3] U.J.A., Vol. III, p. 225 et seq., and vide supra p. 25.
[4] Portarlington Registers.
[5] Notes supplied by the kindness of a descendant of the Duron family.

Army for the Irish Campaign he joined Schomberg's Horse, and as a Captain he fought at the Boyne. In 1693 he was in Dublin, where he served as elder in the French Church of St. Patrick's, and thence removed to Portarlington in 1698, where he died in 1709. The editor of his " Mémoires " states " on voyait encore il y a peu d'années, son épitaphe en langue française sur l'une des pierres sépulcrales du cimetière," but by 1904[1] this had entirely disappeared. One of his daughters, Judith-Julie, was married in Portarlington to Guy Auguste de La Blachière, Seigneur de Coutiers, on April 2nd, 1700. There were three daughters and one son of the marriage. The son, Isaac-Philippe, was baptized by Monsieur Abbadie "Doyen de Kilalou." In 1735 he was a Captain in the Infantry Regiment of Colonel Wentworth,[2] and he died in Portarlington in 1751. De Bostaquet gave his farm in Portarlington to his daughter and her husband, but the latter did not live long to enjoy it, dying in Portugal in 1707 while serving as Lieutenant in Sankey's Regiment, and the former married, as her second husband, the minister de Bonneval.[3]

As to the marriage of a second daughter, Marie Madeleine, some confusion seems to have arisen. The editor of the "Mémoires" states that she married a Monsieur de Vignoles, thus accounting for the presence of the de Bostaquet papers in the possession of the Dean of Ossory. Agnew[4] maintains that she could not have married into the Vignoles family, and believes that the papers were given to de Bonneval and passed on to successive ministers. As has been seen, Major James Louis Vignoles married Anne Marie, daughter of de Bonneval, and so the Vignoles' possession of the papers is not so difficult to understand. . Wagner states that she married the Dublin merchant, Bonvillette,[5] but actually, as

[1] When a survey was made of the tombstones.
[2] "Mémoires Inédits."
[3] Hug. Soc. Proc., Vol. XIV, No. 2, p. 224.
[4] Vol. II, Ch. 22, p. 259.
[5] Hug. Soc. Proc., Vol. VIII, p. 380.

pointed out by Mr. Le Fanu,[1] Marie Madeleine, who only came to Portarlington after her father's death, married Jean Auguste de Claverie in 1725, and died there a widow in 1776. The last French descendant of Dumont de Bostaquet, the Marquis Dumont de Lamberville, died in 1847.[2]

Other tombstones beside that of de Bostaquet must have suffered with time. "What strikes one as strange," says a writer on the Portarlington graveyard, in the "Journal of the Association for the Preservation of Memorials of the Dead,"[3] "is that the earliest slab is only dated 1737, and what is stranger still is that only one inscription is in French and that of the nineteenth century though services in French were held in the Church as late as 1817." The inscription referred to commemorates "Antoine Fleury, pasteur de la Paroisse de Coolbanagher pendent plus de 40 ans décédé le 6e Avril 1801. Aussi Richard Dowdall, Ecuier décédé le huitieme juillet 1804."

Most of the other inscriptions have already been mentioned. Some of the remainder give no hint of a French origin, such as those to members of the Elrington, Ransford and Leak families. The Fleurys were connected with Waterford rather than Portarlington, and so were the Grueber family, although a tombstone marks the grave of Isabella Grueber, née Bonafous, wife of Lieutenant Grueber, who died at Urlingford in 1798, and of her son John and daughter Mary.[4]

The Portarlington Settlement had been recruited by officers on pension after Ryswick and again after the Peace of Utrecht, but even with this the French element would have become absorbed there as in other colonies had it not been

---

[1] Hug. Soc. Proc., Vol. XIV, p. 225.
[2] "Mémoires," Introduction.
[3] Vol. VI, 1904-6, p. 131.
[4] *Vide* p. 100.

for the famous schools established there in addition to those already mentioned as having been built and endowed by the Earl of Galway. These served the double purpose of bringing prosperity and fame to the settlement and of preserving its characteristics. Children were sent from all over Ireland to imbibe French culture as well as classical learning, and Portarlington could claim men as distinguished as the Marquis of Wellesley and his brother among the pupils of the schools.[1]

The original education in Lord Galway's School must have been purely elementary, says Mr. Le Fanu, as the two earliest schoolmasters mentioned in the registers had been a shopkeeper and a bootmaker,[2] but according to Smiles, a Monsieur Le Fèvre, described as a "Lieutenant à la pention," was the first schoolmaster in Portarlington.[3] One of the Cassels and a Monsieur Durand were also masters, as were Messieurs Macarel, Bonafou (or Bonnevaux), Terson and La Cam, with others of Irish descent.[4]

The tombs of a John Bonafous and Thomas Terson, who died in 1803 and 1808 respectively, are amongst those in the burial-ground at the rear of the French Church. The former must have been a connection of the Isabella Grueber mentioned above, and the latter was a descendant of a refugee of the same name from Puilaurens in Languedoc who served as a Captain during the campaigns in Ireland and Portugal, and on retirement settled at Portarlington, where he died in 1749.[5] The Madame Terson at whose scholastic establishment at Clontarf Lady Morgan was educated, may have been the widow of the second Thomas, or at least a relative. She prided herself on the discipline of her school, writes Lady Morgan, founded on that of St. Cyr "so far as a Huguenot

---

[1] Smiles, p. 305.
[2] Hug. Soc. Pub., Vol. XIX.
[3] "Huguenots in England," p. 305.
[4] U.J.A., Vol. VI. Art. "Portarlington."
[5] J.K.A.S., Vol. XI, No. 4.

establishment could be compared to one founded by that fatal she whose influence let loose the dragonnades."[1]

Private enterprise was responsible for much of the scholastic fame of Portarlington. Thus in 1714 a school was kept by Madame de Champlorier, wife of Marc Champlorier who had served as an Ensign under La Melonière, been wounded at the Siege of Limerick,[2] and died in Dublin in 1727; a Mademoiselle Lalande maintained an infant school before the middle of the century, in which she was later succeeded by the Misses Towers;[3] and there were at one period no less than sixteen schools in the neighbourhood, the most famous being kept by the Rev. Thomas Willis in the house which had once belonged to Daniel Du Petit Bosc.[4] In all these establishments French was the common language, and thus the schools filled the need for a cosmopolitan education at a time when England's constant warfare with France made it impossible to send children abroad. The rebellion of '98, however, with the subsequent Union, struck a blow at the schools from which they never fully recovered, since from that date children of the better class were more commonly sent for their education to England.

Not all the Huguenots were educated at their own schools. Edmund Burke found many of them as companions at Ballitore, the famous Quaker School of the Shackleton family. Such names as Audebert, Joubert, Dulamon, Dubedat, Laporte, Lescure, Fontblanque, Zouche, Libert, Chaigneau, Chaunders and Aimée appear in the school lists of his contemporaries,[5] and Mrs. Leadbeater records that " Several French men and boys came here (to Ballitore) in the time of my grandfather to learn English, and they left the name of 'the French Room' to a large apartment in which they

[1] " Memoirs," Vol. I, p. 103. The reference is to Madame de Maintenon.
[2] Hug. Soc. Pub., Vol. XIX, p. 17.
[3] U.J.A., Vol. VI. Art. "Portarlington."
[4] Hug. Soc. Pub., Vol. XIX, p. 17.
[5] " The Early Life of Burke," A. P. Samuels, p. 39.

slept."[1] The French element was not always popular in the school, if Burke's letters to his friend, Richard Shackleton, are any criterion of the general feeling. He writes in 1744 of two unfortunate scholars, " So the two boobies have left Ballitore as they did Edenderry, as its probable will soon quit Portarlington, and then where the devil will they go? Their travels are thus. The boobies, finding France too hot for 'em, they retired to Holland, from thence to London, thence to Dublin, thence to Edenderry, thence to Ballitore, then to Portarlington—and where next? "[2] The boy Louis Aimée, possibly a descendant of Cornet L'Amy who is given by de Bostaquet as having been pensioned in 1692, who entered Ballitore in 1743, seems especially to have aroused Burke's contempt, who does not spare satiric references to the "noble Chevalier Aimé " and his broken English.

By the middle of the nineteenth century very little trace of the French settlers remained, although it is true that the Portarlington Settlement preserved its characteristics far longer than did any other colony. Writing in 1837, Lewis remarks, " The French language continued to be spoken among the refugees for a considerable time but at present they are scarcely to be distinguished from the other inhabitants except where the names afford evidence of their foreign extraction."[3]

The scarlet cloaks of Ruvigny's ex-officers had long disappeared with the swords, diamond knee-buckles and stocks of the original settlers;[4] their language had ceased to be spoken except, as the writer is informed by the descendant of one of them, as a kind of family " slang "; their church was closed in 1841;[5] their bricked recesses for beehives, "Espaliers,"

[1] " The Leadbeater Papers," Vol. I, p. 43.
[2] *Ibid.*, Vol. II, pp. 18 and 28.
[3] " Topographical Dictionary."
[4] *Vide* the description of the Vicomte de Laval in U.J.A., Vol. VI. Art. " Portarlington."
[5] It is now used as the Parish Church.

Italian walnut trees and Jargonelle pears[1] were things of the past; but in the dignified houses, the spacious market square and the old graveyard some traces of the settlement still remained to distinguish Portarlington from an ordinary Irish town of secondary importance.

[1] U.J.A., Vol. VI. Art. " Portarlington."

CHAPTER VII

In dealing with Ireland at the period of the Huguenot immigration it is not always easy to remember that the artificial division between North and South was then non-existent, and that Dublin, in addition to its position as capital, held the chief trade and industry of the country. Until the coming of the Huguenots the northern counties knew little of the linen trade which was to make of them a unit of such political as well as industrial importance, and therefore it has seemed more in keeping with the period to group all those refugees who settled north of the capital under the one heading rather than to observe the arbitrary political division of to-day.

The most important settlement north of Dublin, and perhaps the most important in Ireland where that country is concerned, was established in the ruined village of Lisnagarvey in 1698; and other colonies, more or less offshoots of this, are to be found in Dundalk and Lurgan, but lesser settlements occur in Castleblayney, Lambeg, Killeshandra and Collon, while Belfast afforded a home for the troopers of Schomberg's army. Some Huguenot names may also be traced in the two Meaths, in Louth, Down and Armagh.

When William III, in the spirit of the Bill of 1697 passed by the Irish Parliament to foster the linen trade,[1] invited Louis Crommelin from the Low Countries with his seventy-

---

[1] *Vide* p. 19.

five French families and one thousand looms to encourage and superintend the industry, Lisnagarvey, or Lisburn, was chosen as their place of settlement. The history of the village had been a chequered one. It was burnt by the insurgents in the 1641 rebellion and had surrendered to Cromwell in 1650. Charles II, to reward the fidelity of the inhabitants to his father, had conferred the right upon them of sending two representatives to the Irish Parliament and had erected the church into a cathedral for the united dioceses of Down and Connor. On the landing of Schomberg near Bangor in 1689 it had been the rallying point of some of the forces of James, but it was abandoned by them without a struggle, and William passed through it peacefully shortly before the Boyne.[1] Despite the grant of Charles II the village had remained in a half ruinous condition, but to Crommelin it seemed excellently suited to the requirements of the refugees. Houses were erected for them, with a church for the French minister; the first factory was established at the foot of the wooden bridge over the Lagan, and a bleaching green was laid out at Hilden.[2]

The details of Crommelin's undertaking have already been noted.[3] He invested £10,000 in machinery and raw material, and received a salary of £200 a year for life, and interest at 8 per cent. per annum on the capital invested for twelve years. He was appointed "Overseer of the Royal Linen Manufactory of Ireland" and undertook to instruct the Irish in technical knowledge of the manufacture. To aid him in this he was given three assistants, at a salary of £120 per annum, and these he sent through the country to superintend the cultivation of flax and the finishing of the fabric.[4] One of them, Jean La Trobe, as has already been seen,[5] settled in

---

[1] Lewis, "Topographical Dictionary."
[2] Smiles, "Huguenots in England," p. 296 note.
[3] *Vide* p. 19.
[4] Smiles.
[5] *Vide* p. 108.

Waterford; another, William Crommelin, in Kilkenny.[1]
Crommelin introduced improvements into the machinery
which he had imported. He gave a premium of £5 for every
loom kept going, and in 1705 published in Dublin an " Essay
towards the Improving of the Hempen and Flaxen Manufactures of the Kingdom of Ireland."[2] In the same year the
Irish House of Commons declared that the linen weavers of
Lisburn should be made freemen wherever they chose to
reside,[3] and, to mark its appreciation of his services, Parliament voted the public thanks to Crommelin in 1707. Under
his fostering care Lisburn became a model and thriving town.
Fifty families came later to join the original seventy-five, and
the total strength of the Huguenot colony in Ulster soon
numbered some five hundred persons.[4] Crommelin's salary
was continued to his death, and the Linen Board, in recom-
mending the continuance of his grant after 1712, stated that
" The said Crommelin and Colony have been very serviceable
and greatly instrumental in the improving and propagating
the flaxen manufacture in the north part of this Kingdom."[5]
By 1727, when he died, Antrim, Down, Armagh, Tyrone and
Derry were fully embarked on the manufacture of linens.[6]

No one better fitted as " Overseer of the Linen Manufactory " could have been found by William than Louis
Crommelin, descendant of a wealthy and influential family
which had been engaged in the linen trade for nearly five
hundred years. The family estates were at Armandcourt,
near St. Quentin in Picardy, but the Crommelins had been
wise enough to realize their wealth and establish themselves
in Holland before the Revocation. Here they became great
merchants and, like the La Touches in Dublin, combined

[1] *Vide* p. 126.
[2] Smiles.
[3] Lane Poole, " History of the Huguenots of the Dispersion."
[4] McCall, " Our Staple Manufactures." Quoted Gill.
[5] Quoted, " Rise of the Irish Linen Industry," p. 19.
[6] Dobbs, " Essay upon the Trade and Improvement of Ireland." Quoted
Gill.

trade with banking. Their wealth enabled Louis to guarantee
the £10,000 necessary for the Irish undertaking; and his two
brothers, William and Samuel, to follow him there each with
a like sum. They were joined by their sisters, Jeanne and
Anne, wife of Isaac Cousin of Meaux,[1] and later by a third
brother, Alexander, while another sister, Marie, who had
married in Holland Major Nicolas De La Cherois, brought
their children, Samuel and Madeleine, to join their relatives
after his death.[2]

Burke[3] states that the Crommelins had been originally
Dutch with estates near Courtrai in the Low Countries, and
that in consequence of the persecutions of Alva they had
sought refuge in France. The original owner of the Armandcourt estates was Jean, son of Armand Crommelin. His
grandson, Louis, was born at St. Quentin in 1625, and married
Marie Metayer in 1648. By her he had eight children, who
nearly all fled to Holland before 1685. Of these, Louis
Crommelin, born 1650, married his cousin Anne in 1680 and
settled in Amsterdam. When he removed to Lisburn he was
accompanied by a son, who predeceased him there, and a
daughter Madeleine, who married Captain de Bernière from
Alençon, whose name is also found among those of the
Lisburn settlers.[4]

Alexander Crommelin, who had married Mademoiselle de
Lavalade in Holland, had two children, Charles, who died
unmarried, and Madeline, who married Archdeacon Hutchin-
son.[5] Burke speaks of another daughter, Mary, who married
Daniel De La Cherois of Donaghadee, but there would seem
to be a confusion here with Marie, granddaughter of Samuel
Crommelin and therefore grand-niece of Alexander, or with
Angelique Marie, daughter of Abraham Crommelin.

[1] Wagner MSS.
[2] *Ibid.*
[3] "Landed Gentry of Ireland."
[4] Wagner MSS.
[5] U.J.A., Vol. I. Art. "Lisburn."

Samuel married first Judith Truffet and secondly Louise de Belcastel, probably a sister of Pierre Belcastel Seigneur de Montvaillant, Marquis d'Avèze, a refugee officer from Languedoc, who obtained the Colonelcy of Caillemotte's Regiment after the death of that officer at the Boyne, took a prominent part in the Irish Campaign of 1690-91, was raised to the rank of Major-General in the Dutch Army, and was killed in the war in Spain in 1710.[1] By his first wife he had four sons, whose descendants, now extinct in the male line, are best illustrated by a tree:[2]

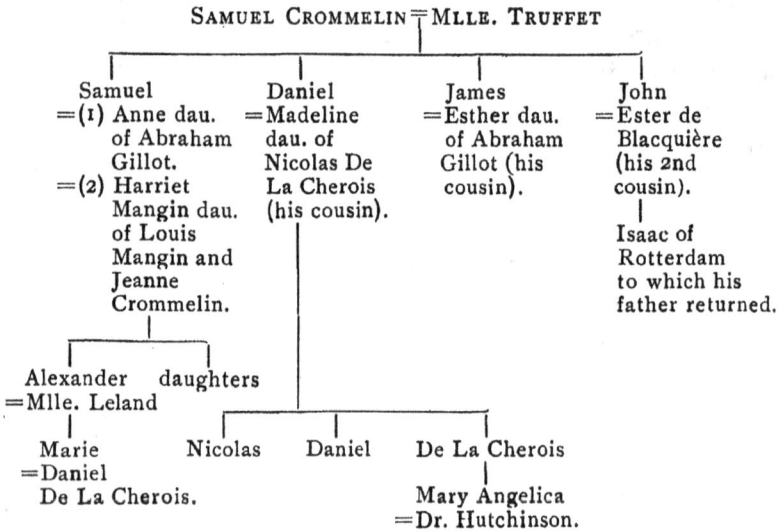

```
                SAMUEL CROMMELIN ╤ MLLE. TRUFFET
                                 │
    ┌───────────────┬────────────┼─────────────┬──────────────┐
  Samuel          Daniel        James          John
 =(1) Anne dau.  =Madeline     =Esther dau.   =Ester de
   of Abraham     dau. of        of Abraham     Blacquière
   Gillot.        Nicolas De     Gillot (his    (his 2nd
 =(2) Harriet     La Cherois     cousin).       cousin).
   Mangin dau.    (his cousin).                 │
   of Louis                                   Isaac of
   Mangin and                                 Rotterdam
   Jeanne                                      to which his
   Crommelin.                                  father returned.
    │
  ┌─┴──────────┐
 Alexander  daughters
=Mlle. Leland
   │
 ┌─┴──────┬─────────┬──────────────┐
Marie    Nicolas   Daniel       De La Cherois
=Daniel                             │
 De La Cherois.              Mary Angelica
                            =Dr. Hutchinson.
```

William Crommelin, as has already been stated, settled in Kilkenny and married Miss Butler, a connection of the Duke of Ormond. They had two children, a son Louis, who died unmarried, and a daughter Marianne.[3]

Of the Crommelin sisters, Jeanne married Abraham Gillot from Alençon, who also settled in Lisburn, and their daughter

---

[1] Lart, "Huguenot Pedigrees," Vol. II, p. 6.
[2] Based on details in the Wagner MSS.
[3] U.J.A., Vol. I. Art. "Lisburn."

married James, the son of Samuel Crommelin.[1] Anne is said by Burke to have married secondly at Lisburn Daniel De La Cherois, but left no descendants.

According to the Wagner Manuscripts the first Samuel Crommelin had a daughter Madeleine who married Captain Paul Mangin, though on this point some confusion occurs. Burke does not mention her, and Smiles states that Mangin married Louis Crommelin's daughter. Born in 1700 he came to Ireland from Metz,[2] and settled first in Lisburn, later removing to Dublin. He married twice, his second wife being Anne, daughter of Henri d'Aulnis de Lalande of the latter city,[3] and had three children, Alexander, Samuel and Harriet, who married the younger Samuel Crommelin.[4]

In the French Cemetery of Peter Street in Dublin a tombstone marked the resting-place of " Paul Mangin, Esq., Capt. in his Majesty's 46th Regiment of Foot who was born at Cologne-sur-Laspree adjoining to the City of Berlin the 5th day of June 1700, and departed this life in the City of Berlin the 17th day of April 1797. Also of his excellent and well beloved wife, Anne Henrietta d'Aulnis de Lalande, who was born in the City of London August 1714 and died in the City of Dublin January 1779."[5] Another stone in the same graveyard recorded the death of Colonel Samuel Henry Mangin in 1798 who left "a widow and eight children to deplore his loss," and of Alexander Mangin in June 1802.[6]

Marie De La Cherois, née Crommelin, the youngest sister, as has already been stated, brought her son and daughter to Lisburn. Here Madeleine married her cousin, Daniel Crommelin; while the son Samuel married Mademoiselle Sara

---

[1] Burke.
[2] " Huguenots in England."
[3] *Vide* p. 166.
[4] U.J.A., Vol. I. Art. " Lisburn."
[5] J.A.P.M.D., 1912.
[6] *Ibid.* Smiles states that many Huguenots of this name came to Ireland. It is also found in Waterford.

Cornière in 1734. Their third son, Samuel, born in 1744, assumed the additional surname of Crommelin, and became the head of the De La Cherois—Crommelin family of Carrowdore Castle, County Down; his son Nicolas being appointed J.P., D.L. and High Sheriff of the County.[1] The eldest son, Daniel, married Mary, daughter of Alexander Crommelin, and had three sons and a daughter. His eldest son and namesake was, like his cousin, J.P., D.L. and High Sheriff, but he died without issue, and the family descends from Samuel Louis, the second son, who died in 1836.

The Crommelin family has been treated of at length because it provides an admirable example of the intermarriage which took place amongst the Huguenots, both on the Continent and later in the Irish Settlements. Here alliances are made over and over again between the branches of the family, and the De La Cherois connection, formed in Holland, is made stronger by intermarriage among the junior members of the families in Ireland.

The De La Cherois came from Ham in Picardy, whence two sons of Claude De La Cherois, Nicolas and Bourjonval, who had been officers in the French Army, fled at the Revocation to join William of Orange. They both distinguished themselves during the Irish Campaign; Bourjonval was killed in a skirmish near Dungannon, but Nicolas, pensioned as a Major in Lifford's Regiment in 1698-99, survived. For his gallantry in an engagement he was made Lieutenant-Colonel, and was presented by the Government with a substantial monetary reward. He died curiously, "poisoned by the apothecary's mistake" in Lisburn in 1702. He married Marie, sister of Louis Crommelin, and his descendants have been dealt with among those of that family.[2] Daniel, a third son of Claude De La Cherois, came also to Ireland. He served in William's army and was pensioned as a Lieutenant in

---

[1] Burke, and Wagner MSS.
[2] Wagner MSS.

Lifford's Regiment.[1] He also married into the Crommelin family, his wife being Angelique Marie, daughter of Abraham Crommelin, who seems to have been another brother of Louis. They had an only daughter, Mary Angelica, who married Thomas Montgomery, last Earl of Mount Alexander, but left no descendants. Daniel De La Cherois seems to have been appointed Governor of Pondicherry by William III, and amassed a considerable fortune, although he is recorded as having drawn his pension as Lieutenant as late as 1727.[2] Two Mademoiselles De La Cherois followed their brothers to Ireland, having escaped in disguise from France to Leyden. Judith, who lived to the age of 113, died at her niece's residence of Mount Alexander.[3]

The Gillot family into which Jeanne Crommelin married has already been mentioned in connection with Portarlington.[4] Several Gillots were officers in the Navy of Louis XIV, and these emigrated to Holland at the Revocation, and were given commissions by William III. Their descendants settled at Lisburn.[5] The name Jellet, also found in this district, is French, but this family had made its home in Ireland before 1685. A William Jellet, born in England in 1632, settled in Dromore, County Down, and a Captain Henry Jellet served in Monk's Army in 1642.[6] An Edward Gillett was Mayor of Youghal in 1721, and a Richard Gillett Lieutenant of one of the Militia Companies in 1660;[7] while two Peter Guillots, probably father and son, obtained the Freedom of Cork as Protestant Strangers in 1699. It would thus seem that the family had become widely scattered throughout Ireland. A

---

[1] " Hiberniæ Notitia."
[2] Hug. Soc. Proc., Vol. VI, pp. 309-12, and MS. Pension List in Nat. Mus., Ire. This puzzling circumstance may perhaps indicate that there were two men of the same name.
[3] " Huguenots in England," Appendix.
[4] *Vide* p. 151.
[5] Smiles.
[6] U.J.A., Vol. I. Art. " Lisburn."
[7] *Vide* p. 71.

writer affirms that all four forms of the name Gillett, Gillot, Guillot and Jellet probably come from Gillot, the diminutive of Gilles (Giles).[1]

The family of de Blaquière, with which John Crommelin allied, came originally from Limousin. John de Blaquière fled to England in 1685 and married Mary de Varennes, the daughter of a refugee. One of his sons became a merchant in London, another settled in Lisburn with a sister who married John Crommelin, and the fifth son, John, Lieutenant-Colonel of the 17th Light Dragoons, became Secretary to the Legation in Paris, and subsequently Secretary to the Lord-Lieutenant in Ireland. Smiles states that he was made a Baronet in 1784, and in 1800 was raised to the Peerage as Lord de Blaquière of Ardkill,[2] but he must have achieved a very great age before receiving these dignities.

When Alexander Crommelin and his wife came to Lisburn they brought with them from London[3] Monsieur Charles De La Valade, brother of Madame Crommelin, to minister in the church which had just been erected for the settlement. De La Valade came of a family which had possessed large estates in Languedoc, but which had been forced to seek refuge in Holland.[4] Several members came thence to Ireland, and a second pastor of this name seems to have officiated in Lisburn for the two years between the ministries of Charles De La Valade and Saumarez Dubourdieu,[5] though it has not been possible to trace him. De La Valade's ministry lasted for forty years. He left an only daughter, Anne, who married in 1737 George Russell of Lisburn.[6]

Saumarez Dubourdieu was, Agnew[7] asserts, a grand-

[1] U.J.A., Vol. I. Art. "Lisburn."
[2] "Huguenots in England," Appendix.
[3] Hug. Soc. Pub., Vol. XXIX, p. 72.
[4] "Huguenots in England," Appendix.
[5] Hug. Soc. Proc., Vol. VI. "Projet de Colonisation."
[6] Smiles.
[7] "Protestant Exiles from France," Vol. II, p. 249.

nephew of Monsieur De La Valade, which probably accounts for his call to the ministry. His grandmother, a sister of the first pastor, married Jacques, Seigneur Du Bourdieu, who died before the Revocation. The widow escaped in disguise with her son to German Switzerland and thence to England, where she found refuge with her brother-in-law, the Rev. Jean Dubourdieu. The son, Jean Armand, who became a minister of the Savoy Church in London, married as his first wife Charlotte, said to have been Comtesse d'Espnage, and had an only child, Saumarez, born in London in 1717, who was educated in Trinity College, Dublin, and became the third and last minister of the French Church in Lisburn.[1] Jean Dubourdieu with whom Madame Jacques sought refuge, was the son of Isaac Dubourdieu who had been pastor of a church in Montpellier and had fled to England at the Revocation, where he officiated at the Savoy. His son was also a minister of this church, and served as chaplain to the three Dukes of Schomberg, attending the old Duke at the Boyne.[2] He was the author of many sermons and of " An Appeal to the English Nation," published to confute calumnies which had been levelled against the Huguenots in 1718, two years before his death.[3]

Saumarez Dubourdieu served the French Church in Lisburn for forty-five years, and when it was closed he joined the Established Church as Rector of Lambeg. His popularity in the neighbourhood is evinced by the fact that his life is said to have been the only one that the Insurgents of 1798 had agreed to spare.[4] He left three sons, John, Shem and Saumarez. The last became a military surgeon and died unmarried. Shem's descendants settled in Dublin; and John, who became Rector of Annahilt, County Down, was

[1] Wagner MSS.
[2] *Ibid.*
[3] " Huguenots in England," p. 259 and Appendix.
[4] Smiles, p. 298 note.

the author of the " Statistical Surveys " of the counties of Derry and Antrim, and the father of a family well represented in the British Army.[1]

The French Church at Lisburn continued, according to Dr. De La Cherois Purdon,[2] until 1798; according to Burn[3] until 1818. Writing in 1837 Lewis[4] states, " A large and handsome edifice now used as the Court-House of the Manor and for holding the petty sessions and other public meetings, was originally built and supported by Government as a Chapel for the Huguenot emigrants, whose descendants, having attached themselves to the Established Church, the ministers stipend has been discontinued, and the building appropriated to the above purpose."

As has already been stated in Chapter IV, the name Dubourdieu is noted by Gimlette in his article on Waterford, as is that of Perrin, though both belong to the north rather than to the southern settlements.

The Perrins were first represented in Ireland by Count Perrin who fled from Nouère where the family held estates. He settled in Lisburn, but later removed to Waterford, and there founded the family to which the Right Honourable Justice Perrin of the Irish Bench belonged.[5]

Another family of note in Ireland which originally settled in Lisburn was that of Saurin. It derived from Charles de Saurin of Calvisson near Nismes, who was an officer in the French Army. His great-grandson, an advocate at Nismes, fled at the Revocation to Geneva, but his three sons all took refuge in England.[6] One served as a Captain in William's army; Jacques, in 1701, became a minister of the French Church in Threadneedle Street,

---

[1] Agnew, Vol. II, p. 179, and Wagner MSS.
[2] U.J.A., Vol. I. Art. "Lisburn."
[3] " History of the Refugees."
[4] " Topographical Dictionary."
[5] " Huguenots in England," Appendix.
[6] U.J.A., Vol. I. Art. "Lisburn."

London, and then of that of the Hague,[1] where he died in 1730.

Louis, who died in Dublin in 1749, had been minister of the French Church in the Savoy and was recommended in the spring of 1727 to Archbishop Boulter by the Archbishop of Canterbury and the Bishop of London. " On Monday last," writes the Primate, " Mr. Saurin came to me with your Grace's letter. I recommended him to the Bishop of Kildare who installed him on Thursday in the Chantorship of Christ Church and is ready to do him what service lies in his power. I am glad to hear so good a character of this gentleman from your Grace and hope he may be of service in this Church. I shall very readily show him what favour I can."[2] Saurin also obtained the Deanery of St. Patrick's, Ardagh. He married Mademoiselle Cornel De La Bretonière,[3] and their son, James, born 1729, also took Holy Orders, and was appointed Vicar of Belfast. His sons were educated by Monsieur Dubourdieu in Lisburn. William, born 1758, entered Trinity College, Dublin, in 1775, was called to the Irish Bar, and in 1798 was offered the Solicitor-Generalship. This he declined as he wished to oppose the Union, and for the same reason refused to become one of the Union Peers, but in 1807 he accepted the position of Attorney-General for Ireland. He retired in 1831 and died eight years later. He had married Mary, sister of the Marquis of Thomond, and their son became Admiral Edward Saurin, R.N.[4] James Saurin rose to as high a position in the Church as his brother had held at the Bar. In 1783 he was ordained, and in 1800 was Rector of Resenallis, Queen's County. Seven years later he was appointed Rector of Donaghmore, and in 1819 rose to the Bishopric of Dromore,

---

[1] " Huguenots in England," Appendix.
[2] " Letters," Pub. Oxford, 1769.
[3] Hug. Soc. Pub., Vol. XXVI, pp. 35 and 152.
[4] U.J.A., Vol. I. Art. " Lisburn."

having been successively appointed Dean of Cork, Archdeacon of Dublin, and Dean of Derry. He died in 1824 and left descendants, one of his sons becoming Archdeacon of Dromore.[1]

Besides those of civilian settlers, some military names are found in the Lisburn colony. Thus Captain St. Sauveur of La Melonière's Regiment died of fever there during the Irish Campaign,[2] and Captain Desbrisay settled there,[3] although he appears later in Dublin, where Captain Theophilus Desbrisay is recorded as having been interred in the Boileau tomb in the Merrion Row French Cemetery in 1722, probably owing to the fact that Madeleine Desbrisay married Simeon Boileau of that city.[4] Louis Geneste Peteras de Cajarc, who fled from his estates in Guienne to join the army of William of Orange and fought in Cambon's Regiment at the Boyne, also made Lisburn his home, save between the years 1724 and 1731, when he resided in the Isle of Man. He left two sons, Louis and Daniel, the former of whom settled in the Isle of Man, and a daughter, Margaret.[5]

But the greater number of settlers in Lisburn were of the manufacturing class, who had come with the Crommelins to Ireland, or had been attracted there later by the growth of the linen trade. Of these Mark Henri Dupré was of importance, since he introduced reed-making as a branch of the industry. He had escaped at the Revocation to the south of Ireland, was resident in Dublin in 1690, and subsequently followed the Crommelins to Lisburn. His descendants were still to be found in Belfast at the end of the last century.[6]

[1] *Ibid.*
[2] Agnew, Vol. II, p. 183.
[3] U.J.A., Vol. I. Art. "Lisburn."
[4] J.A.P.M.D., 1912, and *vide infra* p. 216.
[5] Agnew, Vol. II, p. 233, and Smiles, "Huguenots in England," Appendix.
[6] Gill, p. 71 note, and the U.J.A., Vol. I. Art. "Lisburn."

Another follower of the Crommelins was the manufacturer Louis Roché, who died in Lisburn in 1726. His two daughters, Marie and Alice, married respectively Valentine Jones and Edward Masslin in the year of their father's death, and the descendants of the elder daughter were resident in Belfast when Smiles compiled his work.[1] At one period the Lisburn community appears to have had a French school or at least instruction in its native tongue, for the *Dublin Gazette* of December 1st, 1741, reports from Lisburn the death of Monsieur Nagons, " a French Schoolmaster of this town," who " was educated in France to be a Priest about 26 years ago," and when the Huguenot school in Dublin needed a master Monsieur Isaac Dufour of Lisburn was appointed.[2] He may have been the now unknown Huguenot who gave his name to Dufour Court near Weavers Square in that city, and he seems to have established a family in Dublin where his son, John Moses, was apprenticed in 1748 to the goldsmith James Vidouze.[3]

The author of the article on Lisburn, already so extensively quoted, from the old Ulster Journal of Archæology appends to his paper a list of settlers taken from the vestry books and registers. He states, however, that nothing further may be ascertained about them there, and some of the names listed by him, such as Birrell, Domville or Lascelles, are certainly not Huguenot. Amongst the more authentic is that of Blosset, and this is probably a connection of the Colonel of that name, who settled in Dublin during the reign of Anne. " Several Blossets," Smiles asserts, " fled to Holland and England at the Revocation." Chartres also occurs, which is found as a Huguenot name in Bandon and Belfast. Hignet belongs to Limerick as well as to Lisburn, as does Taverner;

---

[1] " Huguenots in England," Appendix, and U.J.A., Vol. I. Art. " Lisburn."
[2] *Vide* p. 228.
[3] C.H. & A.J., Vol. VIII, No. 53. " The Goldsmiths Co. of Dublin."

Valentin is localized also in Kilkenny; while Le Fevre and Du Four are found in Cork. Covert, too, belongs to this city, while Perdu is found in Youghal as well as Lisburn.

The Lisburn manufactory attracted, as was natural, most of the textile workers amongst the French settlers in the North, but in a lesser degree Dundalk and Lurgan also became centres of Huguenot industry.

With the encouragement of the Linen Board a colony of weavers under the brothers de Joncourt settled in the former town in 1736 to engage in the manufacture of cambric.

They had been recommended to Primate Boulter by Horace Walpole and the Duke of Dorset, and in a letter to the former dated April 28th, 1737, the Archbishop tells of the steps taken towards the organization of the settlement.

" Mr. de Joncourt has lately brought me the favour of yours of the 4th instant. On account of your former recommendation, I did him what service I could at the linen board, where we agreed with him and his brother on the terms for which they are to carry on the cambric manufacture; and gave one of the brothers money to go to France and bring over skilful workmen. Before his return we had fixed upon Dundalk for the place to settle that manufacture in, with the approbation of his brother, and since his return we have advanced money to send the workmen thither to begin their business."[1]

The Board promised to pay the de Joncourts £80 each for seven years " provided that they give satisfaction and that they are capable of improving the Linen manufacture "; £12 a year each for five years to two flax dressers and two weavers; and £8 per annum each to two spinning mistresses. They also undertook to provide a bleach-green with land and seed for flax growing.[2] A voluntary subscription was raised

[1] " Letters."

[2] Journals of the Linen Board, Dublin, 1784, under date April 24th, 1736.

and the manufactory was established on the estate of Lord Limerick,[1] who made himself responsible for the housing of the workmen.[2]

The de Joncourts seem to have been men of some resource, for in addition to cambric they further proposed to make in Dundalk large quantities of black soap " in a good and merchantable manner,"[3] and a grant was made to them for this purpose. No further mention, however, is made of the industry, and it does not seem to have met with the success which attended the cambric manufacture.

By 1739 this enterprise was bearing fruit, and in the *Dublin Gazette* for February 19th-23rd of that year a notice is printed calling " A General Meeting of the Governor and Company for carrying on the Cambric Manufacture in Dundalk or elsewhere in the kingdom of Ireland . . . in order to chuse a Governor and Assistants for the ensuing year as by their charter they are directed." The cambric found a ready market and seems to have been sold in Dublin by 1740 by the Misses Donaldson, " Milleners," on Essex Bridge,[4] although, according to Mr. Gill, " its manufacture made no great headway until after the middle of the century,"[5] and on November 7th, 1739, the Archbishop of Armagh, with Viscount Limerick, the Earl of Kildare and others, are found as sponsors for a petition for aid submitted to Parliament " on behalf of the Governor and Company for carrying on a manufacture for making cambric, black soap and bleaching linen in Dundalk or elsewhere."[6] It was " thriving " by 1770 as stated in a contemporary note by the editor of Archbishop Boulter's letters, but the French

---

[1] Note in Faulkner's Edition of " Letters of Archbishop Boulter," 1770.
[2] Journals of the Linen Board (Royal Irish Academy).
[3] *Ibid.*
[4] *Vide* advertisement in Faulkner's *Dublin Journal*, Dec. 13th-16th, 1740.
[5] " Rise of the Irish Linen Industry," p. 154.
[6] H.C.J., Nov. 7th, 1739.

element seems early to have disappeared, for John Arbuthnot, in making his report to the Linen Board in 1784, only mentions the thread works of a Mr. Wright and "linens and keatings" manufactured by Messrs. Page & Co. in the vicinity,[1] and Dalton, writing of Dundalk in 1864, states that "the place where the manufactory was located is now occupied by the Cavalry Barracks and few traces exist of what must at one time have been a very extensive establishment." He adds that "The Parliament granted bounties for the encouragement of this branch of industry which gave the name of 'Parliament Square' to the locality."[2]

Another proof that the French colonists made no very lasting impression on the neighbourhood is evinced by the fact that, after 1782, no separate pastor was appointed for them. From 1737 until that year Henri David Petitpierre, who had come from Tournai as minister at a salary of £60 per annum, served the congregation, but after his death or retirement the post was given to the Portarlington minister, Antoine Desvoeux, who, like his successors, must have held it merely as a sinecure in conjunction with his work in the Portarlington Church. He was succeeded on his death in 1792 by Jean Vignoles, also of Portarlington, and in 1813 Charles Vignoles succeeded to both churches. As late as 1801, however, the Treasury were authorized by an Act[3] to continue the allowance of £60 Irish paid to the minister. This Charles Vignoles continued to draw, even after becoming Dean of Ossory, until his death in 1877, when the allowance was abolished by the Treasury on the ground that the congregation had long ceased to exist.[4]

No record has survived of any of the settlers who accompanied the de Joncourts, but in the Dublin Diocesan Grant

---

[1] "Journals of the Linen Board."
[2] "History of Dundalk," pp. 184 and 331.
[3] 41 Geo. III, c. 32.
[4] From notes very kindly supplied by Mr. T. P. Le Fanu.

Books Mr. Le Fanu, to whose manuscript notes on Dundalk the present writer is greatly indebted, has been able to trace the marriage licences of a Magdelaine de Joncourt and John Briluin in 1739; of Isaac de Joncourt and Mary Hamilton in 1779, and of Anthony de Joncourt and Amelia Owens in 1799. Other marriages took place in the following century, the last mentioned occurring in 1836 between Mary de Joncourt (alias Cluff) and Alexander Patterson. It will be seen that in only one of these unions the principals seem both to have been of French extraction, and this intermarriage with Irish families may be one reason for the early disappearance of the colony. Further proof that this may have been the case is found in a reference made by Dalton to an old weaver named Flannegan, whom he encountered in Dundalk, who stated that his mother was a Frenchwoman, daughter of one Stephen Gidleau who had come to Ireland with the refugee weavers.[1] If these were typical of the marriages made by the colonists it is not surprising that the French names have disappeared.

Another cambric manufactory, with that of silk, was established by the Huguenot Goyer at Lurgan.

Peter Goyer, a native of Picardy, where he owned a farm and an extensive manufacture of cambric and silk, was forced to fly to Holland at the Revocation. His brother, less fortunate, was martyred during the Dragonnades. From Holland Goyer removed to England, and thence to Lisburn. Here, says Smiles, he established his cambric manufacture, which was later removed to Lurgan. His silk manufacture was destroyed in the Rebellion of 1798, but that of cambric survived.[2] One of his sons was a master in the Belfast Academy.[3]

---

[1] " History of Dundalk," p. 331.
[2] " Huguenots in England," p. 299.
[3] U.J.A., Vol. IX, p. 143. Art. " Belfast."

Lurgan was visited in 1690 by Dumont de Bostaquet in Schomberg's army, and here his relative, Captain Dumont of La Caillemotte's Regiment, died "avec une très grande résignation." "Je priai le squire Bromelay, seigneur de lieu, de trouver bon qu'on l'inhumât dans l'église." This was effected on payment of eight shillings for the minister and poor of the parish. Dumont himself nearly succumbed to the fever which carried off so many of Schomberg's men, but as he writes, "Dieu m'ayant comme fait descendre au tombeau m'en tira."[1]

Castleblayney in the County of Monaghan is given as a place of settlement in the "Projet de Colonisation" already quoted. A colony is said to have been established there from 1694-1695 under the care of a Monsieur Labat, perhaps an ancestor of the Labats of Youghal.[2] That this settlement was chiefly agricultural is proved by a Memoire contained in the Court collection in the library of Geneva. Monsieur Labat, it is there stated, "devra fournir du blé aux gens qui sont dans cette colonie, le don du roi," and the refugees were ordered "de vivre paisiblement et religieusement, d'être dociles et confiants envers leurs commissaires, de faire valoir les terres qu'ils recevront, avec défense de vendre ou tuer les chevaux ou bestiaux qu'on leur remet."

Houses were also provided and a minister was promised to the colonists, but care was taken that they should realize their responsibilities and that they should not abuse the indulgence shown to them. "S'ils se conduisent mal et qu'ils soient en scandale et non en edification aux naturels du pays, Mr. Blaney sera prié de faire mettre en prison les blasphémateurs, déserteurs ou dissipateurs des biens du roi ou de les faires travailler dans des carrières jusqu'à ce qu'ils aient rendu les avances qu'ils auront reçues." Despite or

---

[1] "Mémoires Inédits," pp. 263 and 264.
[2] *Vide* p. 77.

perhaps because of these careful regulations, however, the colony was one of the most short-lived in the history of the refugee settlements. Whether the settlers failed as agriculturalists or as examples of noble living to the neighbourhood, no further record remains of them. No minister seems to have held office amongst them, and by 1696 the colony had been broken up.[1]

That of Lambeg succeeded no better, though in this case a different type of settler was involved. It was made up of workmen who soon were attracted to the more prosperous Lisburn.[2] One of these settlers was René Bulmer who fled just before the Revocation, found his way to Lambeg and resided there in the Priory House. After the manner of the Irish in dealing with these foreign names, René became changed to Rainey and Bulmer to Boomer.[3]

A small settlement at Killeshandra is also mentioned in the "Projet de Colonisation," and among its members was a physician named Lanauze, much famed for his public spirit.[4] The name occurs again in Dublin, where a Mrs. Martha Lanauze, née La Pierre, who died in 1756, was buried in the French burial-ground near St. Patrick's. She was interred in the tomb of Mr. Stephen La Pierre,[5] a Dublin merchant whose son, George, was apprenticed to one of the city goldsmiths in 1723. The La Nauze family were resident in Dublin up to the present century.

Another colony was formed at Collon, County Louth,

[1] " Mémoire pour le comité d'Irlande," 1693 (MSS. Court). Quoted "Projet de Colonisation," Hug. Soc. Proc., Vol. VI.
[2] *Ibid.* Hug. Soc. Proc., Vol. VI, p. 429.
[3] U.J.A., Vol. I, p. 135. Art. "Lisburn," and "Huguenots in England," Appendix. 1889 Edition.
[4] Hug. Soc. Proc., Vol. VI.
[5] J.A.P.M.D., 1901.

and is mentioned by Arthur Young.[1] "Lord Chief Baron Foster," he writes, "received me in the most obliging manner. He has made the greatest improvements I have anywhere met with. He fixed a Colony of French and English Protestants on the land and they have flourished greatly."

The settlement at Belfast was made up for the most part of the rank and file of Schomberg's army;[2] hence it differed from the industrial communities about it, as well as from the more aristocratic military colonies of Portarlington and Youghal. Belfast had been known as a place of settlement even before the Revocation, and amongst its earliest settlers were the families of Le Burt and de Lolme. That there was much intercommunion between the northern settlements is proved by the fact that many names of the Lisburn Huguenots are also found in Belfast, such as Chartres, Saurin or Goyer.[3] Some of the Huguenots of the South seem also to be connected with this city. Colonel Chartres, who originally settled in Bandon, later moved to the North, and his descendants are found here, while the name Godsell, found in Belfast, is also localized in Cork in the eighteenth century.

Amongst the Huguenots in or near Belfast were the important families of Gaussen and Dolling. The last-named settler was descended from the younger son of Count Dolling, who fled from Toulouse to England about 1580. He settled in the Isle of Purbeck, but his descendant, Robert Dolling, removed to London. Here the family became localized until the great-grandson of Robert Dolling, the Rev. Boughey William Dolling, born 1782, was made Rector of Magheralin, County Down, and Precentor of Dromore. He died in 1853,

[1] " Tour in Ireland," p. 34.
[2] Agnew, Vol. III, p. 240, and Hug. Soc. Proc., Vol. VI, p. 428.
[3] U.J.A., Vol. IX, p. 142. Art. " Belfast."

having ministered at Magheralin for over forty-six years.[1] The article on Belfast in the Ulster Journal of Archæology[2] places the Dollings among the original settlers, but this is disproved by Burke.

The Irish branch of the Gaussen family is descended from David Gaussen of Lunel in Languedoc who fled from France in 1685. It is said that he wished to emigrate to England, but the ship in which he escaped was driven by a storm into Carlingford Bay, and he eventually settled in Newry where he died in 1751. He married Dorothy Fortescue, daughter of the then Vicar of Dundalk, and had three daughters and a son. The son, David, also resided at Newry, but his son, a third David, who died in 1832, moved to County Londonderry whence his second son, Charles, removed to Greystones, County Wicklow. The elder son, David, of Lakeview House, County Derry, was J.P. for the county.[3] Many members of the Gaussen family also settled in England and Geneva, and there were several branches of the family in France. Haag[4] mentions those of Saumur, Burgundy and Guienne, as well as that of Languedoc, and a Roman Catholic branch continued to hold land near Montpellier. Of the English settlers the most famous was Jean Pierre, Governor of the Bank of England, who died in 1778. They allied both in Geneva and England with the Bosanquet family, and this is cited by Smiles as a " singular illustration of how the Huguenot families kept together," since " the Gaussens, while neighbours of the Bosanquet family in France, twice intermarried with them there, and have, since the families settled in England, intermarried with them no less than four times."[5]

In addition to the names already mentioned, the writer on Belfast in the Ulster Journal gives others which are less easy

[1] Burke, " Landed Gentry."
[2] Vol. IX, p. 142.
[3] Burke, " Landed Gentry."
[4] " La France Protestante."
[5] " Huguenots in England," Appendix.

of proof. Some indeed are definitely not Huguenot, as Delap, a family which is stated by Burke to be Scottish in descent. The French settlers in Belfast had no church nor meeting-place of their own, and it would be an almost impossible task to trace them in the various parish registers.

Apart from these communities, the names of individual Huguenot settlers are found scattered over the north of Ireland. Thus Samuel Burdy of Dromore, County Down, the biographer of the Rev. Philip Skelton, was descended from a Huguenot soldier who was wounded at the Boyne. In his " Monody on the death of Mr. James Agnew, linen draper of Moss Vale near Lisburn," who died in March 1798, he states this in a burst of poetical autobiography:

> " Our common grandsire left fair Gallia's land
> Forced from her plains by Louis' stern command,
> Joined Great Prince William on Batavia's shore,
> At Boyne's fam'd waters heard the cannon roar."

Burdy entered Trinity College, Dublin, as a sizar in 1777 and graduated in 1781, being ordained two years later and appointed to the curacy of Ardglass. He came to know Skelton in 1781 and compiled the " Life "[1] that won Macaulay's praises in 1792. He published a " History of Ireland " in 1817, and died in 1820, being interred in Kilclief, where he had been a minister. " Bishop Reeves," says the Editor of Burdy's " Life of Skelton," " expressed the opinion that Burdy was probably an altered form of the name Dubourdieu."

The two Meaths seem to have been greatly favoured by foreign settlers. Under James I, Peter Boix and Thomas Petit held lands in Meath and Westmeath respectively;[2] while during the Viceroyalty of the Duke of Ormond, Gabriel Barbour, Thomas Francke, John Vye, William Lemon,

---

[1] " The Life of Philip Skelton," by Samuel Burdy. Dublin, 1792. Reprinted with Introduction by Norman Moore.

[2] " Huguenot Settlers," p. 148.

Richard De La Roche and John Fountain were all landholders in Meath.[1] At the same period Gimlette gives Philip Vientore as settled in County Louth and Ambrose Aungier and Nathaniel Philipot in Longford.

The Jourdain family was localized in Meath, where a John Jourdain, who married Blanche, daughter of Elie Bouhéreau of Dublin, was Rector of Dunshauglin in 1703;[2] and another Huguenot family to settle here was that of Beaufort.

Its members had originally resided in London where Daniel Augustus de Beaufort, born at Wesel in 1700, was pastor of the French Church of New Patent in 1728 and of the Savoy from 1732 to 1741.[3] In 1742 he was naturalized by Act of Parliament, and in the next year came to Dublin as chaplain to the Duke of Devonshire, then Lord-Lieutenant. He was appointed Vicar of Athlumney, and Rector of Navan, County Meath, and in 1758 Provost of Tuam. He had also held a ministry in the French Conformed Church in Dublin, succeeding Jean Pierre Droz in 1752, but this he resigned on his appointment to Tuam. He died at Mountrath in 1788.[4] He married Esther Gougeon and their son Daniel succeeded him as Rector of Navan and Athlumney in 1765, and held the living until 1818. He died in Cork and was buried in Brinny in 1821. Brady supposes him the father of William Lewis Beaufort, Rector of Brinny in 1810, who died in 1849, and gives a William Augustus Beaufort who was also Rector of Brinny in 1836.[5] In England, Admiral Sir Francis Beaufort, Hydrographer Royal, was a representative of the family.[6]

Another Huguenot family of Athlumney, County Meath, was that of Peter Metge (or De La Metgee) of Navan who escaped from Brittany, where he had large estates, at the

---

[1] *Ibid.*, p. 193, and Hug. Soc. Pub., Vol. XXVI, pp. 73-84.
[2] Lieut.-Col. Jourdain, " Ranging Memories," p. 9.
[3] " Huguenots in England," Appendix.
[4] Hug. Soc. Proc., Vol. VIII, p. 129. " Huguenot Churches of Dublin."
[5] Brady, " Records of Cork, Cloyne and Ross."
[6] " Huguenots in England," Appendix.

Revocation and settled at Athlumney. He married Joyce Hatch and had four daughters, who married into Irish families, and a son, Peter. The elder Peter died in 1735, the younger in 1774, leaving four sons and eight daughters. The elder son, Peter, Baron of the Exchequer and M.P. for Boyle, married the second daughter of Sir Marcus Lowther Crofton, Bart., and had a daughter and an only son, Peter, who died unmarried in 1794. The second son, John, was Captain of the 4th Dragoons, M.P. for Dundalk in the Irish Parliament and for Boyle in the Imperial Parliament, and Deputy Auditor-General of the Irish Treasury. He married a daughter of Francis, Baron of Athenry, and secondly Henrietta, daughter of Henry Cole Bowen of Bowen's Court, County Cork, by whom he had three sons and two daughters. Two of the sons dying without issue, the present representatives of the family descend through the second son.[1]

No record of the Huguenots in the north of Ireland can omit the name of Dean Drelincourt of Armagh. Born in Paris in 1644, he was the son of Charles Drelincourt, the famous Huguenot Pastor of Charenton, who, Gimlette states, had become so intimate with Ormond in France that on the latter's return to Ireland he had entrusted his youngest son to his care.[2] Agnew, however, asserts that his employment by the Duke may have been due to the services of his brother Charles, who held the post of physician to William III.[3] However he obtained the position, Pierre, who was educated at Geneva,[4] entered the Church of England and became chaplain to the Duke and tutor to his grandson, and in this capacity he was chosen by the Huguenots of Dublin to present their thanks to Ormond for his reception of the refugees in 1681. In the same year, having graduated M.A. in Dublin

---

[1] Burke.
[2] " Huguenot Settlers," p. 238.
[3] " Protestant Exiles," Vol. III, p. 195.
[4] " Huguenots in England," Appendix.

University, he was made Precentor of Christ Church, and in 1683 Archdeacon of Leighlin, obtaining the rectories of Shankill and Powerstown in that diocese. He became Dean of Armagh in 1691, with the rectories of Armagh and Clonfeacle,[1] and died at the age of seventy-six in March 1720, as stated on the monument placed in Armagh Cathedral by his wife to record a name " Victorious over death and dear to fame." Since his preferments were not filled, however, until two years later, Agnew thinks that some mistake as to the date may have been made on the monument.[2]

The Drelincourt generosity was well known. The Blue Coat Hospital, established in Dublin by Charter of Charles II, owed much to the Dean, who left it £800 on his death; and the French Church in Dublin obtained a legacy of £500. In 1732 his widow founded and endowed a school called the " Drelincourt Charity " in Armagh, and in Wales a chapel and school were also founded by her known as Birse-Drelincourt. This, with other evidence, has given rise to the supposition that she was probably an heiress of that country. The Drelincourts' only child, Anne, was married in 1739 to Lieutenant-Colonel Hugh, last Viscount Primrose, who died two years later. She died in London in 1775, but she forgot neither her ancestry nor her father's deanery, for amongst her bequests was £200 Irish " for the marrying or settling in any way of business four young women, those of Armagh or of French extraction to have the preference."[3]

Another Huguenot cleric who obtained preferment in Armagh was the Rev. Pierre Bouquet de St. Paul. He was ordained priest at Fulham in 1711, ministered to the French congregation in Wexford and then in St. Patrick's, Dublin, and resigned this post on being appointed Rector of Carling-ford, County Louth, in 1735. He married Marianne Darassus

[1] Gimlette, p. 238.
[2] " Protestant Exiles," Vol. II, p. 222.
[3] Ibid.

in Dublin in 1716, and the last of their children died in 1787.
He obtained the D.D. degree of Dublin University in 1727.[1]
Gimlette[2] assigns a Huguenot ancestry to the Margetson
family, of which a member was Primate during the Viceroyalty of Ormond. Dr. Margetson, his son, represented
Armagh City in the Irish Parliament and was instrumental
in the establishment of the first French Church in St. Patrick's,
Dublin, of which he became churchwarden. "The name
was originally Argesson, so called from their place in France.
John d'Argesson in 1499 married Louisa Du Puy and had two
sons, John who fought at Pavia, and Peter who fled to
England on account of his religious opinions, in the sixteenth
century," and became the ancestor of the Irish Archbishop.
The family, adds Gimlette, now reside in Sussex.

Little now remains to mark the Huguenot settlements in
the North. The "trim cottages, shaded by trees which they
had planted to remind them of the villages they had left in
Sunny France,"[3] are no longer to be distinguished around
Lurgan; their gardens, which Skelton instanced as affording
the Irish "a useful example of neatness and good economy,"[4]
have disappeared; and a serious fire in Lisburn in 1707[5] must
have removed all traces of the original houses built for the
reception of the refugees. Nevertheless the linen trade
remains as their best monument in Ireland. "Was it not
God who gave you a peace of sixty-four years and the French
Refugees?"[6] asked Skelton in 1751. . . . "The men who
planted this trade among us which in the space of half a
century hath turned our wilderness into a garden."

---

[1] Hug. Soc. Proc., Vol. VIII, p. 87. "The Huguenot Churches of
Dublin and their Ministers."

[2] "Huguenot Settlers," p. 232 note.

[3] Sermon of Professor Savory delivered at a Huguenot commemoration
service at Carrickfergus, Oct. 25th, 1931. Reported in Hug. Soc. Proc.,
Vol. XIV, p. 426.

[4] "The Case of Protestant Refugees from France Considered."

[5] Lewis, "Topographical Dictionary."

[6] "The Case of Protestant Refugees."

CHAPTER VIII

THE WESTERN SETTLERS

As might be expected, the Huguenots chose the line of least resistance in forming their settlements, and either remained in the ports at which they had arrived or went to special towns, such as Portarlington or Lisburn, which had been prepared for their reception. Few penetrated to the west of Ireland, which was both difficult of access and lacked the advantages for trade which their geographical position gave to the eastern counties; nevertheless a few French names are connected with Limerick, Galway, Sligo and Mayo.

Smiles states that Huguenot settlers in Limerick established the lace and glove trade,[1] but Mrs. Hall in speaking of the city, mentions that its famous lace was introduced by a Mr. Walker from England in 1829, who brought over lacemakers from Nottingham to instruct the Irish in the art;[2] and no mention of Limerick as a place of settlement is made in the " Projet de Colonisation," nor by other writers.

It is possible that the lengthy siege which the city sustained made the Huguenots more unpopular here than elsewhere in Ireland, and Lenihan states that in 1698 " To the great relief of the citizens such Dutch Guards and French Refugees that had remained were ordered away."[3] There are, however, some isolated instances of settlers here, such as the Le Froys, the Delmeges and the D'Esterres.

[1] " Huguenots in England," p. 299.
[2] " Tour in Ireland."
[3] " History of Limerick."

The Lefroy family seems to have come originally from Picardy; but an Antoine Lefroy of Cambrai, flying from the persecutions of Alva, settled in England during the reign of Elizabeth. He joined the refugee congregation in Canterbury, where his descendants were silk dyers until the death of Thomas Lefroy in 1723. The latter left a son, Anthony, of Canterbury, who died in Leghorn in 1779; and his son, Lieutenant-Colonel Anthony Lefroy, settled in Limerick. Another son, Isaac, Fellow of All Souls and Rector of Ashe and Compton, re-established the English branch of the family.[1] Lieutenant-Colonel Lefroy was born in 1742 and died in 1819. He married Anne, daughter of Colonel Gardiner, and had four sons and five daughters. His daughters married into various county families, and of his sons, one became Captain in the 65th Regiment, another, Benjamin, was a Captain in the Royal Artillery and J.P. for County Kildare; the fourth was killed in action as a midshipman on the *San Fiorenzo* in 1805; and the eldest, Thomas Langlois, of Carriglas Manor, born in 1776, became Lord Chief Justice of Ireland, having been called to the Bar in 1797 and appointed a Bencher of the King's Inn in 1819. He represented Dublin University in Parliament from 1830 until 1841, when he was appointed Baron of the Exchequer, and he became Lord Chief Justice in 1852. He married, in 1799, a daughter of Jeffry Paul of Silver Spring, County Wexford, and left four sons on his death in 1869.[2]

The family of Delmege of Castle Park and Rathkeale, County Limerick, was Alsatian in origin and, according to Burke, descended from Adam Dolmage who fled from France to Ireland during the reign of Louis XIV. His brother, Julius, sought refuge in Jamaica, and there founded a family which became extinct in 1835. Adam Dolmage settled in Rath-

---

[1] "Huguenots in England," Appendix.
[2] Burke, "Landed Gentry of Ireland."

keale and had a grandson, Adam John, Captain of the Loyal German Fusiliers in 1778. He married Eliza Powell and had five sons. The third son, Christopher, born in 1783, married Martha, daughter of John Yielding, and, establishing himself at Castle Park, founded that branch of the family. The eldest son, Julius, a Captain in the 4th King's Own Regiment, born in 1772, succeeded his father at Rathkeale and married, in 1799, Susanne de Gorrequer of Brittany. He died in 1849, leaving two sons and three daughters.[1]

The D'Esterres are of noble origin and claim descent from the Counts of Aix. At the Revocation Henri D'Esterre was forced to seek refuge in Holland. Here he married a Dutch lady of noble birth, Annie Amy Van Boffar, and with her removed to Ireland, where they purchased an estate in County Clare named by them Castle Henry. They are reported to have sailed up the Shannon bringing with them an immense amount of treasure in money, jewels and valuable china and table linen, " enough to supply twenty families," and thus seem to have been more fortunately circumstanced than the majority of the refugees. Possibly because of this they early became part of the Irish gentry around them. Their son Henry married, in 1724, Lucia Norcott at Springfield, County Cork, and their only daughter Mr. Darby of Leap Castle in the King's County. Henry D'Esterre died in 1752 aged sixty-six, and was buried at Six Mile Bridge in County Clare. He left two sons, Norcott and Henry, and three daughters. Of these Annie married Michael Parker of Hilbrook in 1761, and her brother, Norcott, married her husband's sister, Annie. Norcott had two sons, William, the Captain of an Indiaman, and Captain Norcott D'Esterre of the Royal Marines, who lost his life as the result of his famous duel with Daniel O'Connell.[2] Henry D'Esterre the younger was Sheriff of

---

[1] *Ibid.*

[2] Notes on the Family of D'Esterre (MS.), compiled in 1892, in the possession of Miss D'Esterre of Dublin.

Limerick in 1789 and Mayor in 1793.[1] Members of the family removed to England and Canada, and the remaining representatives of the Irish branch are now resident in Dublin, by whose kindness the writer has been permitted to utilize the above notes.

Nicholas Bonfoy, who resided in Limerick in the eighteenth century, may have been of Huguenot origin. He obtained the Freedom of the City in a silver box, the gift of "The Corporation of the City of Limerick to Nicholas Bonfoy, Esquire." "Neither McGregor nor Ferrar's History of Limerick mentions Bonfoy," writes Mr. Day of Cork, "but he must have been a Huguenot."[2]

Other names that may represent Huguenot refugees are those of Councillor John Tounadine, who was Sheriff of Limerick in 1764; Isaac Clampett who was Mayor in 1739; John Tavernor who was Sheriff in 1751,[3] and whose surname occurs amongst the Lisburn Huguenots listed by Dr. Purdon;[4] and Daniel Hignette who was Sheriff in 1671,[5] and who is recorded by Gimlette as a foreign settler and the owner of lands in County Cork.[6] This name also occurs amongst those of the Lisburn Huguenots.

Some important Huguenot names are connected with Killaloe, where James Abbadie held the Deanery from 1699 to 1724 and Dr. Richard Chenevix the Bishopric before his translation to that of Waterford in 1745, where the history of his family has been recorded.

James Abbadie was born at Nay in Bearn in 1654. He took the degree of Sedan, one of the four Huguenot Universi-

---

[1] Lenihan.

[2] C.H. & A.J., Vol. V, No. 44. Article by Robert Day on "The Freedoms of the City of Cork."

[3] Lenihan.

[4] U.J.A., Vol. I. Art. "Lisburn."

[5] Lenihan.

[6] "Huguenot Settlers," p. 194.

ties of France,[1] in his eighteenth year, and subsequently settled in Berlin. This he left to accompany Schomberg to England and thence on the Irish Campaign, during which he was one of the chaplains present at the Boyne. He was appointed minister of the Savoy Church in London and was honoured by being selected to preach the funeral oration on the death of Queen Mary.[2] In 1699 he received the Deanery of Killaloe, which he held for twenty-five years, and would have obtained that of St. Patrick's had he been proficient in English. Failing this, and considering "the small remainder of life he is likely to live," the Primate, in the summer of 1726, furnished him with letters of recommendation to Lord Carteret and to Dr. Gibson, then Bishop of London, in which he states "The bearer is Mr. Abbadie, Dean of Killaloe, one who for many years has made a figure in the world by the writings he has published. I find upon enquiry he was by King William recommended to the Government here for somewhat considerable and would have had the Deanery of St. Patrick's but that, having no knowledge of our language, it was thought improper to place him in the greatest preferment in this city.—He has firmly adhered to His Majesty's family here in the day of trial, and is every way a worthy man."[3] The writings referred to are possibly the "Defence of the British Nation," published in 1693, and "L'Art de se Connaitre Soi-même." He also published in Berlin a treatise on "The Truth of the Christian Religion" which caused Madame de Sevigné, although an enemy of the Huguenots, to declare that she did not believe "that any one ever spoke of religion like this man."[4] A copy of this book is preserved

[1] The others were at Montauban, Nismes and Saumur.

[2] Smiles, pp. 252, 253.

[3] "Letters of Hugh Boulter, Lord Primate of Ireland." "It is a curious illustration of the manner in which Church patronage was dealt with in Ireland," writes Lecky, "that Abbadie was promised the first considerable preferment that fell vacant although he was entirely unable to speak English." "History of Ireland," Vol. I, p. 353.

[4] Quoted Smiles, p. 252.

in Marsh's Library in Dublin with the interesting inscription "Don de l'auteur—Bouhéreau" recorded on its fly-leaf.[1] Abbadie received the desired position in London and died at Marylebone in his seventy-third year in 1727.[2] While in Ireland he resided occasionally at Portarlington, where reference occurs in the registers to "le Doyen de Cilalou," and where a Cornet Daniel d'Abbadie of the Earl of Galway's Horse, who was pensioned on the Irish Establishment from 1699 to 1727 and who may have been some connection of the Dean, was living about 1719.[3]

Paul Amyrault, who has been dealt with in connection with Carrick, was Chancellor of Killaloe in 1667, and Joseph Amyrault, who was probably his son, was Archdeacon of the same diocese in 1690.[4]

Two other French clerics of importance in the west of Ireland were the Rev. Theophilus Brocas, D.D., and the Rev. Peter Maturin.

Brocas came of a noble family which held an estate at Casteljaloux in Guienne. Gabriel La Motte Brocas, the founder of the Irish branch of the family, escaped at the Revocation, served in the army of William of Orange and settled in Ireland in 1704.[5] His son, Theophilus, who was born a year later, was educated at the Cathedral School in Dublin and entered Trinity College.[6] He took Holy Orders and was appointed by the Crown to the Deanery of Killala and to the Vicarage of St. Anne's, Dublin, where he died in 1766. For his valuable work in promoting the arts and manufactures of Ireland he was presented with the Freedom of the City in a gold box. He left one son, the Rev. John Brocas, D.D., who succeeded him in the Deanery and was

---

[1] U.J.A., Vol. III. Art. "Portarlington."
[2] This date is given by Smiles. Agnew gives 1737.
[3] Agnew, Vol. II, p. 102.
[4] *Vide* p. 121.
[5] Hug. Soc. Proc., Vol. I, p. 334, and XXVII, p. 223.
[6] Parish Register Society, Vol. II, 27.

also appointed Rector of Monkstown, County Dublin, and chaplain to the Military Chapel at Ringsend. He died in 1806 leaving an only son, the Rev. Theophilus Brocas, Rector of Strabane, Derry, who died without issue, and a sister, Georgiana, who married in 1804 Robert Lindesay, Esq., Captain of the Louth Militia, through whom the family survives.[1]

The Rev. Peter Maturin was the son of Gabriel Maturin, a French pastor who, after an imprisonment of twenty-six years in the Bastille, escaped to Ireland a cripple. The son was made Dean of Killala, and his son, Gabriel Jacques, born in Utrecht in 1700, was appointed to the Deanery of St. Patrick's, Dublin, in succession to Dean Swift.[2] From him descended the Rev. C. Maturin, Senior Fellow of Trinity College and Rector of Fanet, and the Rev. C. R. Maturin, author of " Bertram."[3]

Besides deaneries the West afforded two earldoms to French refugees. The history of the Earl of Galway has already been traced in dealing with Portarlington.[4] It remains to mention the Trench, or La Tranche, family whose descendants became the Earls of Clancarty and Ashton.

Many inconsistencies have arisen in the varying accounts of this family. Smiles states that it derives from Frédéric De La Tranche, who fled to England after the Massacre of St. Bartholomew from the Seigneury of La Tranche in Poitou, and settled in Northumberland.[5] Gimlette suggests that John Trench, who in Elizabeth's reign engaged in the manufacture of textiles with the La Cocque brothers, was an ancestor of the family, but points out that he is described as a " Norfolk gentleman " and that the name occurs in the

---

[1] " Huguenots in England," Appendix.
[2] Gilbert, " History of Dublin," Vol. III, p. 197.
[3] " Huguenots in England," Appendix.
[4] *Vide* p. 138.
[5] " Huguenots in England," Appendix.

Registry of the French Church at Norwich.[1] A tombstone in Clongill old churchyard near Kells marked the grave of "Thomas Trynch, Clerk, Rector sometime of this Church," who died in March 1631, and described him as "born of an illustrious and unconquered Scottish family";[2] and, lastly, one tradition states that Frédérick fled at the Massacre of St. Bartholomew, while another maintains that he gained distinction in the Siege of La Rochelle.[3]

Mr. Austen Leigh in his article on the Trench family, in Volume VIII of the Proceedings of the Huguenot Society, based largely on the "Memoir" compiled for private circulation by Mr. Thomas Cook Trench, inclines to the belief that they may not have been Huguenots at all since a family of the name was existing in Scotland in the fifteenth century and Trenches were resident in Gressenhall, Norfolk, long before 1572.

The Earl of Clancarty, however, who compiled a Memoir of his family in 1802,[4] seems to have had no doubts as to their French origin.

According to the Memoir Frédérick De La Tranche fled after 1572 to Northumberland, as stated by Smiles, who may have quoted from it. He there married Margaret Sutton and had three sons, Thomas, James and Adam. He later crossed into Scotland, where he died in 1580, and thus his son, who removed to Ireland and held the living of Clongill, is described as Scotch. This son is called "Thomas" on his tombstone, but it was James Trench, according to Mr. Austen Leigh, who took Holy Orders, married Margaret, daughter of Lord Montgomery, and came to Ireland in 1605, where he was given the Rectory of Clongill by the Bishop of Meath, Lord Montgomery's brother. His daughter married her first

---

[1] "Huguenot Settlers," p. 186.
[2] J.A.P.M.D., Vol. III.
[3] Hug. Soc. Proc., Vol. VIII, p. 356.
[4] Printed in Playfair's "Family Antiquity."

cousin, Frederick, son of Thomas Trench, who also settled in Ireland, purchasing Garbally Castle, County Galway, which remained the seat of the elder branch of the family until 1810. The latter died in 1669, leaving three sons, Frederick, John and William. Frederick and John both served as guides to the army of William III in the Aughrim Campaign of 1691, and the house at Garbally was lent as a military hospital. John became Dean of Raphoe.

The great-grandson of Frederick, the Dean's brother, Power Keating Trench, born in 1741, M.P. for Galway and Colonel to the Galway Militia, was raised to the Peerage in 1797 and later advanced to a Viscounty and Earldom with the title of Earl of Clancarty. He died in 1805. His fourth child was Power Trench, later Bishop of Waterford and Archbishop of Tuam.

The grandson of the Dean of Raphoe married Mary, heiress of Francis Sadleir of Sopwell Hall, County Tipperary, and his son Frederick, M.P. for Portarlington, was created Baron Ashton of Moat in 1800. A younger son, Richard, married in 1803 Melesina, granddaughter of the Right Rev. Richard Chenevix, Bishop of Waterford,[1] and was the father of Richard Chenevix Trench, Archbishop of Dublin.[2]

At one period of its history Sligo was governed by a French refugee. This was René De La Fausille of Anjou, who before the Revocation had been Captain of the Royal Regiment of La Ferté. He emigrated to Switzerland and thence to Holland, where he entered the service of William of Orange. He was made Captain of Grenadiers in Caillemotte's Regiment and was so severely wounded at the Boyne that he was rendered unfit for further military service. In reward for his conspicuous bravery Smiles states that William appointed him Governor of Sligo Port, Town and County,

[1] *Vide* p. 95.
[2] Hug. Soc. Proc., Vol. VIII, p. 370.

with a pension of ten shillings a day.[1] He could not, however, have obtained this post immediately, for he does not
appear in the list of Governors and Deputy Governors compiled by Crossly in 1699 from a commission of William III,[2]
and he was, in fact, kept on full pay till this date as is evinced
in the Return of French Pensioners on the Irish Civil List in
1702. He is there described as Deputy Governor of " Slegoe "
with a pension of six shillings a day, and it is stated that he
had served in Holland and Ireland for twelve years and was
disbanded as " lamed " in 1699. He is given as possessing
£700 and a farm of £15 a year, and as having " a numerous
family." He had married outside the Huguenot circle, his
wife being a Miss Jane Feltman, and the " numerous family "
consisted of four daughters and two sons. The elder, John,
was a Brigade-Major and fought at Fontenoy and Dettingen.
He later became Major-General and Colonel of the 66th
Regiment and died on board H.M.S. *Marlborough* off Cuba
in 1762. He left only one child, a daughter, and as his only
brother died unmarried the family became extinct in the
male line.[3]

Hardiman, the historian of Galway, makes no reference
to any French settlers residing in that town, but in the list
of Mayors and Aldermen quoted by him occurs the name of
James Ribet Vigie, who seems to have found his way to
Galway from Cork. In the latter city, as has already been
shown, he was sworn free gratis amongst other refugees on
February 18th, 1685, as a " poor distressed French Protestant
forced to flee by reason of ye persecution."[4] Nine years later
he appears as Sheriff in Galway and, in 1703, as Mayor. A
Commission of Array of three Foot Companies, drawn up on

---

[1] " Huguenots in England," Appendix; also Hug. Soc. Proc., Vol. VI,
p. 318, and IX, p. 588.
[2] *Vide* article by H. A. S. Upton in Journal R.S.A.I., Vol. LV, Part I.
[3] " Huguenots in England," Appendix, and Hug. Soc. Proc., IX, p. 588.
[4] *Vide* p. 30.

the accession of the Queen, includes him as Lieutenant, and, in 1715, another Commission of Array of five Companies returns Alderman Vigie as Captain of the 2nd Company. He was dead by 1740, but he left a son to fill his place, for in the Militia Returns of that year James Ribett Vigie, Esq., is Captain of the 5th Company "vice J. Ribett Vigie, Senior, deceased."[1] The son may have been that "James Ribett" who was Sheriff in 1722, although this name may be a misspelling of Rivett or Revett found in the list of Mayors in 1692, 1727 and 1761, and amongst the Sheriffs in 1673, 1725 and 1773.[2] He cannot, however, have held his position in the Militia for any length of time, for in the Dublin newspaper, *Pue's Occurrences*, dated April 1741, occurs the entry "died James Ribet Vigie, Esq., Barrick Master of Gallway."

Hautenville and Feuquire are other Huguenot names found in the list of Aldermen of Galway. In 1719 a John Hautenville appears as Sheriff, and at the same period this name may be traced amongst the Huguenots of Dublin, where a Daniel Hautenville was living in 1720.[3]

Agnew gives a Feuquire in a list of Huguenot merchants of London under date 1744,[4] but the name appears at an earlier period in Ireland, for in Galway a John Feuquire (or Fenquire) served as Sheriff in 1701 and again in 1703, and at the same time was included as an officer in the Militia. By 1740 he, like Vigie, was dead, for in the Militia Returns made at that date Robert Cook, Alderman, is recorded as First Lieutenant in the 4th Company "vice J. Feuquire, deceased."[5] The name does not reappear, and it is possible that, if he had descendants, they removed to London.

Other names which may be Huguenot, but whose origin it has not been possible to establish, are Amory, Cambie,

[1] Hardiman, " History of Galway," Part I, Ch. 7.
[2] *Ibid.*, Part II.
[3] *Vide* Registers of the French Churches.
[4] " Protestant Exiles," Vol. III, p. 212.
[5] Hardiman, Part II.

Camel, Dorsay and Semper, all to be found among the Aldermen of Galway;[1] while a William De La Mere is recorded by Gimlette as the holder of a property of 2,472 acres in the county under the Duke of Ormond.

Apart from those mentioned in the foregoing pages, it has proved impossible to discover anything further of the Huguenots in the West. If other refugees sought shelter there they must have early intermarried with the Irish families around them, and thus lost their individuality; a supposition which is all the more likely when the isolation of the western districts at that period, which would tend to cut the settlers off from the other French colonies in the country, is taken into account. No reference is made to them by any contemporary historian; Young,[2] who refers to the Palatines in Limerick, completely ignores the Huguenots, and writers on the western counties of Ireland have followed in his steps.

[1] *Vide* Hardiman, Part II.
[2] " Tour in Ireland."

CHAPTER IX

THE HUGUENOTS OF DUBLIN AND ITS ENVIRONS

WHEN in 1733 the Portarlington Huguenots petitioned the Lord-Lieutenant for an increase in the salary of their minister, they stated that their settlement was, with the exception of Dublin, the most considerable in Ireland;[1] it would thus seem that by this date the French colony in the latter city had established itself as the largest and most influential in the kingdom.

Refugees of all classes, trades and professions found their way to Dublin, and formed themselves into Calvinistic or conforming congregations according to the strictness of their belief. Thus immigrants from Spitalfields removed there to engage in the manufacture of tabinets, as the weavers from Norwich and Canterbury had come to Carrick and Clonmel. Officers on pension made their home in the capital as others had done in Portarlington and Youghal; business and professional men flourished in Dublin as in Waterford and Cork; and the linen weavers of the North were anticipated by the colony at Chapelizod established by the Duke of Ormond.

Dublin, therefore, provides a model in miniature of every type of Huguenot community throughout the country, and has been placed at the close of these chapters on their history as a summary of the whole.

As in Waterford and Cork, a foreign element, other than

---

[1] *Vide* p. 149.

that provided by the Danes, had existed from an early period among the citizens of Dublin, and the Vicus de la Rochel, mentioned in the records of Christ Church,[1] proves the presence of merchants from La Rochelle, even before the Huguenot immigration.

Of the earlier Huguenots connected with Dublin, Jean de Beaulieu, who brought with him some of the refugees from the Southampton colony, was perhaps the most important. He had escaped to Valenciennes from Poitou and thence to England, and the baptism of a son of " Jehan de Beaulieu de Valentienne " et de " Sara Van Houen de Londres sa femme " is recorded in the Southampton Register in 1567.[2] Later he removed to Ireland and settled in Dublin, but on the passing of the Edict of Nantes he seems to have returned to Languedoc, whence other members of the family fled when the Edict was revoked.

Jacques de Boileau, Seigneur de Castelnau and Councillor of Nismes, born 1626, died, after nearly eleven years' confinement in a French prison, in 1697. His son, Charles, fled to England and served as a Captain of Infantry under Marlborough at Blenheim. He left the Army in 1711 and lived at Southampton till 1722, when he settled as a wine merchant in Dublin. He had married Marie Collot d'Escury (or Descury) in that city in 1703, and on his death there in 1733 he left, amongst eighteen children, a son, Simeon, to carry on his business,[3] a daughter, Margaret, who married the Rev. Jean Pierre Droz, and Marie, who became the wife of Henry Hardy of Cork.[4] Simeon, who married Madeleine Desbrisay, died in 1767 and was buried in the Merrion Row cemetery.[5] He was succeeded by Solomon Boileau, born 1745, who, like his grandfather, had an army career before

---

[1] Harris, " History and Antiquities of Dublin," quoted Gimlette.
[2] Hug. Soc. Pub., Vol. IV, p. 39.
[3] Lart, " Huguenot Pedigrees," Vol. II, p. 13.
[4] *Vide* p. 53.
[5] J.A.P.M.D., 1912, and *vide supra*, p. 188.

entering business, having served as a Lieutenant in the 76th Foot before becoming a bank clerk. He was later appointed cashier in Finlay's Bank in Dublin, and in 1810 was drowned in the Dee at Chester. He married Dorothy Gladwell in 1766 and had nine children, amongst them Simeon Peter, who married a descendant of the De Renzy family and was the father of Major-General Boileau. John Peter, a younger brother of Solomon Boileau, who settled at Barnes, was the father of Sir John Boileau created a baronet in 1869.[1]

Marie Collot d'Escury, with whom Charles Boileau allied, was the daughter of David d'Escury, a fellow officer from Azuy-le-Rideau in Touraine who, at the beginning of the persecutions, escaped with his father as an orange seller to Holland. The latter entered the Dutch Service and the son became a Major in Schomberg's Regiment and fought at the Boyne. He served for thirteen years in Holland, Ireland and Flanders, and was disbanded " leamed " in 1698-9, when he received a pension of five shillings a day. The family for generations held positions in the English Army.[2] They intermarried with the La Rives, and a memoir of the escape of the original settler was preserved amongst the papers of Henry La Rive of Castlecomer already mentioned.[3]

Another of these early Huguenots was John, the son of Raphael Thorius, who had escaped from France to England, where he died in 1625. John studied medicine at Oxford and became a Fellow of the College of Physicians in Dublin in 1627.[4]

But although these settlers with others from the United Provinces were of importance, it was not until the restoration

---

[1] Lart, Vol. II, pp. 13-14, and C.H. & A.J., Vol. I (2nd series), No. 1, p. 36. " Old Dublin Bankers."

[2] Hug. Soc. Pub., Vol. VII, p. 108, and Hug. Soc. Proc., Vol. VI, p. 301. Also " Huguenots in England," Appendix. 1889 Edition.

[3] *Vide* p. 128.

[4] " Huguenots in England," Appendix.

of Charles to his kingdom and Ormond to power and position in Court circles that the real history of the Huguenots of Dublin as a definitely recognized body may be said to have commenced.

As has already been stated, Ormond was deeply interested in the establishment of a linen manufacture in Ireland,[1] and in order to effect this he set apart houses and land at Chapelizod in 1667 for the use of weavers whom he hoped to import from the Continent. Sir William Temple, then Ambassador at Brussels, was directed to send over five hundred families from Brabant. These were joined by refugees from La Rochelle and the Isle of Rhé, and Sir George Carteret sent men from Jersey and the neighbouring parts of France. Houses were provided for them as for the settlers in Clonmel and Carrick, and soon, under the supervision of Colonel Richard Lawrence, three hundred hands were at work in making cordage, sailcloth, ticking, and " as good linen cloth and diaper of Irish yarn as was made in any country of Europe."[2] Lawrence also introduced wool combing and the manufacture of friezes and blankets, and the venture for a time met with such success that he " did not question but posterity would own their future affluence to be a blessing they derived from His Grace's wisdom and excellent government."[3]

By the early eighteenth century, however, the manufacture at Chapelizod had failed,[4] and the colonists, like those of the small settlement later formed in Wicklow under William III, were too near to the Metropolis to keep a distinct character of their own for any length of time. They worshipped at the French Church of St. Patrick's, and soon became indistinguishable from the Dublin Huguenots.

---

[1] *Vide* p. 13.
[2] Carte, "Life of Ormond," Bk. VI, p. 343.
[3] *Ibid.*
[4] Gill, "Rise of the Irish Linen Industry," p. 9.

Those of Wicklow, like the Lefebure family,[1] scattered also to other parts of Ireland, and thus the history of neither colony can satisfactorily be traced. A more enduring monument to Ormond's " excellent government " where the Huguenots were concerned, is found in the patronage he extended towards the French congregation which at his instigation was granted in 1665[2] the Chapel of St. Mary in St. Patrick's Cathedral in which to worship. This, says a writer in 1681, was " une preuve solide et parlante de son Excellente charité."[3]

On December 23rd, 1665, the Dean and Chapter of St. Patrick's drew up the conditions on which the chapel was granted to the French refugees. It was to be preserved entire and the Dean and Chapter were to have the privilege of burying there. This was also extended to the French ministers and church officers gratis, but to no other member of the congregation without licence from the Dean or Proctor. The French service was not to interfere with those in the choir of the cathedral, and the bishops were to have liberty to meet there as in times preceding. Repairs were to be at the charge of the French congregation, but the Chapter inserted a clause of resumption at any time on a three years' notice. Most important of all these clauses was that which laid down that the French congregation should be bound by the discipline and canons of the Church of Ireland, under the jurisdiction of the Archbishop of Dublin.[4]

James Hierome and Elias de Ruinat, clerks; Dr. Dudley Loftus; Sir Peter Harvey; Edward Denham, M.D.; John Herault and James Fontaine " on behalf of the French and other nations intending to join in the French Liturgy of

---

[1] Hug. Soc. Proc., Vol. VI. " Projet de Colonisation," and *vide* p. 119.
[2] Hug. Soc. Proc., Vol. VIII, p. 95. " The French Churches of Dublin."
[3] " De l'État Present d'Irlande." Pamphlet. Dublin.
[4] Hug. Soc. Pub., Vol. VII. " Registers of the Fr. Conformed Churches, Dublin." Ed. J. J. Digges La Touche.

the Church of Ireland "[1] took part in the transaction, and the House of Commons interested itself in the matter, appointed a committee to discuss it, and proposed to contribute twenty shillings per member for the repairing of the building. This, however, was found insufficient, and it was ordered that " The Sergeant-at-Arms attending this House be appointed to receive from the several members of this House such voluntary contributions as they shall think fit to give for, and towards the repairing and finishing of a church within this city or liberties thereof, wherein the liturgy of the Church of England translated into French shall be constantly read."[2]

By April 1666 the building was restored and ready for use, and on the 29th of that month the inaugural service was held. Ormond's chaplain, Jacques Hierome (or Hierosme or Jerome), officiated as minister and " made an excellent sermon upon the occasion."[3]

The service was an auspicious one, attended by the Lord-Lieutenant, " his Guard and Gentlemen preceding him, with the maces and sword carried before him, accompanied by the Lord Primate of Ireland, the Lord Archbishop of Dublin, Lord High Chancellor of Ireland, the Council of State and several great Lords and other persons of quality of both persuasions, followed by the Lord Mayor, with the Sheriffs and Officers of the City, who had the sword and mace likewise carried before him." The Duchess of Ormond, the Countess of Arran and "a great train of ladies of quality "[4] were also present.

The Primate at this period was Margetson, himself, as has been already noted,[5] of Huguenot stock, and the Lord Mayor was John, son of Lewis Desmynieres, of Utrecht, who with other Dutch merchants had been naturalized by an Act of

[1] Hug. Soc. Proc., Vol. VII, p. 94.
[2] H.C.J. (Ireland), Feb. 1st and 26th, 1665.
[3] London Gazette, May 21st, 1666.
[4] Ibid.
[5] Vide p. 202.

1662.[1] Henry Desmynieres, a grandson of Lewis, took Holy Orders, and was a prebendary in the three dioceses of Ossory, Emly and Kildare.[2] This Dutch family must have been connected with the French one of the same name represented by Daniel and John Desminieres from "Roan in Normandy," who obtained their Letters of Denization in Ireland at the same period.[3] The Huguenot representative, John Herault, cannot have been naturalized until 1667, when he "took the Oaths" as a native of the "Isle of Olerone, France,"[4] and the James Fontaine, who also represented the French congregation, must have been the Chirurgeon-General who obtained his patent in Dublin in 1661 and has already been mentioned in the chapter on Cork.[5]

Hierome came to Ireland as chaplain to the Duke of Ormond, and took the necessary Oaths on March 9th, 1665.[6] He was a Doctor of Divinity and had been minister of Fécamp, and now, in 1666, was ordained a minister of the Church of Ireland and licensed for the new French Church. In June of the same year he was installed as Precentor of Waterford and later as Treasurer of Lismore. Two years afterwards it is recorded in the Chancery Rolls that "The King in consideration that James Hierome, clerk, had brought the French congregation at the Savoy to conform to the Church of England and in consideration of his learning, piety and being a stranger, presents him to the vicarage of Chapel Izod, with liberty to graze two horses and eight cows in the Phœnix Park, free."[7] In 1671 he was installed as

[1] H.C.J. (Ireland), July 10th, 1662.
[2] *Ibid.*
[3] Hug. Soc. Pub., Vol. XVIII, p. 336.
[4] *Ibid.*, p. 340.
[5] *Vide* p. 39.
[6] Hug. Soc. Pub., Vol. XVIII, p. 340.
[7] Gimlette, p. 235. The Phœnix Park was made by Ormond in 1663 as a deer park for the residence of the Lord-Lieutenant, and the vicars of those parishes affected as to tithes by its creation were compensated. Hence the necessity for the grant to Hierome. Litton Falkiner, "Illustrations of Irish History," p. 55.

Prebend for Donoughmore in the Chapter of St. Patrick's, and he died in 1682 in Carrick-on-Suir, having retired from the ministry of the French Church six years before his death.

He married three times, his third wife, Martha Le Roy, surviving him, and had at least five daughters, four of whom married into the Huguenot families of de Massas, Prevost, La Pierre, Chabrier and La Nauze.[1] In 1689 a John Jerome of Kilkenny was attainted by the Parliament of James II, but his connection, if any, with the minister is uncertain,[2] as is that of Stephen Jerome, the fanatical preacher who had been chaplain to the Earl of Cork[3] and Rector of St. Bride's, Dublin, in 1635.[4]

The Savoy Church in London seems, through Hierome, to have been brought into connection with the congregation of St. Patrick's; thus the French Churches in Ireland were constantly supplied with ministers from the London Church, such as Abbadie, Séverin, Saurin, Susy Boan, Dubourdieu, Durand and Pons.[5]

Four Huguenot Churches in all were established in Dublin, those of St. Patrick's and St. Mary's which conformed to the Established Church and eventually united in 1716, and those in Peter Street and Lucy Lane which were Calvinist and united under one Consistory in 1707.

Much confusion has arisen owing to the varying names given to the churches in the registers. Thus the congregation of St. Mary's Chapel in St. Patrick's is distinct from that of the French Church of St. Mary's later formed in St. Mary's Abbey, and the registers of the Nonconformist Churches of Lucy Lane, Wood Street and Peter Street, which were

---

[1] Hug. Soc. Proc., Vol. VIII, p. 92, and J.A.P.M.D., Vol. XI, p. 362.
[2] Gimlette, p. 259.
[3] *Ibid.*, p. 178.
[4] Sir William Brereton, "Travels in Ireland." Ed. C. Litton Falkiner, in "Illustrations of Irish History."
[5] Burn, "History of the Foreign Refugees."

deposited in the Public Record Office in 1896,[1] included a Register of Marriages, Baptisms and Burials of the French Church of Golblac Lane from 1701-1732. "No reference has been found to indicate the locality of this street," writes the Deputy Keeper of the Records, and suggests, though wrongly, according to Mr. Le Fanu, that it was " off Lucy Lane or was an alias for it." In the same way Wood Street was only another name for the Peter Street congregation which had met in this locality before the church in the latter street was built. It will be best for the sake of clearness to take the history of each group of churches in order before dealing with the ministers of both.

The church in St. Patrick's continued to increase in numbers, and though, under James II, the minister, Rossel, was imprisoned and service was for a time suspended, the congregation grew so large on the accession of William that five galleries were at various times added to the church. Overcrowding still occurring, however, the chapel in St. Mary's Abbey was leased in 1700 from Sir Humphrey Gervais as a Chapel of Ease, and services were instituted here from 1701. In 1704 a difference of opinion arose on the question of the appointment of a minister, and the new church (variously styled " St. Mary's," or " Mary's Abbey," or " Little St. Patrick's ") established its independence with its own ministers, *anciens* and Consistory, which met for the first time on January 1st, 1705. It retained its independence until 1716, when once more it became united to the French Church of St. Patrick's with one Consistory, one Treasury and five ministers, three to represent St. Patrick's and two for St.

---

[1] 28th Rep. Dep. Keep. Rec., 1896. They were fortunately edited, before their destruction in the Four Courts, by Mr. T. P. Le Fanu, and appear amongst the publications of the Huguenot Society, Vol. XIV. From 1732-1771 the registers are missing since, according to an entry made by the minister, Subremont, in the existing register, thieves broke into the vestry on Jan. 16th, 1771, and failing to find the Communion Plate " vented their rage upon some of the Church books which were then there and burnt same," among them being the registers.

Mary's.[1] The united churches were to be governed by the "Discipline" of the French Church of St. Patrick's, which had been drawn up in 1694 with the approval of Archbishop Marsh. This had been compiled, writes Mr. Le Fanu,[2] owing to the necessity felt by the Conformed Church of establishing its French nature in view of the competition of the new Calvinistic Church of Bride Street; since the great number of indigent refugees flocking into the City made it necessary to stress its responsibility as a charitable organization; and since the constitution of the French Church of the Savoy on which that of St. Patrick's had been modelled contained much that was unsuitable for Dublin.

By it the Consistory had power to refuse admission to outsiders, but could not excommunicate, and the church was free to choose its own ministers. It was French in tone, but the promise made by Ormond to the Archbishop of Dublin in 1665 that the new church would be "governed wholly according to the discipline and rites of the Church of Ireland and the Canons of the same strictly and indispensably"[3] was not forgotten; and that the ministers were in close touch with the dignitaries of the Cathedral is attested by Dean Swift, who kept up his knowledge of French by "reading or gabbling with the French clergy who come to me about business of their Church."[4]

Now both churches came under this discipline, and from this date one set of registers alone was kept. In 1740 St. Mary's was closed and the congregation joined in the service in St. Patrick's. This service ended in 1816, says Dr. La Touche, when the congregation had dwindled to about twenty persons, but Mr. Le Fanu states that the last service was held

[1] Hug. Soc. Pub., Vol. VII. "Introduction to Registers of Conformed Churches."
[2] Hug. Soc. Proc., Vol. XII, p. 245. "Archbishop Marsh and the discipline of the Fr. Ch. of St. Patrick's."
[3] Quoted *ibid.*
[4] Letter, Dec. 5th, 1721. "Letters," Ed. Hill, p. 106.

on Christmas Day, 1817.[1] On January 1st, 1833, Messrs. Richard Espinasse and François Bessonet, the treasurers of the Church Funds, met; and in signing their statement noted " that once numerous congregation of respectable men is now alas! represented by the above two functionaries."[2] The burial-ground connected with the church, which had been established on the north side of " The Cabbage Garden " cemetery in 1681, was closed in 1858, and was purchased for the Consistory in 1876 by Messrs. Bessonet and La Touche.[3]

The registers of the Conformed Churches were deposited by the elders in the Record Office, Dublin,[4] and were most fortunately edited *in extenso* by Dr. La Touche for the Huguenot Society before the destruction of the Four Courts. They extend (with the exception of the Baptisms of St. Patrick's from 1687-1716) from 1668 to 1830.

There were many, however, who found with De Bostaquet that the Anglican form of service was " très opposé à la simplicité de notre reformation," and who, like him, " were not edified."[5] Thus Gimlette[6] states that a Calvinistic congregation met at Lady Ossory's house under Ormond, and immediately after the passing of the Act of 1692, which allowed complete freedom of worship to Protestant Strangers, a Nonconformist Church was formed under the protection of the Lord-Lieutenant, but without a Government grant for its ministers.[7] " It is not possible," writes Mr. Le Fanu, the editor of the registers, " to form an accurate estimate of the comparative size and importance of the two bodies, but the number of Baptisms seems to show that at least

---

[1] Hug. Soc. Proc., Vol. VIII, p. 133.
[2] Quoted *ibid.*
[3] J.A.P.M.D., 1901.
[4] 26th Rep. Dep. Keep. Rec., 1894, also the Minute Book of St. Mary's, 1704-1716 (37th Rep.).
[5] " Mémoires Inédits."
[6] " Huguenot Settlers," p. 173.
[7] Weiss, Bk. III, p. 279.

half of the Dublin refugees did not conform."[1] Lord Galway endeavoured to form a union between the churches but failed.

The founder of this new church began by renting a house from Councillor Thomas Whitshed in Bride Street, and the congregation also acquired ground for a cemetery near St. Stephen's Green, now known as that of Merrion Row. The church was variously styled " L'Eglise recueillie proche St. Brigide," or "L'Eglise qui se recueillit en Bride St." In 1699 it became established in an ancient chapel on a site known as Jesuits' Lands on the west side of Lucy Lane, where the Huguenots, as in Portarlington, were tenants of the Hollow Sword Blade Company who obtained the fee simple in 1703. Later, in 1701, a difference of opinion caused part of the congregation to secede and to establish another church in a house in Wood Street with a cemetery near Newmarket on the Coombe, which seems to have formed part of St. Luke's churchyard. Here it continued from 1701-1711, and in 1707 the Lucy Lane congregation joined that of Wood Street under one Consistory, when four ministers served the united churches.

In 1711 a church with a burial-ground attached was built by subscription. It was situated in Peter Street, and the Wood Street congregation became that of " L'Eglise Françoise de St. Pierre."

The church in Lucy Lane was sold in 1773 to a Presbyterian congregation and was pulled down about 1825. That of Peter Street continued until 1814.[2] In 1806 " comme notre troupeau est presque annihilé " the church was closed in winter, and on the death of the last minister, Monsieur Subremont, service was abandoned, and the building was

---

[1] Hug. Soc. Pub., Vol. XIV. " Introduction to Registers of the Nonconformist Churches." Ed. T. P. Le Fanu.

[2] Smiles's statement (" Huguenots in England and Ireland," p. 295) that the building then became the Molyneux Asylum for the Blind is erroneous. The original asylum was on the other side of the street.

demolished in 1838. The site, however, still belongs to the trustees of the church.

The burial-grounds continued in use, and a mortuary chapel was erected in the Peter Street cemetery "par acte de Consistore" in 1840. The last entry of a burial in this cemetery is in 1879, and in that of Merrion Row in 1901, special clauses for their protection having been inserted in the Burial-Grounds Act of 1856.[1] Mr. Le Fanu proves from the registers that from 1717-1721, for the sake of economy, one burial-ground, that of Merrion Row, alone was used.[2]

Burn[3] states that the hostility of the Government, especially in Ireland, to any dissent allowed small favour to these Calvinistic Churches, and to this assigns their "early disappearance," but it will have been seen that in Dublin at least the Nonconformists held their own until the nineteenth century. There was little friction between the Conformed and Nonconformed Churches. Sometimes the ministers of one attended at the other and, as in the case of the marriages made by the daughters of Jean Darassus, members of one family might belong to each church. In matters of discipline also each congregation helped the other in placing the same ban on an offender. A good example of the amicable relations of the churches and the equal respect with which they were regarded by the refugees is found in the will, already mentioned, of John Galtier of Waterford,[4] who bequeathed an equal sum to each of the four Dublin churches.

This friendly spirit is also seen in the rules of the "Societé Charitable des Réfugiés,"[5] which was founded in 1719 to care for the poorer refugees and to educate and supply work for their children. To this end a day school was established in

---

[1] The above notes are taken from Mr. Le Fanu's invaluable article on the Dublin churches. Hug. Soc. Proc., Vol. VIII, p. 87.

[2] Hug. Soc. Pub., Vol. XIV.

[3] "History of the Refugees," p. 250.

[4] *Vide* p. 112.

[5] *Vide* Hug. Soc. Proc., Vol. VIII, p. 126.

1723, and a school house built in Myler's Alley in 1732. The children were expected to attend each of the French Churches on successive Sundays. In 1736 the school grew by the addition of boarders,[1] and in 1753, in an effort to encourage the textile industry, three looms were presented to it by the Linen Board. By 1770, however, it had lost its distinctive French character with the death of Mr. Isaac Dufour, who had come from Lisburn to teach there; and in 1822 it was closed. The last charity sermon for the Society was preached by Jean Letablère in 1813. In 1823 the funds were merged with those held by the representatives of the French Church of St. Patrick's, and thus have existed to the present day.

A second Society was formed to assist those refugees who flooded Dublin in 1751. Its principal object was to assist the attempted settlement at Innishannon,[2] and when this failed the affairs of the Society were wound up. In a Memorial to the Lords Justices in 1752, it was stated that "The Society has taken and furnished a large house in Dublin in which they (the refugees) are to lodge, and be maintained until they are enabled to exercise their respective trades and manufactures."[3] This house was in Chequer Lane and seems to have been the tardy outcome of a discussion engaged in by a Committee of the Privy Council in 1681 or the result of a revival of the proposal then made as to the advisability of having "une maison toute prête et fournie des choses nécessaires pour leur réception," and of taking "grand soin de leur subsistence et de leur établissement; soit en leur fournissant des outils pour leur travail ou métier; soit en leur donnant une assistance conforme à leur condition."[4]

The new colonists took the Oaths at the Court of

---

[1] They were required, possibly for economy, "to let their hair grow, and not to wear wigs," and were to be provided by the institution with pocket handkerchiefs.
[2] *Vide* p. 82.
[3] Quoted Hug. Soc. Proc., Vol. VIII, p. 87 *et seq.*
[4] "De l'État Presente d'Irlande," Dublin, 1681. Pamphlet.

Exchequer in July 1752, and they seem to have excited some popular interest, for in the *Dublin Journal* of August 29th of that year, it is recorded that " Sunday last arrived here from Rotterdam, 96 foreign Protestants, men, women and children; they all seemed in good health and spirits, and went in the afternoon to the French Church in Peter Street where there was a large collection made for them." " Ten French Protestant Families," it is later stated in the same paper, " arrived here from Bordeaux," and in the *Dublin Gazette* of July 25th-28th, 1752, it is thought worthy of notice that " last Wednesday a gentlewoman upwards of 50 years of age who fled lately from France on account of the persecution against the Protestants now carrying on in that Kingdom, was baptised before a numerous audience at the French Church in Peter Street."

The ministers of both the Conformed and Nonconformist Churches have been dealt with by Mr. T. P. Le Fanu in the already extensively quoted article in the proceedings of the Huguenot Society.[1] Here it is only possible to list them with a few facts from the lives of the most important. Some, it will be seen, as Caillard, Des Voeux, Gillet, Mont Cenis or de Villette, officiated in other churches in the provinces and have already been treated of there, and a glance at the list below will show that there seems especially to have been much intercourse between the ministers of the Calvinist Churches of Dublin and that of Portarlington.

Ministers of the Nonconformist Churches

Joseph Lagacherie	1692–1694
Barthelemy Balaguier[2] (also officiated at Portarlington)	1693–1724
Jean Darassus (also officiated at Portarlington)	1696–1716

---

[1] Vol. VIII, pp. 87-139.
[2] Or Belaquier, as the name is sometimes spelt.

J. Gillet (also Portarlington) . . .	1701 (Visitor only)
— Pons	1701–1718
Jean de Durand	1704–1744
Paul de St. Ferreol	1717–1755
Paul De La Douespe	1717–1720
Gaspard Caillard (also Portarlington) .	1720–1739
Jacob Pallard	1724–1736
— Baby	1736–1739 (?)
Antoine Des Voeux (also Portarlington)	1737–1760
Jacques Pelletreau (left for church in St. Patrick's)	1740–1758
Louis Ostervald	1744–1754
Pierre Hobler	1760–1765
Isaac Subremont	1760–1814
Louis Campredon	1766–1770
François Bessonet (left for church in St. Patrick's)	1771–1781
François Campredon	1781–1784

(During the ministry of Monsieur Balaguier, two assistants, De La Chapelle and De La Roche, probably his pupils, took over some parochial duties.)

Ministers of the Conformed Churches

Jacques Hierome	1666–1676
Moses Viridet	1676–1685
Josué Rossel	1685–1691
Charles Rossel	1692 (Resigned same year)
Gabriel Barbier	1692–1710
Jean Severin	1693–1704
George Louis De La Sara . . .	1700–1701
Charles De La Roche	1700–1702
Abraham Viridet (first appointed lecteur but resigned 1705 and reappointed 1712) .	1712–1738
Louis Quartier	1701 (Resigned same year)
Pierre Degalinière (officiated St. Mary's) .	1701–1721

Henri de Rocheblave	1701–1702 (Retired. Later appointed Lucy Lane)
Reappointed	1706–1709
De La Mothe (elected but never took up his duties)	1704–
Alexandre de Susy Boan	1710–1741
Pierre Bouquet de St. Paul (also Wexford)	1715–1735
Pascal Ducasse (at St. Mary's, also officiated at Portarlington)	1701–1730
Amaury Fleury	1716–1734
Antoine Fleury	1730–1736
Louis Scoffier	1736–1781
Jean Pierre Droz	1737–1751
Charles de Villette (also Carlow)	1737–1783
Daniel Beaufort	1752–1758
Jacques Pelletreau	1758–1781
Jean Lescure. (Served as Reader only for six months)	1778
François Bessonet	1781–1788
Justin de Mont Cenis (also Cork)	1786–1795
Jean Letablère	1795–1816

Most of the "Conformed" and many of the Calvinist ministers were beneficed in the Church of Ireland. De St. Paul, Beaufort and the Fleurys have already been mentioned in this respect,[1] and the family of Letablère affords another good example.

René De La Douespe, Sieur de Letablère in Lower Poitou, fled to Holland in 1685 and became an Ensign in Du Cambon's Foot. He fought at the Boyne and continued to serve in the same regiment under Lifford until 1699. In 1723 he revisited Poitou but returned to Dublin, where he died six years later.[2] His son, Daniel, born in Dublin in 1709, was educated by Dr. de St. Paul, entered Trinity College, Dublin, and was

[1] *Vide* pp. 101, 199, 201.
[2] "Huguenots in England," Appendix.

appointed Vicar of Larabryen in 1742. In 1749 he was made a Prebendary of Kildare, and in 1759 Dean of Tuam. He died in 1775.[1] As a promoter of the Dublin Silk Manufactory, he was presented with the Freedom of the Weavers' Guild in a silver box in 1769.[2] He married Madeleine Vareilles and on her death Blanche Jourdan, and had a son, Jean, who graduated from Dublin University in 1773 and was Curate of St. Nicholas' in 1781 before obtaining his appointment to the French Church. His youngest daughter, Esther, married Edward Litton, who served in the American War of Independence, and was the ancestor of a notable Irish family. A monument to the Dean of Tuam was placed in St. Patrick's Cathedral. Two other sons of the original settler joined the Goldsmiths' Guild of Dublin. René was apprenticed in the year of his father's death to Daniel Pineau, and John, who was apprenticed in 1726, became a Warden of the Company in 1750.[3]

Of the other French clergy employed in the Church of Ireland, the Viridets, Rossel, Dégalinière, de Rocheblave and Caillard may be cited as further examples; and the career of de Rocheblave exemplifies also the close connection between the Calvinist and Conformist Churches.

Born in France in 1665,[4] he studied theology at Schaffhausen and fled to England at the Revocation, when he became chaplain to Ruvigny at Greenwich. Having served in various London churches, he was collated to Narraghmore in 1696, and to Usk in 1700. He resigned the French Church at St. Patrick's a year after his appointment in order to reside on his benefice, which in the following year he also resigned to become minister at Lucy Lane. He later went to London,

---

[1] Hug. Soc. Proc., Vol. VIII, p. 87.
[2] J.R.S.A.I., Vol. XLIX. Stubbs, "The Weavers' Guild." Not of the Masons' Guild as stated by Smiles, "Huguenots in England," Appendix.
[3] C.H. & A.J., Vol. VIII, No. 53. "Dublin Goldsmiths."
[4] Agnew, "Huguenot Exiles," Vol. II, p. 246.

whence he was recalled, in 1706, to the Conformist Church of Dublin. He was buried in St. Patrick's in 1709, leaving a wife, Isabeau La Caux, and three children.[1]

Dégalinière owed his clerical appointments to his friendship with Pepys. Through Thomas Gale, Dean of York, and a relative of the diarist, he was made Vicar of Mohill in 1699, and of Drung and Larah in 1700.

Charles, son of the Josué Rossel who had been imprisoned by James II, was curate to Viridet at Arklow and later Vicar of Drumlane and Killesherdiney. He had a son, Charles, father of the Dublin merchant, and a daughter who married Jerome Brodin. The elder Rossel had been Pastor of Vigan and had presided over a meeting of the Reformed Churches of the Cevennes at Colognac in 1683.[2] For this he was ordered to be broken on the wheel, but he escaped to Ireland, where, under James II, he was subjected to a new but short-lived persecution. Under Charles Rossel, the Minute Book of the Conformed Church began in 1692.[3]

Moses Viridet was the son of Jacob Viridet, an officer of the Duke of Orleans, and probably for this reason did not lose his French property, although residing abroad. He was twice married, first to the Lady Dorothy Coote, daughter of the Earl of Mountrath, and secondly to Françoise, daughter of Benjamin de Mazières, Sieur du Passage et de Voutron. By her he had a son, Moses, born in 1684, and a daughter, Susanne, who married, in 1708, Anthony Rafugeau, a Huguenot merchant of Dublin, whose father had fled from Poitou.[4] With the children of his first marriage he was made a denizen of Ireland in 1678, and in 1682 was appointed to the Chapter of St. Patrick's as Prebend of Kilmactalway. In 1685 he resigned the ministry of the French Church owing, Gimlette

---

[1] Hug. Soc. Proc., Vol. VIII, p. 117.
[2] Ibid.
[3] Ibid.
[4] Ibid., p. 99.

surmises, to the attack made on it by James II, but more probably, as Mr. Le Fanu remarks, on his being collated to Arklow. His descendants seem to have followed him in the ministry, for an Abraham Viridet served in the French Church from 1703 to 1738, and in 1778 his son, the Rev. Daniel Viridet, was Prebendary of Kilmeen. Another Abraham Viridet, Comptroller-General of the Revenue for Ireland, was buried in the French Cemetery near St. Patrick's Cathedral in 1797.[1]

Abraham Viridet, the cleric, studied at Geneva and Trinity College, Dublin, whence he graduated in 1702. In 1703 he was ordained deacon in St. Canice's, Kilkenny, and priest in St. Patrick's Cathedral in 1707. He kept a school and was licensed as a teacher of Latin by the Archbishop in 1716. He married Mary Vivian and had two sons, Daniel, mentioned above, and John, who died in 1738.[2]

The ministers Balaguier, Darassus and Ducasse are of interest as having been connected with Portarlington as well as Dublin.

Balaguier was a native of Puylaurens and had been minister of Aiguefonde. He fled to England and served in the church of La Patente, whence he was sent with the necessary service books for the new church in Dublin, where he died in 1725. He married Marie Perer and had two daughters, Marie and Pauline, who married Daniel Gervais, and two sons, Jean Antoine, born in London in 1689,[3] and Jacques, apprenticed in 1707 to the goldsmith Daniel Pineau.[4]

Jean Darassus had been chaplain to the Earl of Galway in Piedmont and returned with him to Dublin. He married Elizabeth, daughter of Colonel de Romagnac, and had five children : Jean; Elié, who became a Captain and died in 1699;

---

[1] Gimlette, p. 237.
[2] Hug. Soc. Proc., Vol. VIII.
[3] Hug. Soc. Pub., Vol. XI, p. 8.
[4] C.H. & A.J., Vol. VIII, No. 53. "Dublin Goldsmiths."

Charles, who was appointed chaplain to Colonel Du Bourgay's Regiment and died in 1731; Marianne, who married Monsieur de St. Paul of the French Church of St. Patrick's; and Henriette, who married Paul de St. Ferreol, the Calvinist pastor. Darassus died or resigned, states Mr. Le Fanu, in 1717. The former is the more likely, as in the will of the Earl of Galway, who died in 1720, a legacy of £100 is left to "John Darasus, son of Madame Darasus of Dublin," and an equal sum "to her daughter Henriette," and no mention is made of the father.[1]

Ducasse was a protégé of Abbadie and had been chaplain to Colonel Echlin's Regiment in Dublin, where he married Catherine Dumeny in 1700. He was the son of Pascal Ducasse, Seigneur de Meyrac, and a native of Pontar in Bearn. He obtained his degree of D.D. in 1722 and the Deaneries of Ferns and Clogher successively in 1724 and 1727.[2] The name also occurs in Portarlington, where Jacques Ducasse, from Guienne, who served as a Lieutenant in the English Army, seems to have been resident about 1720.[3]

By 1733, as has already been stated, the colony of Huguenots in Dublin had firmly established itself. As early as 1704, when Philip Legendre published in Rotterdam his "Histoire de la Persécution faite à l'église de Rouen sur la fin du dernier siècle," Dublin was fully recognized as a place of settlement, the only one in Ireland to be mentioned by him. "Fine and flourishing families," he states, were to be seen "at Amsterdam, Leyden, at the Hague, at Berlin, at London, Dublin, Rotterdam and elsewhere that had no reason to repent that they forsook their native land to follow the torch of the Gospel." They were assisted by both Government and Corporation. In 1681 the Lord-Lieutenant and Privy Council "of their accustomed pitty and charity to the afflicted"

---

[1] Agnew, "Henri de Ruvigny."
[2] Hug. Soc. Proc., Vol. VIII, p. 120.
[3] Registers of the French Church.

recommended that a collection should be made for them and suggested, as has already been stated, that they should be assisted towards practising their several trades; and the Corporation ordered that French artisans and craftsmen should be admitted to the Freedom of the City, and should escape all taxes for five years. This " Act of Assembly " was renewed for seven years after the Revocation and again in 1692,[1] and although the proceeds of the collection did not all go to the French, the charitable organizations of the Huguenots themselves soon took the place of State aid and many of the refugees, who came chiefly from Aunis, Saintonge, Guienne and Poitou, soon became wealthy and influential Dublin citizens.

The French workmen who came to Dublin to engage in the weaving of tabinets settled for the most part in the " Liberties " of St. Patrick's, and the Earl of Meath; and street names like " Pimlico " or " Spitalfields " bore witness to the fact that many of them came from these districts of London where the Huguenot weavers had become localized.[2] It has been stated that they at first obtained a factory in High Street;[3] and by 1682 a Weavers' Hall was in existence. In 1745 a new Weavers' Hall was erected on the Lower Coombe, £200 for the undertaking being advanced by James Digges La Touche, Master of the Guild. An almshouse was formed by the Weavers in 1767, and a charity school was also maintained.[4]

The refugees founded a Dublin Florists' Club in the reign of George I, as a copy of the Floricultural Society which they had maintained in England. They held their meetings in the Rose Tavern in Drumcondra Lane,[5] and though by the nineteenth century the Club was gone, it was still re-

[1] Hug. Soc. Proc., Vol. VIII, p. 100.
[2] " Huguenots in England," p. 294.
[3] Correspondent, *Irish Times*, March 20th, 1933.
[4] J.R.S.A.I., Vol. XLIX, Pt. I. Stubbs, " The Weavers' Guild."
[5] Burn, p. 248.

membered when Warburton's "History of Dublin" was compiled.[1]

To the La Touche family is attributed the establishment of the silk and poplin weaving industry in Dublin. David Digues des Rompières De La Touche was born in 1671. His elder brother, Paul, conformed to the Roman Catholic faith, and thus was granted the family property, of which the principal estate was La Touche near Blois on the Loire. He was instrumental in gaining for David a Cadetship in the Corps of Gentlemen of Valenciennes, but in 1686 the latter fled to join an uncle, Digues De La Brosse, who had settled in Amsterdam. He entered Caillemotte's Regiment and fought at the Boyne, subsequently obtaining a commission in Princess Anne of Denmark's Regiment of Foot. He was pensioned as a Lieutenant after Ryswick and found himself in straitened circumstances in Galway at the conclusion of the Campaign.[2] From here he made his way to Dublin, and in 1699 married Martha Judith, daughter of Noë Biard, a refugee from Bellême in the Department of Orne.[3] Engaging in the weaving industry, he joined the Guild of Weavers in 1701, by 1706 was a member of the Council, and was elected Master in 1708. By 1717 he had become a prominent member of the Trinity Guild of Merchants, which controlled most of the commerce of the City, and his integrity was so well known that their money and valuables were entrusted to his care by other Huguenots who came and went through Dublin. This led to his joining Nathaniel Kane, who was also connected with the weaving industry in the Coombe, and two other merchants in the establishment of a bank,[4] and thus the famous La Touche Bank originated. In 1722 it was removed to Castle Street,

---

[1] "History of Dublin," 1818, Vol. II, p. 841. Warburton, Whitelaw & Walsh.
[2] Hug. Soc. Proc., Vol. XIV. Lunel MSS.
[3] On her death in 1713 he married Wilhelmina Sanbregan.
[4] Hug. Soc. Proc., Vol. XIV. Lunel MSS.

where it existed until the nineteenth century. Long before his death, La Touche had realized over £10,000, and when he died in 1745 he left all his property to his elder son, David, subject to certain legacies including £3,000 for the younger, James.

The elder dropped the patronymic Digues, taking La Touche only as surname, and in the name of the younger "Digues" became corrupted to "Digges." The second David, who married Mary, daughter of Gabriel Canasille, had seven sons, three of whom were partners in the bank. He built the mansion Bellevue, near Delgany, where he was buried in 1785, and where his fifth son, Peter, erected a church. The second son, David, had Marley, near Rathfarnham, as a residence. He played an important part in the establishment of the Bank of Ireland in 1782, and was appointed Governor for the first three years, his brothers being among the directors. He was a Privy Councillor and represented Belturbet in Parliament, while John, the fourth son, who possessed the estate of Harristown, was M.P. for County Kildare.

Their uncle, James Digges La Touche, the merchant prince of Dublin, married twice, his first wife being Elizabeth, daughter of David Chaigneau, who was Sheriff of Dublin in 1717. By his second wife, Martha Thwaites, he had five sons. William, born 1746, who was Writer to the British Resident at Bussora, married Miss Grace Puget, daughter of the London banker of Huguenot descent, and built the house in Stephen's Green which Arthur Young found "well contrived and finished elegantly."[1]

The history of the younger branches of the family is too well known to need repetition here. Some members married into the nobility and others held important positions both in Ireland and abroad. The public spirit and generosity of the

---

[1] " Travels in Ireland." The above notes are taken from a " Biographic Sketch of the late James Digges La Touche," by William Urwick, D.D., and supplemented by information kindly supplied by Mr. T. P. Le Fanu.

La Touches was characteristic. Burdy[1] recalls, as an instance of it, that when in 1783 a famine, "the most severe that history records," occurred, John La Touche carried a message from his father to Philip Skelton stating that "if he wanted money to buy meal for his poor, he might draw on his Bank for any sum he stood in need of." Skelton's first toast after dinner was invariably "The family of La Touche," since he maintained that they "had souls of a superior nature to the generality of men."

Another Dublin weaver, though a far less successful one than David La Touche, was the Huguenot Nicholas Du Pin, who in 1692 endeavoured to establish a linen manufactory in the City.[2] Its history is summed up by William Molyneux in a letter to John Locke written in September 1696.[3] "About the year 1692 one M. Du Pin came to Dublin from England and here, by the King and Queen's Letter and patents thereon, he set up a Royal Corporation for carrying on the Linen Manufactory in Ireland. Du Pin, himself, was nominated Under-Governor, and a great bustle was made about the business. At length, artificers began to set to work and some parcels of cloth were made," but, by quarrels with rival companies in London and Drogheda, "all is blown up and nothing of this kind is carried on but by such as, out of their own private purses, set up Looms and bleaching yards."[4]

Some Huguenot names appear in the list of Masters and Wardens of the Weavers' Guild, and amongst them may be quoted:

Lewis Larowe (or Leroux), Warden in 1693 and Master in 1708;

[1] "Life of Skelton."
[2] Gill, p. 44.
[3] "Letters between Locke and his Friends," p. 166.
[4] Du Pin may have been connected with the John Du Pin, merchant, from Anjou who took the Oaths in Dublin in July 1669. Hug. Soc. Pub., Vol. XVIII, p. 342.

Francis Lattore, Warden in 1694 and Master in 1699;
Isaac Dezouch, Warden in 1727;
James Digges La Touche, Master in 1745;
John Lartigue, Warden in 1760 and Master in 1763;
Francis Ozier, Warden in 1761;
Thomas Angier, Warden in 1778 and 1779 and Master in 1787.[1]

Although the poplin manufactory grew to considerable proportions, and the numbers of Dublin weavers were greatly increased by the new influx of refugees in the middle of the eighteenth century, strikes eventually spoilt the industry; the Bounties, which for some time had been keeping it alive, were withdrawn in 1786, and by the nineteenth century the Liberties "instead of the richest became one of the poorest quarters of Dublin."[2]

Besides employing themselves in textile industries, the Huguenots in Dublin, like those in Cork, were numerous and influential members of the Goldsmiths' Guild which was chartered in 1637.

"A perusal of the names (in the Journals of the Guild) brings to one's notice the extent to which the craft in Dublin was enriched by French Huguenots, and other continental Goldsmiths," writes Sir Charles Jackson,[3] " of whom a large number were driven by persecution from their native countries, which thereby lost many talented workmen which Ireland gained."

Many of these names have already been noticed in the foregoing pages. Amongst the rest appear:[4]

Adam Soret, Master in 1686 and 1691;

---

[1] Taken from the lists printed J.R.S.A.I., Vol. XLIX, p. 80.
[2] Smiles, p. 295.
[3] " English Goldsmiths and Their Trade Marks," p. 325.
[4] Taken from the lists compiled from the Journals of the Company by H. F. Berry, and published in C.H. & A.J., Vol. VIII, No. 53.

Abraham Soret, Watchmaker, probably his son, Warden
   in 1702-1705;
Benjamin Racine, Warden 1705-1708, Master 1710-1711;
   whose son, Peter, was apprenticed to the trade in 1718;
John Pallet, Warden 1712-1714, Master 1716-1717;
Noah Vialas, Warden 1730-1733, Master 1741, Clerk of the
   Guild in 1755;
Isaac d'Olier, Warden 1739-1741, Master 1752-1753;
Jeremiah d'Olier, Master 1781;
Thomas de Limarest, Warden 1743-1746, who may have
   been descended from the Jacques Limarest, a cornet
   in Miremont's Dragoons, who was pensioned after
   Ryswick;[1]
Daniel, nephew of the Sheriff William Onge, Warden 1748,
   Master 1751;
James Vidouze, Master in 1773;
Bartholomew de Landre, Warden 1785-1788, Master 1788.

In the apprentice lists appear:

Abraham Voisin, who with others was prosecuted by the
   Guild for working bad silver;[2]
Matthew La Roch;
James Moussoult;
Joseph Malbon, of London;
Francis Bovet, of Rochelle;
John and Francis Gerrard;
Samuel Ruchant;
John Paturle, who " served in France ";
John, son of Aymé Fourreau, " Gentleman of Dublin ";
Benjamine Boové;
Stephen Delile;
Esias de Lorthe;

---

[1] Hug. Soc. Proc., Vol. VI, p. 305.
[2] Sir C. J. Jackson.

Abraham Mondet;

Thomas Jolly, possibly a descendant of the Dublin minister under Cromwell who lost his living at the Restoration;

Peter, son of Lamotte Desinards;

George Lapier;

Daniel Beringuier;

Charles Boucher, of Rochelle;

Samuel Goodeau;

Philip de Glatigny, son of Adam de Glatigny, a Lieutenant in La Melonière's Regiment, pensioned after Ryswick;[1]

Lawrence Darquier;

Isaiah Dezouche, son of the silk weaver;

John Davisson;

David and Peter Riausset;

William Soubiran;

Daniel Pineau, to whom so many of the Huguenot craftsmen were apprenticed.[2]

To these may be added the names of two Huguenots who figured amongst the Dublin pewterers, James Audouit and Bertrand Piggenitt, who, as French refugees, obtained their Freedom in 1682 and 1685 respectively.[3] The d'Olier family came from Toulouse. Charles Edouard d'Olier, who was French Ambassador at Constantinople in 1673, had a grandson, Isaac, who fled at the Revocation, entered the service of William of Orange, and eventually settled in Dublin. He obtained the Freedom of the City of Amsterdam in 1686, and that of the Irish capital in 1697. In 1721 his son, Isaac, was apprenticed to the goldsmith Williamson, and his subsequent history in the Guild has been

---

[1] MS. List of Pensioned Officers in Nat. Mus., Ire.

[2] It was possibly his widow who was buried in the French Cemetery near St. Patrick's in 1747. (J.A.P.M.D., 1901.)

[3] Proc. R.S.A.I., Vol. XLVII, p. 47. H. Cotterell and M. S. D. Westropp, " Irish Pewterers."

already noted. His son, a third Isaac, was also apprenticed as a goldsmith in 1747. Jeremiah d'Olier, too, entered the Guild, was High Sheriff of Dublin in 1788 and one of the founders and early Governors of the Bank of Ireland.[1] D'Olier Street still memorializes his name.

Other trades besides these found their French representatives; thus Pierre Le Clerc, Daniel Guyon and Raymond Pennete figure as wine merchants,[2] while Claude Duplaix advertises himself as a manufacturer of gold and silver lace "at the Blue Door in Fleet Street."[3] Of these Guyon took the Oaths as a Protestant Stranger from St. Savinien in 1704.[4]

The woollen draper, Charles Daulnis, may also be mentioned. He was partner to Digby Tarlton in this trade, and seems to have carried on his business at the sign of the "Green Man and Wool Pack" in Dame Street, whence his partner transferred to the "Sign of the Squirrel" in High Street on his death in September 1740.[5] The name is also localized in Portarlington, where a Captain Pierre D'Aulnis was one of the early settlers. Another woollen draper was Alexandre Pelissier, patronized by some of the Portarlington colonists,[6] who has already been referred to in connection with that settlement;[7] while Peter Lunel, who so vividly lives in the account of the family compiled by his grandson,[8] cannot be omitted.

Born at Havre in 1652, he was educated in Amsterdam, but returned to France in 1669. Nine years later he appeared in England, and, in the regiment of Horse Guards, fought at the Boyne. Soon after the Campaign he took smallpox, which

[1] "Huguenots in England," Appendix.
[2] Hug. Soc. Proc., Vol. XIII, p. 560.
[3] Peter, "Dublin Fragments," p. 23.
[4] Hug. Soc. Pub., Vols. XVIII and XXVII.
[5] *Pue's Occurrences*, Dec. 1740. Advertisement.
[6] Hug. Soc. Proc., Vol. XIII, p. 560.
[7] *Vide* p. 168.
[8] Written in 1807 and edited by Mr. Le Fanu in Hug. Soc. Proc., Vol. XIV, p. 20.

" broke out so violently " that he left the Army. He had saved 300 guineas and in 1691 had married Kiturah Low, and he now took a farm of 300 acres at Raharah in County Roscommon. He had three daughters and two sons, George and William, the latter of whom he sent to boarding-school at Athlone. " Mind your learning, William," he is reported to have said, " 'tis all, my dear child, I have to give you." The farming project evidently proving a failure, Lunel removed to Dublin, where he " attempted a little business in the mercantile trade." " My grandfather," writes his biographer, " used to call upon his acquaintances among the French Protestants, many of whom settled in Dublin. They were all respectable, strove to help themselves, lived on very little, were always decent and some of them even showy in their appearance." Amongst these may be instanced an acquaintance of Lunel's from Havre, whose career provides an excellent example of the ingenuity of the Huguenots. He had possessed property and wealth in France, but, when destitute in Dublin, turned to the making of button moulds, a trade which he informed Lunel he had learnt as a childish hobby from the gate porter in his French home.

William Lunel set up in business as a draper in Francis Street. His father died in 1720 and was buried in the Merrion Row cemetery, and for seven years the son struggled against difficulty and poverty; eventually succeeding in building up a flourishing wholesale trade with the Norwegian vessels that visited the port. To do this he had mastered Danish, and another proof of his initiative is afforded in the story told by his son that in the early days of this business, when he had lacked the capital to lay in a sufficient stock, he had made sham packets of stuff to fill his shelves in order to give his shop a well-stored appearance.

In 1766 he migrated to Bristol, where he died in 1774. He married three times, his first wife being Charity, daughter of John Bagnall, and of his sons the eldest, William

Peter, his biographer, remained in Bristol, while the second, George, born in 1761, returned to Dublin and set up business in Capel Street. He became a director of the Bank of Ireland in 1793 and held this post until his death in 1811, when his son, a second William Peter, succeeded him.

Amongst the other Huguenot families engaged in trade in Dublin those of Raboteau, Le Fanu and Du Bedat were the most important. John Charles Raboteau, whose parents fled to Ireland from Pont Gibaud, near La Rochelle, was descended from Josué Raboteau, Procurier au Présidial to Saintes in 1615. He was born at Carlow, but settled as a wine merchant in Dublin, where he established a consider-able trade, and where he married a Miss Thornton, the daughter of an Irish clergyman. His sisters married into the Phipps family of Sligo, and his daughter, Rebecca, married Samuel D'Arcy at Carlow. He was instrumental in the escape of two young cousins[1] from France, one of whom married Stephen Chaigneau,[2] the other, about 1725, Pierre Barré, afterwards Alderman of Dublin.

She must have known this family before her flight, for the Barrés also came from Pont Gibaud. Peter established himself about 1720 as a linen draper in Dublin, with a ware-house in Fleet Street and a country house at Cullen's Wood. He died in 1776,[3] leaving a son, Isaac, who was educated in Trinity College, Dublin, joined the Army and was Adjutant-General under Wolfe at Quebec. He later entered Parlia-ment, where he won fame for his spirited opposition to the Stamp Act. In 1776 he was appointed Vice-Treasurer of Ireland and a Privy Councillor, and later Treasurer of the

---

[1] Agnew, Vol. II. Smiles states that they were nieces of Raboteau ("Huguenots in England," Appendix), but Mr. Le Fanu notes: "Com-paring the facts collected by Agnew with the family papers in my posses-sion, it is clear to me that ladies of the family escaped from France on more than one occasion, and that their stories became confused."

[2] *Vide* p. 73.

[3] Agnew, Vol. II.

Navy and Paymaster of the Forces. He died in 1802.[1]

Two nieces of John Charles Raboteau, Henriette and Marie Esther, the latter of whom died soon after arrival, also escaped from France and were brought to Ireland concealed in sails or apple casks on one of his ships. Tradition states that they were wrecked on the coast of Wexford, but they eventually reached Dublin, where they were aided by Monsieur Miot, also a Huguenot, and placed under the care of Gaspard Caillard, the minister.

Henriette married William Le Fanu in May 1734. He was the son of Philippe Le Fanu who fled to Ireland about 1731 and settled in Dublin, possibly at Ballsbridge, where he died in 1743. Other members of this family had already made Ireland their home. Jean de Secqueville served through the Irish Campaign and was pensioned on the Establishment, and his cousin, Charles Le Fanu de Cresserons, who had escaped at the Revocation to Holland, joined William of Orange and fought at the Boyne under La Melonière. Later he accompanied Lord Rivers to Spain, but returned to settle in Dublin in 1710. He married Marguerite de Graindorge and established himself in a house in Stephen's Green, which he obtained from Colonel Solomon de Blosset de Loche. On his death in 1738 he left all his property, save for some legacies to the French Churches, to his cousins Jacques, who was naturalized in Ireland in 1710, and Philippe.

A daughter of Philippe Le Fanu married Charles Barbe of La Patente, Spitalfields, and her son, William Barbe, who married Henrietta Hardy,[2] also settled in Dublin as a merchant, where he died in 1749.

William Le Fanu, who was born in 1707, maintained a warehouse behind his house in Stephen's Green. He seems

---

[1] "Huguenots in England," Appendix. He was presented with the Freedom of the City of Cork in a silver box. (Tuckey, "Cork Remembrancer.")

[2] *Vide* p. 53.

to have been interested in the manufacture of coarse linen and was granted a premium by the Linen Board in 1749. Like the La Touches his wealth enabled him to engage in banking, and he held lands in King's County and Westmeath as well as house property in Dublin.[1]

Two of his sons, Joseph and Henry, married the two sisters of the Right Honourable Brinsley Sheridan. Joseph's son, Thomas Philip, became Dean of Emly, and his son, the famous Joseph Sheridan Le Fanu, was born in 1814.[2] The name is now extinct in France and is confined in England and Ireland to the descendants of the Dean of Emly and of his first cousin, the Rev. William Joseph Henry Le Fanu.[3]

The Du Bedats came originally from Agen in the province of Guienne. Jean, a son or grandson of Matthew Du Bedat, born at Lacepede in Guienne, was sent to the Quaker school in Ballitore. He founded the first sugar refinery in Ireland and became a wealthy Dublin merchant and a leading member of the Peter Street congregation. He died in 1780. His daughter Anne married Elias Tardy in 1771; and one of his grandsons was William Du Bedat, Transfer Officer of the Bank of Ireland.[4]

The Tardys came from La Tremblade in Saintonge, and although they were not refugees they were so intimately connected with the other French Protestant families in Dublin that they may be mentioned here. Elias Tardy served in the French Navy under Admiral Conflans and was taken prisoner by the English at Belleisle in 1759. Remaining under British rule he settled in Dublin in 1766 and engaged, like the Du Bedats, in sugar refining, being made an *ancien* of the French Church and a trustee of the chapel

---

[1] T. P. Le Fanu, "Memoir of the Le Fanu Family."
[2] Agnew.
[3] "Memoir of the Le Fanu Family."
[4] Agnew, Vol. II, p. 267.

and burial-ground in Peter Street. He married twice, his first wife being Anne Du Bedat, who died in 1786, and his second Alice, widow of John Chaigneau.[1] Of his children, his eldest son, Francis, died in 1836, unmarried; Elias, the second son, born in 1777, left the country to set up a medical practice in London; and James devoted himself to the study of natural history. He became the father of the Rev. Elias Tardy.[2]

Besides the Le Fanus many Huguenots who were officers of William's armies or descended from them, or who themselves entered the Service, were eminent in Dublin. Thus Captain de Questebrune was buried there in 1699; Charles de L'Isle, a Captain of Horse and a native of Valenciennes, died in the capital in 1693; and Lieutenant Elie De La Catherie, Estienne Seve, described as " officier à la pension "; Captain Claude La Ramière from Guienne; and Captain Maurice La Primaudaye may also be mentioned. Among the most important of these early settlers was Jacques de Belrieu, Baron de Virazel, Seigneur de St. Laurans, who has been so often referred to in connection with Lord Galway's plans for the Irish Settlements. He, like La Ramière, was a refugee from Guienne, and he died in Dublin in 1720. His son, Daniel, born at Bordeaux and naturalized in 1702, married in Dublin in 1705 Catharine, daughter of Pierre Vatable.[3]

The histories of three other Huguenot families, those of de Pechels, Gualy and Ligonier, may be given in more detail.

The representative of the last-named family descended from Jean Ligonier, Consul de Castres in 1584. Abel, Sieur de Rogues, pastor at Labastide de Leran in 1681, fled to England and was naturalized in 1697. His sister, Marie Marguerite, born in 1657, married her cousin, Abel de Rotolp de

---

[1] *Vide* p. 73.
[2] Agnew, Vol. II, p. 270.
[3] Hug. Soc. Proc., Vol. IX, p. 584.

Ladaveze, Pastor of Castres. They also escaped to England, and two of their children, Abel and Anthony, were naturalized in 1707. Abel married a Dutch lady and returned to Holland. Anthony became Lieutenant-Colonel of the 19th Foot and died in Dublin in 1771. He married Emilie, daughter of Colonel John Trapaud, a refugee from Guienne, and left two sons, John and Abel. John, a Captain of Dragoons, married Maria Dejean and died in 1804, and Abel became Archdeacon of Cashel before his death in 1767.

Sir John Louis Ligonier, who became Field-Marshal, a Privy Councillor and Knight of the Bath, was a son of Louis de Ligonier, Seigneur of Montaquet, who married Louise Du Poncet. John Louis came to England in 1697, entered the Army in 1702, fought in Marlborough's campaigns, and was knighted at Dettingen. In 1757 he was created Viscount and Baron Ligonier of Enniskillen, and later Viscount Ligonier of Clonmel. He died in 1770. His nephew, son of Colonel Francis Ligonier, who died in 1746, fought as a Captain at Minden and succeeded his uncle as Viscount Ligonier of Clonmel in 1770. He married Penelope Rivers and died in 1782.[1]

Louise du Poncet had a brother who was a Lieutenant-Colonel of Foot under William in Ireland. Two brothers of this name from Castres settled in Dublin in the early eighteenth century. One of them, Captain William Du Poncet, married Susanne Baudry, and his daughter married Pierre Besnard of Angers, possibly a connection of the Cork settler.[2]

The Gualys came from Rouergue whence Peter, son of the Sieur De La Gineste, fled to England at the Revocation, with his children Paul, Francis and Margaret. Paul and Francis entered the Army, Paul becoming a Major-General

---

[1] Hug. Soc. Proc., Vol. VIII, p. 373. Wagner, " The Ligonier Family," and Agnew, Vol. II, pp. 193-9.
[2] *Vide* p. 56.

and Francis eventually settling in Dublin.[1] Here Peter de Gualy, probably his son, died in 1764, and Charles, the latter's only son, in 1774. On their tombstone in the Peter Street French Cemetery was the quaint inscription, "They were worthy among worthies."[2]

Samuel de Péchels de la Boissonade of Montauban was imprisoned and transported to America, but escaped to Jamaica and, obtaining a passage to England, arrived one month after the landing of William of Orange. He was given a commission in Schomberg's Regiment, but fell ill at Newry and was invalided to London, where he was joined by his wife who had escaped from France through Geneva. He was pensioned in London, but later transferred to Ireland and settled in Dublin in 1692, where he died forty years later. His son, Jacob, entered the English Army, fought under Marlborough and was made a Colonel. He married Jane Boyd,[3] a descendant of the Earls of Kilmarnock.

Colonel de Romagnac and Colonel de Blosset de Loche with his sons Paul and Solomon were amongst the Dublin military pensioners, and their relative, the minister Jean de Durand, who died there in 1744, was attracted to the settlement by their presence therein. Another minister, Paul de St. Ferreol, was also connected with the military settlers, since he was a relative of Charles de St. Ferreol, a native of Dauphiné, who fought through the Irish Campaign, subsequently retiring to Dublin.[4]

The professions as well as the trades in Dublin had their Huguenot representatives. Many of those connected with the Church have already been noted, but mention must be made of Jean Pierre Droz and of Elie Bouhéreau.

---

[1] "Huguenots in England," Appendix.
[2] J.A.P.M.D., 1912.
[3] Smiles, "Huguenots in England," Appendix. For an account of the reminiscences of the elder de Péchels see the same author's "Huguenots in France," p. 285.
[4] Hug. Soc. Proc., Vol. VIII, p. 109.

The former, as has been stated, was minister of the French Church in St. Patrick's from 1737 to his death in 1751. He was a native of Neufchatel, had been ordained deacon in 1734 and priest in 1735 in St. Paul's Cathedral, and married in 1737 Margaret Boileau de Castelnau.[1] But more important than his clerical career was his institution of the first original, critical and literary periodical to appear in Ireland. He kept a bookshop in College Green (later removed to Dame Street),[2] and established a library, and besides writing for his *Literary Journal*, which appeared in 1744,[3] he published several works of the French refugees in Ireland.

Elias Bouhéreau was one of the most important of the Dublin Huguenots. He was the son of one of the Protestant pastors of La Rochelle, and Haag states that he was born in that town in 1642 and that he eventually became D.D. of the University of Orange. This has been corrected by Dr. Newport White[4] from the Bouhéreau Manuscripts, who states that he was born in 1643. At the Revocation he left France and served as secretary to Thomas Cox, Envoy to the Swiss Cantons, and then to Ruvigny in Piedmont, later accompanying the latter to Ireland and acting as his secretary when he held the post of Lord Justice from 1697-1701. Bouhéreau settled in Dublin and was appointed Librarian to the Library of Archbishop Marsh. No record exists of his having been made a Doctor of Divinity, although this has been stated, and he was never a minister of any of the French Churches[5] although he officiated as Precentor of St. Patrick's from 1709-1719.

One of his sons, John, was ordained in 1709, eventually obtained a Doctorate in Divinity and was appointed as the first Assistant-Librarian of Marsh's Library, a post which he

---

[1] *Ibid.*
[2] Gilbert, "History of Dublin," Vol. II, p. 272.
[3] Madden, "Irish Periodical Literature," Vol. I, p. 338.
[4] Proc. R.I.A., Vol. XXVII, p. 141, and Hug. Soc. Proc., Vol. IX, p. 20.
[5] As stated by Smiles. "Huguenots in England," Appendix.

held until 1725. Another son, Amateur, was a Major in General Otway's Regiment and died in Limerick. A third, who had fought through the Williamite wars and had lost an arm at the Siege of Ehernburg, became Town Major of Dublin and left descendants, amongst them being Sir E. R. Borough, who was born in 1800 and died in 1879.

Of his daughters, Blanche married John Jourdain, who, as has already been mentioned, held a living in Meath,[1] and Marguerite married the French minister, Louis Quartier,[2] the son of Jacques Quartier, minister of the French Church of Groningen. They had one daughter, Jeanne, who married in 1730 Jean Freboul, and whose "Recollections" form an invaluable part of the Bouhéreau Manuscripts.

When Bouhéreau fled from France he carried with him the records of the Consistory, of which his father was President, and deposited them in Marsh's Library. When they were opened after his death, a note was found directing their return if they should ever be claimed by a reconstituted Protestant Consistory of La Rochelle. They lay undisturbed in the Library until the nineteenth century, when the papers were forwarded to the Consistory at their request and were utilized by Pastor Delmas of La Rochelle in his history of the Protestant Church of that city.

Amongst the Dublin Huguenots who interested themselves in the arts was Jean Bernard Logier, a teacher of music, who invented the musical notation which bears his name;[3] James Tabarict (or Tarbary) who was admitted to the Freedom of the City in 1682, and carved the woodwork for the Chapel of the Royal Hospital at Kilmainham;[4] and Gabriel Beranger, the artist, who worked in Dublin from 1750-1817. Two

---

[1] *Vide* p. 199.
[2] Proc. R.I.A., Vol. XXVII. Dr. Newport White, "Elias Bouhéreau."
[3] "Huguenots in England," Appendix.
[4] Proc. R.S.A.I., Vol. LIII. Art. by W. G. Strickland on Kilmainham which contradicts the belief that Grinling Gibbons was responsible for this work.

branches of his family had escaped from France, the one to Dublin, the other to Holland, and Beranger, who was born in Rotterdam in 1729, united them by coming to Dublin and marrying his cousin, Louise Beranger, the daughter of the Irish settler. On her death in 1782 he married Elizabeth Mestayer, possibly a daughter of Charles Mestayer, but left no children. Besides being an artist himself he kept a print shop and artist's warehouse in South George's Street from 1766 to 1779,[1] and he was employed by the Antiquarian Society of Dublin to travel through the country with Signor Bigari, an Italian architect, to describe and draw its antiquities. He left some two hundred sketches with a diary of their journeys which Sir William Wilde considered most valuable as an essay on the Ireland of his day. For many years he also held the post of Assistant Ledger Keeper in the Government Exchequer Office. He died in 1817, and was buried in the Peter Street cemetery.

Of the many other French refugees who settled in Dublin or passed through it on their way to the provinces it is not possible here to make a record. In addition to the names already quoted those of Langlois, St. Germain, Rambaut, Racine, Beauchamp, Martinet, Pellisier, Belsonne, Faviere and Maignon were connected with the French burial-ground near St. Patrick's;[2] Jonglas, Martineau and Dupee with that of Merrion Row; and Villebois, Battier, Le Bas, Espinasse, Miot, Mestayer, Pommoieu, Corneille and Bourdage with that of Peter Street.[3]

Marshal Schomberg was buried in St. Patrick's, and another notable Huguenot whose remains were said to have been interred in Dublin was the famous Cavalier of the Cevennes,[4] the "baker's apprentice with a genius for war,

[1] Proc. of the Royal Hist. and Arch. Assoc. (later the R.S.A.I.), Vol. I, Pt. I. Sir W. R. Wilde, "Memoir," 1870.
[2] J.A.P.M.D., 1901.
[3] *Ibid.*, 1912.
[4] Smiles, p. 238.

elected brigadier of the Camisards at seventeen to die at fifty-five the English Governor of Jersey."[1] This is an error since the Camisard leader was buried in the churchyard of St. Luke's, Chelsea, but he certainly visited Ireland, after escaping from France and campaigning with the English forces under the Earl of Peterborough in Spain, and at the age of twenty-six, in 1707, settled on half-pay at Portarlington. Here he married Mademoiselle de Ponthieu,[2] from whom he separated after a few years, and wrote his " Memoirs of the War in the Cevennes," which was published in Dublin in an English translation in 1726. In 1727 he was recommended by the Primate to the Duke of Newcastle, then Secretary of State, but it was not until eight years later that his pension was increased by his promotion to the rank of Brigadier. By Royal Commission, dated March 28th, 1738, he was appointed Governor of Jersey, and he was later created a Major-General, but he only enjoyed his honours for a brief period for he died at Chelsea in 1740.[3]

Other names might be listed, but in choosing those mentioned in the foregoing chapters an attempt has alone been made to show the influence of the refugees in each department of Irish Society, and in no case has an exhaustive treatment of their family histories been intended. A sufficient number of Huguenot goldsmiths, pewterers, weavers, wine merchants, sugar refiners and traders generally has been given to prove the business acumen and initiative of the refugees, and those names already mentioned in connection with banking, the Church, the arts and the medical and military professions sufficiently attest the importance of the Huguenot element in Dublin.[4]

---

[1] Stevenson, " Travels with a Donkey in the Cevennes."
[2] *Vide* p. 165.
[3] Grubb, " Jean Cavalier," Ch. 18.
[4] Even as late as 1800 one hundred and two Huguenot names may be traced amongst the shopkeepers and merchants in the City. (Wagner MSS.)

If the capital offered a wide field for enterprise the refugees took full advantage of it, and although their influence may be forgotten in the provinces it was too deep, too widespread and too long continued in Dublin ever to escape a record in the City's history.

CHAPTER X

IN 1697 the writer of the letter addressed to the Right Honourable Robert Molesworth on " The True Way to Render Ireland Happy and Secure "[1] assured him that " The French Protestants have many men of letters among them and they are generally remarkable for their good breeding and civility. 'Tis not to be doubted then that they, living in towns and villages among the ruder Irish, will in time help greatly to improve them both in manners and religion." As regards the linen trade he believes that " this is a manufacture in which the French do excel and therefore the Irish may very reasonably promise themselves great advantages by the coming in of the French and their improving of it," and perhaps the best way of assessing the success or failure of the Huguenot settlements from the point of view of Ireland will be to consider how far his eulogy was justified by subsequent history.

Not all writers of the period were as sanguine. In 1732 a pamphlet, printed by Charles Forman in the form of a letter to Sir Robert Walpole, attacked the Earl of Galway, who, the writer states, " got the Irish establishment reduced so low purposely to make a fund for good pensions for his countrymen the French Huguenots. Many of those self-called gentlemen," he adds vindictively, " were no more than journeymen

---

[1] Pamphlet, Dublin, 1697. *Vide* p. 22.

256

barbers, tailors or footmen in France but amongst us they were immediately vamped up into what not."[1] William III was bitterly attacked for his championship of the refugees. A Bill was passed in the English Parliament to annul the grants, such as that of the Portarlington estate, made by him to foreigners, and in 1698 it was proposed in the Irish House of Commons "That an address be presented to the Lords Justices to intercede with His Majesty that the five regiments of French Protestants should be disbanded."[2] In 1702 an Act to limit commissions to those born in England, Scotland or Ireland so as to cut foreign officers out of his armies was lost by the bare majority of 94 to 91;[3] while in the previous year the Earl of Rochester had attempted to force the officers on half-pay in Ireland to proceed for service to the West Indies.[4] This William could forbid, but he could not alter the attitude of his English subjects.

> " We blame the King that he relies too much
> On strangers, Germans, Huguenots and Dutch,"[5]

wrote Defoe, summing up the situation, and when a Bill for the naturalization of aliens was proposed in the House of Commons in 1694, the Member for Bristol concluded a bitter speech with the vehement appeal, "Let us first kick the Bill

---

[1] Quoted Agnew, " Henri de Ruvigny." The Huguenots seem themselves to have taken precautions against this by obtaining certificates signed by the minister of their last place of residence before moving to a new locality. Thus the De La Cherois sisters procured a certificate at Leyden before coming to Lisburn, and Elie Tardy arrived in Dublin in 1766 with a "certificate de vie et de mœurs " signed by M. Dugas of Saintonge, a leading minister of the Church of the Desert. Tokens were also used as a kind of passport by the refugees. (Vide the U.J.A., Vols. I and VI. Articles on Lisburn and Portarlington.) These were usually of metal and were called " méreaux." (Grant, p. 72.)

[2] " Huguenots in England," p. 231.

[3] H.C.J. Man. 2/13, 1702. Quoted Trevelyan, " Blenheim."

[4] "Protestant Exiles," Vol. II, p. 188.

[5] " True-born Englishmen," Pt. II.

out of the House and then foreigners out of the Kingdom."[1]

Such attacks were as unbalanced as too fervent eulogy and owed their origin rather to English jealousy than to any great fault in the characters of the Huguenots themselves.[2] In contrast to them may be cited a statement by the author of "A History of the Trade in England," published in London in 1702, who asserts that "the English have now so great an esteem for the workmanship of the French refugees that hardly anything vends without a Gallic name." In Ireland, too, the Huguenots found admirers. "Are they not sober, modest, industrious and honest?" asks the Rector of Fintona in 1751.[3] "They confine themselves to their own business which they pursue with admirable address and skill, to the great advantage, not only of themselves, but of the nation in general. They have shown themselves brave and faithful in the army; just and impartial in the magistracy. Have they not brought us a treasure of men—industrious in time of peace and brave in war?"

It is not enough, however, to take the judgment of either camp in this conflict of opinion, and history has proved that there was something to be said for both points of view.

The foreigners certainly cost Ireland much in pensions and grants, but that they had earned the former by their valiant conduct in the armies of William and Anne, and the latter by their assiduity in trade and manufacture, cannot be doubted. They occasionally came into conflict with civic and ecclesiastical authority, as in the case of the Vashon brothers in Waterford and Daillon in Portarlington, and acts of certain individuals such as the De La Croix in Cork might be cited

---

[1] On its publication the speech was ordered to be burnt. Sommer's Collection Tracts, Vol. IV, p. 272.

[2] Some of the Huguenots were accused of treachery during the Irish Campaign, but this charge was brought home to Catholic Frenchmen in William's army. *Vide* Gimlette, p. 268.

[3] Rev. Philip Skelton, "The Case of Protestant Refugees from France Considered." Written as a sermon but never preached.

to disprove Skelton's tribute to their honesty, but on the whole they were amenable to the regulations for public and private life in the cities of their adoption. In 1711 the Houses of Convocation declared that "the French Refugees who, upon their first coming over into this kingdom did all conform to the Established Church and were treated with utmost tenderness and humanity and great numbers of them subsisted at an immense charge for these twenty years past," have "broken into Non-conforming congregations ";[1] and Skelton[2] states that by some it was objected "that these men ought not to be too much encouraged because they increase the number of our dissenters in proportion as they settle among us." Yet, he remarks, "they seldom or never communicate with our native dissenters, but either keep up their own congregations that they may afford their new countrymen an opportunity of serving God in the only language they understand, or come over to the Established Church by hundreds every year," and in their "Apology "[3] the Huguenots themselves raised a spirited defence against such attacks. As will have been seen, many indeed conformed, but those who remained in the Calvinistic congregations maintained amicable relations both with the Church of Ireland and their fellow countrymen in the Conformed Churches. In the North they were especially welcomed by the Presbyterians, who found the religious principles of "this poor distressed people" similar "both with respect to the substance of discipline and worship as well as of doctrine " to their own,[4] but throughout the country they seem success-

---

[1] "A Representation of the Present State of Religion," etc. Drawn up and agreed to by both Houses of Convocation in Ireland. Pamphlet, Dublin, 1711.

[2] "The Case of Protestant Refugees from France Considered."

[3] "An Apology for the French Refugees Established in Ireland." Pamphlet, Dublin, 1712.

[4] Reid, "History of the Presbyterian Church in Ireland," Vol. III. pp. 26 and 27.

fully to have avoided religious differences with their neighbours, and a striking proof of their popularity is evinced in the fact that, while Quakers and Wesleyans were everywhere subject to petty persecution, and sometimes even open violence, the Huguenots were left unmolested.

Not all of them, save perhaps for the Crommelins, were rich. "They come with their lives you have so generously preserved but I can't say with their fortunes," wrote Drelincourt;[1] and when the monetary affairs of the Huguenot pensioners were make the subject of inquiry in 1702, only four admitted to the possession of £1,000.[2] Some, indeed, like the Labatts of Youghal, went bankrupt; but the majority fully proved Skelton's prophecy, "If, after supplying the necessities of the Refugees, we give them never so small a beginning to trade on these poor men will soon make us rich,"[3] since they possessed an aptitude for business and a power of application that raised many of them to wealthy and influential positions in a surprisingly short time. Thus James Ribet Vigie, who is sworn free in Cork in 1685 as "a poor distressed French Protestant," is Mayor of Galway in 1703,[4] and David La Touche, who was left with only a small pension to support him after the Peace of Ryswick, was a wealthy manufacturer and the founder of a leading Dublin bank before his death.[5] Instances such as these could be multiplied from the foregoing account of the settlements as proof that in initiative and energy the French refugees were second to none, and with such men as citizens the Irish towns were certain to benefit.

---

[1] "A speech made to His Grace the Duke of Ormond to return the humble thanks of the French Protestants lately arrived in this Kingdom," by P. Drelincourt, chaplain to His Grace. Pamphlet, Dublin, 1682.

[2] Hug. Soc. Pub., Vol. XIX. Introduction to the French Registers of Portarlington.

[3] "The Case of Protestant Refugees from France Considered."

[4] *Vide* pp. 30, 212.

[5] *Vide* p. 237.

But it is in connection with the linen trade of the North that the faults and virtues of the Huguenots as settlers can best be seen, and here their influence lingered longest.

"The Huguenots," writes Professor Gill,[1] who is here referring to the Crommelins and their following, "brought with them personal and material wealth. They knew the best methods of flax-culture and could teach fine spinning. They had the most efficient looms adapted to the weaving of Cambric, damask and finest broadcloths. They had experience of bleaching, partly gained at Haarlem. They were acquainted with the methods of trade in highly organized markets and the kinds of cloth most in demand in other countries. Many of them were men of substance who were able to invest capital and thus to supply to some extent the greatest of all the economic needs of Ireland." Yet their influence was not wholly good. Crommelin, for instance, tried to make the Irish use a French spinning-wheel which was less efficient than the native machine, and in many of the regulations for the trade, probably initiated by the Huguenots, a selfish spirit is seen. Thus in 1705 and 1709 rules were passed prescribing a five years' apprenticeship, followed by two years' service as journeyman for every master weaver, but exempting foreign Protestants from such restrictions, which were meant to limit the number of workers and prevent the Irish from setting up independently until they had served an apprenticeship to Huguenot masters.[2] In the same spirit the manufacture of cloths narrower than the 22½ inches of Huguenot workmanship was forbidden.[3]

Nevertheless, that they improved the methods of manufacture and established the reputation of Irish linen is beyond question. In 1737 a London merchant, Huey by name, stated that Irish linen was at that time much better in quality

[1] " The Rise of the Irish Linen Industry," p. 16.
[2] *Ibid.*, p. 19.
[3] *Ibid.*, p. 63.

than it had been twenty-five years earlier,[1] and Smith, writing in 1746, exclaims, " To what a noble pitch has our linen manufacture been raised. And for this we are in some measure indebted to foreigners. Witness the order of thanks of the House of Commons given to Mr. Cromlin [sic] a French gentleman naturalized in this kingdom, than actually sitting in the House, and likewise the present of £10,000 as an acknowledgment for the great service he had done this country in establishing that manufacture here. Colour was indeed wanting to our linen but, by the care of the Linen Board and the industry of Dutch bleachers, we have at length surmounted that obstacle."[2]

Once firmly established, the industry outlasted most of those in the South, which failed to survive the change in manufacturing method caused by the introduction of steam-power, but the manufacture of poplins still remains as a witness to the initiative of the La Touches. It may be argued that the linen and silk industries would have prospered in any hands, so carefully were they nursed by a Government which was forced to ruin the woollen trade in order to satisfy the demands of English producers; but no fostering can establish an industry if the skill and energy to carry it forward are lacking, as Fontaine found in his fishing venture at Bearhaven, and the Huguenot manufacturers possessed the required zeal and ability in full measure.

Apart from the textile manufactures, their influence is seen in the work of the Irish goldsmiths, silversmiths and glass-makers. In Dublin and Cork a large proportion of the members of the Goldsmiths' Guild were Huguenot; and although they may not, as some writers have claimed, have established the glass manufactures in Waterford and Cork,

[1] *Ibid.*, p. 20.
[2] " The Ancient and Present State of the Co. and City of Waterford," Introduction.

they set up works near Portarlington which did something to further the industry.

Not only in trade but in culture the Huguenots left their mark. They had been of a higher social standing in Ireland than in England owing to the number of officers, drawn from the French nobility, who had settled there after the Irish Campaign, Ryswick and the Peace of Utrecht; and Portarlington, with its famous schools, flourished as a centre of all that was best in social life until the disruption of 1798.

As has already been stated, they adorned the learned professions. " Eminent preachers, eminent lawyers and clever statesmen, whose names are not unknown to the literature and science of France, occupied high places in their professions in Dublin," wrote Lady Morgan in the early nineteenth century. " Of these I may mention, as personal acquaintances, the Saurins, the Lefanus, Espinasses, Faviers, Corneilles, Le Bas, and many others whose families still remain in the Irish Metropolis."[1] They may not have been invariably popular with the Irish gentry, thus Edmund Burke can make caustic references to the French element amongst his schoolfellows at Ballitore,[2] but that they were fully accepted amongst them is evinced by the positions in Society, in the Church and in the State which they achieved. The Bank of Ireland owes much to its first governor, David La Touche. The first literary journal to be published in Ireland was the work of a Huguenot minister, and the first Librarian of Marsh's Library was a refugee from La Rochelle. With such evidence of the initiative and many-sided abilities of the Huguenots it is hard to agree with Arthur Young that " no country, whatever state it may be in, can be improved by colonies of foreigners."[3]

Young, however, was considering the Palatines, planted

---

[1] " Memoirs," Vol. I, p. 106.
[2] *Vide* p. 174.
[3] " Tour in Ireland," p. 182.

round Limerick in 1709, and while they decayed and became submerged in the life around them, the French Huguenots rose above that life to leave their impress on it. It is true that, by intermarriage with the Anglo-Irish population, and the anglicization of the French names, the settlements grew indistinct, and little now remains to mark them save a few graves scattered throughout the country, with Huguenot burial-places in Dublin and Portarlington; a French Charitable Fund in the former city; the ruined "French Church" in Waterford, and a "French Church Street" in Cork. But many Huguenot names still exist in Ireland, and no survey of the Irish Church and State can be complete without a mention of those refugees who played such a large part in their history.

The Huguenots in Ireland need no panegyrist to justify their citizenship. Their dispersal from France was, as Lady Morgan justly states, "one of the greatest boons conferred by the misgovernment of other countries on our own,"[1] and their sober industry and worth paid, many times over, the debt that they owed to the country which had afforded them protection.

They may have been self-centred in their struggle for success, but what community striving to establish itself among foreigners is not? and with the faults of a minority they combined that courage and strength of will that are among its virtues. The success that attended them in their new home is the proof of their service to the general community; and the salient characteristic that enabled them to succeed is best summed up in the prophecy, so strikingly proved by their history in Ireland, made in the sixteenth century by Ambroise Paré, himself a Huguenot:

"At all events, posterity will not be able to charge us with idleness."[2]

[1] "Memoirs," Vol. I, p. 106.
[2] Quoted Smiles, "Huguenots in England," p. 135.

BIBLIOGRAPHY

GENERAL HISTORY

AGNEW, REV. D. C. "Protestant Exiles from France." 2nd Edition. London. 1871.

BAIRD, H. M. "History of the Rise of the Huguenots." 1880.

BAIRD, H. M. "The Huguenots and the Revocation of the Edict of Nantes." London. 1895.

BULL. "Protestant France."

BURN, J. S. "History of the French and Other Foreign Protestant Refugees in England." London. 1846.

DUNLOP, ROBERT. "Ireland under the Commonwealth." (A selection of Documents relating to the Government of Ireland.) Manchester. 1913.

FALKINER, C. LITTON. "Illustrations of Irish History." 1904.

GILL, CONRAD. "The Rise of the Irish Linen Industry."

GIMLETTE, REV. T., D.D. "The Huguenot Settlers in Ireland." (Unfinished papers privately printed. Waterford. 1888.)

GRANT, A. J. "The Huguenots." Home University Library. London. 1934.

HAAG. "La France Protestante." Paris. 1846.

JACKSON, SIR CHARLES, F.S.A. "English Goldsmiths and their Trade Marks." London. 1921.

LECKY, WILLIAM. "History of Ireland in the Eighteenth Century."

MADDEN, R. R., M.R.I.A. "Irish Periodical Literature." London. 1867.

LANE POOLE, REGINALD. "A History of the Huguenots of the Dispersion." London. 1880.

REID, JAMES SEATON. "History of the Presbyterian Church in Ireland." Belfast. 1867.

SMILES, SAMUEL. "Huguenots in England and Ireland." Revised Edition. London. 1876.

SMILES, SAMUEL. "The Huguenots in France." London. 1878.
WEISS. "Histoire des Réfugiés Protestants de France." Paris. 1853.
WESTROPP, M. S. D., M.R.I.A. "Irish Glass." London. N.D.

LOCAL HISTORY

ALEXANDER THE COPPERSMITH. "Remarks on—Cork." Cork. 1737.
ANON. "A Tour Through Ireland by Two English Gentlemen." Dublin. 1746.
BENNETT, GEORGE. "History of Bandon." Cork. 1862.
BRADY, W. M., D.D. "Parochial Records of Cork, Cloyne and Ross." Dublin. 1863.
COLE, REV. J. H. "Records of Cork, Cloyne and Ross." Cork. 1903.
CAMERON, SIR C. A. "History of the College of Surgeons, Dublin." 1886.
DALTON. "History of Dundalk." Dublin. 1864.
DOWNEY, E. "The Story of Waterford." Waterford. 1914.
EDWARDS. "Cork Remembrancer." Cork. 1792.
EGAN, P. M. "History and Guide to the County and City of Waterford." 1894.
GIBSON, REV. C. B., M.R.I.A. "The History of the County and City of Cork." London. 1861.
GILBERT, J. T. "A History of the City of Dublin." Dublin. 1857.
HALL, MR. AND MRS. "Ireland." London. 1841.
HARDIMAN, JAMES. "The History of the Town and County of Galway." 1820. Reprinted Galway. 1926.
LENIHAN. "A History of Limerick." 1866.
LEWIS, SAMUEL. "A Topographical Dictionary of Ireland." London. 1837.
NIXON. "Cork Almanack."
O'SULLIVAN, FLORENCE. "History of Kinsale." Dublin. 1916.
PETER, A. "Dublin Fragments, Social and Historic." Dublin. 1925.
RYLAND. "History of Waterford." 1824.
SMITH, CHARLES. "Ancient and Present State of the County and City of Cork." 1750. (With MS. Notes by Caulfield and

Crofton Croker. Edited by R. Day and W. A. Coppinger. Cork. 1893.)

SMITH, CHARLES. " Ancient and Present State of the County and City of Waterford." 1746.

TUCKEY, FRANCIS A. " Cork Remembrancer." Cork. 1837.

WARBURTON, WHITELAW AND WALSH. " History of the City of Dublin." London. 1818.

WEBSTER, CHARLES A., B.D., M.R.I.A. " Church Plate of the Dioceses of Cork, Cloyne and Ross." Cork. 1909.

WEST, W. " A Directory and Picture of Cork and Its Environs." 1810.

WINDELE, J. " Historical and Descriptive Notices of the City of Cork." Cork. 1837.

YOUNG, ARTHUR. " A Tour in Ireland." (1776-1778.) Edited by C. Maxwell, M.A. Cambridge. 1925.

BIOGRAPHY

AGNEW, REV. D. C. " Henri de Ruvigny, Earl of Galway." Edinburgh. 1864.

BOSTAQUET, DUMONT DE. " Mémoires Inédits." (1688-1693.) Edited by Read and Waddington. Paris. 1864.

BURDY. " The Life of Philip Skelton." Edited by Norman Moore.

BURKE. " Landed Gentry of Ireland," also " Peerage."

CARTE, THOMAS. " History of the Life of James, Duke of Ormond." 1736.

CROSSLEY. " Irish Peerage " (for note on Ruvigny).

FONTAINE, JAMES. " Memoirs of a Huguenot Family." 1722. Edited by Anna Maury. New York. 1852.

GRUBB, ARTHUR. " Jean Cavalier." London. 1931.

JOURDAIN, LIEUT.-COL. " Ranging Memories." (For note on Jourdain family.)

LART, C. E. " Huguenot Pedigrees." London. 1924.

LEADBEATER, MARY. " The Leadbeater Papers." 1766-1824. London. 1862.

LE FANU, T. P., M.R.I.A. " Memoirs of the Le Fanu Family." Privately printed.

"Miscellanea Genealogica et Heraldica."
MORGAN, LADY. "Memoirs." London. 1862.
PLAYFAIR. "Family Antiquity" (for Memoir on Trench family).
SAMUELS, ARTHUR. "The Early Life of Edmund Burke." Cambridge. 1923.
URWICK, WILLIAM, D.D. "A Biographic Sketch of the late James Digges La Touche." Dublin. 1868.

CONTEMPORARY AND MANUSCRIPT MATERIALS

Publications

"A Representation of the Present State of Religion with regard to Infidelity, Heresy, Impiety and Popery; Drawn up and agreed to by Both Houses of Convocation in Ireland pursuant to Her Majesty's Command." Pamphlet. Dublin 1711.
"An Apology for the French Refugees Established in Ireland." Pamphlet. Dublin. 1712.
Calendar Carew MSS.
Calendar State Papers, Ireland. (Abbreviation in text, C.S.P.)
Council Book, Cork.   Edited by Richard Caulfield, LL.D.,
  „   „   Kinsale.   F.S.A. With Annals compiled from
  „   „   Youghal.   public and private sources.
"De L'Etat Presente D'Irlande et des Avantages qu'y peuvent trouver les Protestants François." Pamphlet. Dublin. 1681.
DRELINCOURT. "A Speech made to His Grace the Duke of Ormonde—to return the humble thanks of the French Protestants." Pamphlet. Dublin. 1682.
DUBOURDIEU. "An Appeal to the English Nation." 1718.
EVELYN, JOHN. "Diary." Edited by William Bray. 1818.
FULLER, THOMAS. "Church History of Britain." Edited by Nichols. London. 1868.
"Hiberniæ Notitia." Pamphlet. Dublin. 1723.
"Journals of the Irish House of Commons."
"Journals of the Linen Board of Ireland."
"Jus Regium—Or the King's Right to Grant Forfeitures." Pamphlet. London. 1701.
"Letters of His Excellency Hugh Boulter, D.D., Lord Primate

of Ireland." Edited by Faulkner. Oxford, 1769; Dublin, 1770.

"Letters Between John Locke and His Friends." London. 1708.

"Letters of Dean Swift." Edited by G. B. Hill. London. 1899.

"Letters of Denization and Acts of Naturalization of Aliens in England and Ireland." (1603-1800.) Edited by W. A. Shaw, Litt.D. Publications of the Huguenot Society of London. Vols. XVIII and XXVII.

LUTTRELL, NARCISSUS. "A Brief Historical Relation of State Affairs." 1678-1714.

"Registers of the French Conformed Churches of Dublin." (1668-1830.) Edited by J. J. Digges La Touche. Publications of the Huguenot Society of London. Vol VII.

"Registers of the French Nonconformist Churches of Dublin." Edited by T. P. Le Fanu, M.R.I.A. Publications of the Huguenot Society of London. Vol. XIV.

"Registers of the French Church of Portarlington." Edited by T. P. Le Fanu, M.R.I.A. Publications of the Huguenot Society of London. Vol. XIX.

Reports of the Deputy Keeper of the Records. Ireland.

SKELTON, REV. PHILIP. "The Case of Protestant Refugees from France Considered." 1751. Published in "Complete Works," Vol. III. London, 1824.

Sommer's Collection of Rare Tracts. London. 1748.

"The True Way to Render Ireland Happy and Secure." Pamphlet in form of letter to the Rt. Hon. Robert Molesworth. Dublin. 1697.

Newspapers

Dublin Gazette.

EXSHAW's *Gentleman's Magazine.*

FAULKNER's *Dublin Journal.*

London Gazette.

Pue's Occurrences.

Manuscripts

"Apprentices of the City of Cork, Enrolment Book of the." Transcribed by Caulfield.

"Besnard Family of Cork, Notes on the." Compiled by Canon T. E. Evans. 1886.

"Court of D'Oyer Hundred Book—Cork." Transcribed by Caulfield.
" D'Esterre Family of Limerick, Notes on the."
De Tuigny Property, Portarlington; Copy of Lease in connection with the.
" Duron Family of Portarlington, Notes on the."
" Freemen of the City of Cork, Register of the." Transcribed by Caulfield.
French Church, Cork; Copy of Lease and Conveyance in connection with the.
" Guerin Family, Notes on the."
Hardy Family of Cork, Original Papers and Documents relating to the.
Officers Pensioned in Dublin in 1727, List of. (National Museum, Ireland.)
" Perrier Family of Cork, Notes on the."
Vestry Books of Christ Church, Cork.
Wagner Collection in the Library of the French Hospital, London.

JOURNALS

	Abbreviation used in text
Cork Historical and Archæological Journal .	C.H. & A.J.
Journal of the Association for the Preservation of Memorials of the Dead . .	J.A.P.M.D.
Journal of the County Kildare Archæological Society	J.K.A.S.
Journal of the Royal Society of Antiquaries of Ireland	J.R.S.A.I.
Journal of the Waterford and South East of Ireland Archæological Society . .	J.W. & S.E.I.A.S.
Proceedings of the Huguenot Society of London	Hug. Soc. Proc.
Proceedings of the Royal Irish Academy .	Proc. R.I.A.
Ulster Journal of Archæology . . .	U.J.A.

INDEX